Cracking Baseball's
Cold Cases

Cracking Baseball's Cold Cases

Filling in the Facts About 17 Mystery Major Leaguers

PETER MORRIS

McFarland & Company, Inc., Publishers
Jefferson, North Carolina, and London

ALSO OF INTEREST AND FROM McFARLAND

*Base Ball Founders: The Clubs, Players and Cities of the Northeast
That Established the Game*, Edited by Peter Morris, William J. Ryczek,
Jan Finkel, Leonard Levin and Richard Malatzky (2013)

*Base Ball Pioneers, 1850–1870: The Clubs and Players Who Spread
the Sport Nationwide*, Edited by Peter Morris, William J. Ryczek,
Jan Finkel, Leonard Levin and Richard Malatzky (2012)

LIBRARY OF CONGRESS CATALOGUING-IN-PUBLICATION DATA

Morris, Peter, 1962–
    Cracking baseball's cold cases : filling in the facts about 17
mystery major leaguers / Peter Morris.
        p.   cm.
    Includes bibliographical references and index.

    ISBN 978-0-7864-7545-2
    softcover : acid free paper ∞

    1. Baseball players — United States — Biography.
    2. Baseball players — United States — Anecdotes.   I. Title.
GV865.A1M665 2013
796.3570922 — dc23
[B]   2013007178

BRITISH LIBRARY CATALOGUING DATA ARE AVAILABLE

Cover images © 2013 Thinkstock/iStockphoto

Manufactured in the United States of America

*McFarland & Company, Inc., Publishers
    Box 611, Jefferson, North Carolina 28640
    www.mcfarlandpub.com*

To Marci Murphy

Table of Contents

Introduction

For the past two decades, I've been part of a small but determined group of baseball researchers who share an unusual goal. The various baseball encyclopedias list complete birth information for the vast majority of the approximately 18,000 men who have played major league baseball and in most cases there is death information for those who have passed away. But there are still a select few whose vital information includes only the word "deceased" where a date and place of death ought to appear. Those men are baseball's cold cases and it is the mission of the members of the Biographical Committee of the Society for American Baseball Research (SABR) to find when and where they died.

Those two decades of digging have produced outstanding results: a "missing player" list that once included more than 500 names has been trimmed in half during that period. The progress is all the more impressive because the death information of another one hundred major leaguers has been determined to be incorrect and either deleted or replaced with the correct information. So that equates to a batting average of around .600 in a sport where .300 is the benchmark of excellence.

But are these elusive players actually worth pursuing? Most of them had brief and undistinguished careers during the early years of professional baseball and have long been buried and forgotten. What reason could there be to try to track them down?

There are a few different ways to answer that question. One is to point out that the pursuit of these "missing players" has enriched our understanding of baseball history in unexpected ways:

- We discovered an obscure 1879 one-gamer named William Edward White, who was the first African American major leaguer.
- The search for a nondescript 1891 player named Patrick Murphy (see

chapter 11) led to such an abundance of revelations that I wrote a book about it.

• We tracked down a Negro League player named Ray Brown who was subsequently inducted into the National Baseball Hall of Fame.

Another approach is to highlight the ways in which these discoveries broaden our understanding of the backgrounds and motivations of the men who played the game during its early years.

These are all important byproducts of our research, yet none of them are what excites me most about the search for missing ballplayers. What truly fuels my passion for this research is the chance to get to the bottom of the mystery behind the "deceased" listing. In many cases, a missing player is found by tracking down a death certificate that reveals little about the man himself. From time to time, however, the search does shed new light on the player's life and it is those revelations that make all of the work seem worthwhile. Here are the stories of how some of the most memorable cold cases were solved.

Chapter 1

Walter Walker

A S THE FIRST "MISSING PLAYER" I helped to track down, Walter Walker
will always have a special significance to me. But Walker would have
been one of my most memorable cold cases under any circumstances because
of his remarkable and tragic life story.

I was born in England in 1962, but when I was still a toddler my family
moved to a suburb of Washington, D.C. I went to kindergarten there and
began to develop an interest in baseball from watching Senators games with
my father. Much of my enthusiasm stemmed from the colorful nicknames
such as "Harum Scarum" Narum and "Wee Willie" Kirkland that we used
when referring to the hometown players. (Only decades later, after I became
friends with Dave Baldwin, a Senators pitcher during those years, did I realize that many of those nicknames were the product of my father's fertile
imagination.)

At the end of that school year, however, we moved to Toronto. There
was no professional baseball team in the city at the time, so before long I
had learned to skate and was collecting and flipping hockey cards. Baseball
occupied a less important place in my boyhood reveries, but it never vanished
entirely. Trips to visit American cousins would bring back memories of the
first sport to have captivated me. One of my relatives even gave me a set of
baseball legend cards and I was introduced to magical names like Babe Ruth
and Christy Mathewson. The rules of the game were still a bit of a mystery
to me, but those cards intrigued me enough that I began asking for baseball
cards for my birthday each year. Before long, I set my sights higher and
requested a copy of the Macmillan *Baseball Encyclopedia*. As a result, I developed a passion for baseball that was the kind of distant affection a child feels
for something far away and seemingly unattainable.

The Blue Jays arrived in 1977 and things began to change when a
hockey-mad city fell in love with the American national pastime. In the

mid–1980s I took a summer job at the Canadian Baseball Hall of Fame, then located near Exhibition Stadium, the original home of the Blue Jays. It was a fateful decision that provided me with my initial exposure to baseball research.

My main responsibility was to act as an usher, but I took an interest in the history of the game in Canada and was soon assigned to answer questions. Most of those inquiries were straightforward, which was fortunate because my knowledge was still very limited. Things changed when I began receiving phone calls from a Chicagoan named Richard Topp.

Topp explained that he was chairman of the Society for American Baseball Research's Biographical Committee and was looking for information on some missing Canadian major leaguers. I wasn't able to be of much help and a less persistent person would have soon given up. But Richard kept calling back and encouraging me to search for information. No doubt he was hoping that I'd dig up the missing information, but more than anything else he seemed intent on getting me to share his passion for the detective work that such research required. And he succeeded — while I never did any significant research on missing ballplayers while working for the Canadian Baseball Hall of Fame, he got me intrigued.

I stayed in touch with Richard Topp and after moving to East Lansing, Michigan, to do graduate studies at Michigan State University, I asked him if he had any leads in mid–Michigan. He gave the name of Walter Walker and that was how my career as a baseball sleuth began in earnest.

It was apt for a Michigan State student to be looking for Walter Walker because Walker's line in the Macmillan *Baseball Encyclopedia* was spartan: his playing record consisted of four games for Baltimore in 1885, while the biographical line stated only that he had been born in Ionia, Michigan. Then came that dreaded word — "deceased." I had little else to go on but Richard Topp had instilled in me the faith that the truth about players like Walker was out there waiting to be discovered. So I called up my friend Dave MacGregor and asked him if he'd like to join me in an adventure. On a bright summer day in 1992 we set off on the thirty-mile drive to Ionia armed with plenty of optimism and a notebook containing a few scribbled clues that Topp had provided, plus the addresses of the county courthouse, the local historical society and public library.

Our first stop in Ionia was the county courthouse where, to use a baseball metaphor, we struck out. There was no death record for a Walter Walker in Ionia and county birth records didn't go back far enough to be of any help. Next it was off to the microfilm collection of the public library to scour the local newspapers of the era for additional clues. We started with the dates of Walker's four games with Baltimore, expecting that his hometown paper would be full of news about the local boy reaching the major leagues. To our disappointment, no mention at all was made of Walker's big league debut during that span, nor did subsequent issues make up for the omission. Worse, an article about a game played in Ionia made it seem as though Walker was not in Baltimore at all. It was an ominous sign, but I was too new at this type of research to recognize it as such.

With our initial efforts having met with failure, Dave and I turned next to the library's local history collection. There we made an exciting discovery: a listing of internments at Ionia's St. Peter and Paul Cemetery that included the burial of a Walter Walker in March of 1922. We returned to the microfilm reader with visions of a full-page obituary of Ionia's only major leaguer, only to once again meet with disappointment. The only reference to our man's passing was a brief piece that announced that "Wallie" Walker had died at his "home" in Pontiac and that his body would be brought home for burial. It seemed likely that we'd filled in the missing death information, but we now had a new mystery: why would Walker's death warrant such scant coverage in his hometown?

Dave and I spent a few more hours at the library without getting any further and then headed over to St. Peter and Paul Cemetery, where we looked in vain for Walter Walker's grave. At last we turned for home, thinking that we'd probably solved the underlying mystery but realizing that there were still many loose ends that would need to be filled in. Little did we know how much there still was to learn about Walter Walker.

When I phoned Richard Topp to update him on my progress, he advised me to obtain a death certificate from the state. He also told me that he would pass my discoveries along to a couple of experts who might be able to confirm my apparent find: Bill Carle, who had succeeded Topp as chairman of the Society for American Baseball Research's Biographical Committee, and a legendary researcher named Joe Simenic. So I filled out the necessary form at the State of Michigan's Public Health Department and waited expectantly for more news.

It didn't take long. Simenic consulted his vast files and passed along a series of notes about Walter Walker. Among them were a couple of articles from the late 1880s reported that Walker had given up baseball to become an attorney. The last one appeared in 1893 and bore the sad news that Walker had been declared insane and was institutionalized at an asylum in Pontiac.[1] Suddenly the brief mentions of his death made sense and the reference to his "home" in Pontiac took on new significance. When Walker's State of Michigan death certificate arrived, it confirmed that he was an attorney who had died at the Pontiac Valley Insane Asylum on February 28, 1922, where he had been a patient for nearly thirty years.

Our research, scant as it was, earned us the Biographical Committee's "Find of the Month Award" and a write-up in that month's newsletter under the headline, "Walter Walker Found!" But the satisfaction was soon tempered when Richard Topp phoned with disturbing news. Remember how the Ionia papers had failed to mention his major league debut and even seemed to state that he was in Ionia at the time? I'd brushed that off as a mistake, but in fact the error was mine. Topp informed me that Joe Simenic had done some more digging and suspected that the Baltimore games belonged to a different player named Oscar Walker. My excitement turned to alarm — could it be possible that I'd helped to track down a missing major leaguer only to have it turn out that he wasn't really a major leaguer at all?

Simenic kept plugging away and soon reported back with more news. Additional sources confirmed his hunch that Oscar Walker was the 1885 Baltimore player, meaning that those games would be eliminated from Walter's record. But it turned out that Walter Walker had played a single game for Detroit — then a National League team — on May 8, 1884. Walter Walker's place in the *Baseball Encyclopedia* was secure and, better still, in future editions the word "deceased" would be replaced with a full listing of his place and date of death.

The task of "finding" Walter Walker was now complete, but my curiosity wouldn't let it end there. The more I thought about the resolution of the Walter Walker mystery, the more I realized that many unanswered questions remained. How much more could be learned about his life? How had the Ionia papers covered his career and his all-too-brief stint as a major leaguer? Most of all, were there any clues as to why a life of such promise had gone so far astray? To try to find the answers, I paid a visit to the State Library of

Michigan, conveniently located in downtown Lansing. Each trip to the State Library offered a few new details and this life story gradually emerged.

Walter Walker had been born on March 12, 1860, the fifth of six children of Archibald and Mary Walker, Scottish immigrants who had initially settled in Hamilton, Ontario. The family had moved to Michigan shortly before Walter's birth and they moved frequently during the next few years. Walter was apparently born during a brief stay in the town of Berlin (which was renamed Marne as a result of the anti–German sentiment of World War I), but the family also lived in the town of Wright before settling permanently in Ionia around 1863. Archibald Walker died while Walter was young, but Mary Walker became proprietress of a successful Ionia hotel and there were no hardships for the youngster generally known as Wallie.

By the 1870s, Ionia had become a baseball hotbed, hosting an annual tournament that attracted top teams from all over Michigan and sometimes much further. At the 1876 tournament, future Hall of Famer James "Pud" Galvin of the Reds of St. Louis tossed the first perfect game in baseball history against the Cass Club of Detroit. His feat attracted scant attention, but one local paper did note: "The game was in some respects one of the most remarkable on record. The Cass boys did not make a base hit or reach first base during the game. Each man of the club batted three times and each was put out three times."[2] Amazingly, it was Galvin's second no-hitter of the day; he had also hurled a no-hitter in the morning game and only three errors by his teammates prevented Galvin from recording two perfect games in one day.

There is no way to be certain that Walter Walker witnessed Galvin's amazing feat, but it seems likely since the 16-year-old Walker was catcher and captain of the Stars of Ionia, one of the entrants in the tournament's junior division. If so, perhaps it inspired the teenager to dream of a career in professional baseball.

What we can safely assume is that that wasn't what Mary Walker had in mind for her son. He was an excellent student and in 1878, after graduating from the local high school, Walter Walker entered Assumption College in Sandwich, Ontario, to study for the priesthood. At some point during the next four years he must have had a change of heart, as he eventually graduated with a degree in "belles letters," the nineteenth-century equivalent of a degree in literature.

After returning to Ionia, Walker became the owner of a local cigar factory and also served as city clerk.[3] Walker also worked briefly for the State Department in Lansing. It was not the last time that a missing player would surprise me by turning up right under my nose. Yet baseball had found a place in his heart and he pursued it whenever possible. He umpired briefly in the Northwestern League, a top minor league, and earned a growing reputation as one of the state's best amateur catchers. In 1883, he caught several games for the Cass Club — the club that had been the victims of Galvin's perfect game — and his work was impressive enough to earn him a contract with the National League's Detroit Wolverines for the 1884 season.

The Wolverines held their spring training workouts in Richmond, Virginia, and initial reviews of his work were glowing. "Walker caught," raved the *Free Press* after his first exhibition game appearance, "and though he never saw [pitcher Dupee] Shaw previous to the first instant he caught him perfectly. Such a performance is wonderful.... It will leave little doubt in the minds of the Detroit people that the club, for the first time in its history, has two efficient batteries." Detroit's starting catcher, Charley Bennett, echoed the praise of his young back-up.[4]

But then a hand injury began to nag Walker and his performance suffered. He was also distracted, as his younger brother James had disappeared while on an outing to Bois Blanc Island in northern Michigan. While the family anxiously awaited word of James's fate, Walter's older brother Archibald, Jr., was severely injured in a logging accident and had to be rushed to the Flint Surgical Institute.

Detroit began the regular season with a long road trip and chalked up four straight losses with Bennett behind the plate. Walker's hand had still not healed, but manager Jack Chapman nonetheless pressed him into duty on a rainy day in New York on May 9, 1884. Shaw's difficult curves proved overwhelming and the rookie was charged with seven passed balls and two errors, although he did manage a single and scored a run. After that inauspicious debut, Chapman sent Walker back to Detroit for the balance of the road trip.

The Ionia papers jumped to Walker's defense, accusing Chapman of playing the young catcher after he had told his manager that he was not well enough to play. Meanwhile Walter's brother Archibald was making great progress toward a full recovery and on May 14 Mary Walker decided that it was safe to return home to Ionia. To her horror, however, she discovered that the train taking her home was also bearing the body of her youngest son James, whose body had at last been found on a remote part of Bois Blanc Island. Walter Walker traveled back to Ionia for the funeral and while he was there the Detroit management heartlessly released him, ending his major league career.

He had stints with several minor league teams over the next few seasons, but never earned a return trip to the major leagues. In the fall of 1885 he began to study law in the office of a local lawyer. He attacked his studies with characteristic diligence and passed the state bar exam on February 20, 1886. One month later he and another new attorney, Fred C. Wallington, opened a practice in Mt. Pleasant, making it look as though Walter Walker's involvement with baseball had come to an end.

Instead business was slow and when an offer to play minor league baseball in New York State arose, Walker jumped at the opportunity. Wallington was miffed by his partner's defection and when Walker returned in the fall he chose to buy him out. Suddenly at a loose end, Walker accepted the Democratic nomination for prosecuting attorney of Isabella County in September and was soon embroiled in a contentious campaign. The Republican nominee was none other than Wallington, who was not shy about warning voters that Walker might desert his responsibilities to play baseball.

Walker nonetheless won and he served the county for two years with distinction, while at the same time building a private practice. Despite his busy schedule, Walker also made frequent visits back to Ionia and these began to become the subject of local gossip. On November 15, 1887, their purpose became clear when Walker returned to Ionia once more to marry 26-year-old Jennie V. Kimball. All in all, these were two years chock full of professional and personal fulfillment.

They came to the end with the election of 1888, as a backlash against President Grover Cleveland, a Democrat, resulted in a Republican clean sweep of Mt. Pleasant. The popular Walker lost his race by the narrowest margin of any Democrat, but that was little consolation. He and his new wife remained in Mt. Pleasant for only a few more months, before relocating to Detroit in March of 1889.[5]

The baseball bug soon bit Walker again and he began playing for the Detroit Athletic Club's baseball team, a squad that also included future

Detroit mayor John C. Lodge. In 1891, Walker became involved with an effort to revive the Northwestern League, a minor league in which he had previously played and umpired. With his usual vigor, he soon was functioning as president, secretary and treasurer of the league, and as secretary and treasurer of the of the Detroit entry.

Key planks of the league included a strict salary cap and Sunday baseball, but both innovations were plagued with troubles. Some clubs circumvented the salary cap, leading to competitive imbalance, while churches and police disrupted efforts to play Sunday baseball. Clubs soon began to drop out and Walker also left before midseason.

The failure must have been devastating and may have contributed to his mental breakdown. On July 13, 1892, Walter Walker was admitted to a private asylum in Dearborn. After ten months, his wife's financial resources were exhausted and Walker was institutionalized in the Pontiac Valley Asylum.[6] Diagnosed with dementia and monomania, Walter never recovered and remained in the asylum until his death.[7]

The terrible sadness of the situation was made worse by his wife's predicament. Rather than seek a divorce, Jennie Walker had stood by her stricken husband and hoped against hope for his recovery, even continuing to list his name in the Detroit city directory. But in 1905 she at last sought a divorce on the grounds of cruelty and drunkenness, only to find that she had fallen into a legal limbo because her husband was unable to respond to the charges.

"The case is surely a peculiar one," explained an unnamed Detroit lawyer. "In Michigan insanity is no ground for divorce and, to obtain a decree, some cause or ground must be found which dates back of the time insanity began. In this case, it is apparent that the charges made in the bill are at least ten years old, a rather odd state of affairs. I understand that cruelty and drunkenness are charged. I have been a friend of Mr. Walker for years and I only want to see him get a square deal."[8]

It appears that Jennie Walker did eventually succeed in obtaining her divorce, since her husband's death certificate lists him as divorced. What became of her remains unknown.

Chapter 2

Seymour Studley

THE RELATIVE EASE WITH WHICH Dave MacGregor and I had tracked down Walter Walker led me to imagine that other cold cases would prove just as easy. Alas, the other missing players from Michigan that Richard Topp suggested I work on had ridiculously common names such as Ed Miller, John Ryan, and Henry Jones. Over the next few years I developed leads on each of these men, only to have them disappear without a trace. Biographical research, I was learning, was not easy.

At times I found these searches frustrating, but what never waned was my fascination with nineteenth-century baseball. Like most baseball fans, I had been fooled into creating an arbitrary line that designated 1900 as the start of "modern baseball." In turn, everything before that date effectively was relegated to second-class status. Once I had the chance to read nineteenth-century baseball reportage for myself, I came to see how misguided that notion was. It was hard to read a single day's baseball coverage without gaining new insights into the game's development and gaining a new appreciation for the unpredictability and sheer fun of early baseball.

My research interests gradually expanded and I published my first baseball article — a profile of Walter Walker, naturally enough — and began working on a book about the history of early baseball in Michigan (which was eventually published as *Baseball Fever* [2003, University of Michigan]). Yet I never stopped pursuing missing players and began corresponding with members of the Biographical Committee all over the country — Carle in Kansas City, Simenic in Cleveland, Bob Richardson in Boston, Bill Haber in New York, Jay Sanford in Denver, Reed Howard in Wilmington, Delaware, and Debi Dagavarian-Bonar in New Jersey, just to name a few. Each of them had their own research interests, their own pet projects, and their own theories as to where a missing player might have gone, which made the exchange of information all the more enjoyable.

Steadily the ranks of baseball's cold cases were winnowed down, but the progress remained slow until the late 1990s when two developments changed everything. The first was the emergence of the Internet as a research tool so powerful that it became possible to find players on the other side of the country without leaving the house. The other was the return to the pursuit of missing players of a New York City researcher named Richard Malatzky who brought two invaluable resources to the committee: a thorough knowledge of how to access New York's wealth of resources and an extraordinary dedication for following up on any lead, no matter how unpromising.

It is not an overstatement to say that these two windfalls revolutionized the way we did research. The majority of our missing players vanished in the late nineteenth or early twentieth century when there was no FBI and few of the forms of identification that we now take for granted.[1] The result was that an American who didn't want to be traced for any reason — criminal activities, a bad marriage, debts, etc. — found it all too easy to disappear. More frustratingly, even a person who relocated without any intention of vanishing could be maddeningly difficult to trace.

Our efforts to track these players down were plagued by the same obstacles, which made the research painstakingly slow and unsystematic. We might discover that a missing ballplayer was from Cincinnati and lived there until 1903, but if he moved at that point we could do little more than guess at where he would turn up next. We knew that the censuses and city directories probably held the solution to the mystery, but these resources were indexed imperfectly, if at all, and had to be searched one at a time. Even if the missing player possessed an unusual name, the hunt was likely to be very time-consuming. Throw a common name into the mix and it became like looking for a needle in a haystack.

A perfect example was a missing one-game major leaguer named Fred Gunkle, who by all rights should have been an easy find: his surname was rare, he worked for the same company for fifty years, and he and his wife enjoyed a marriage of similar length. The lone problem was that he worked as a salesman and moved often enough to make our lives miserable. One step at a time, during the pre–Internet years, we traced his steps from Reading (Pa.) to Chicago to Iowa to South Dakota and at last to Indianapolis, only to conclude after patient inquiry that he didn't die in any of these locales. Then came the Internet and it became a snap to unearth the humdrum solution to the mystery: Gunkle and his wife retired to California and died there.

Then there was the case of Seymour Studley. Despite being a member of one of the first legendary baseball clubs and the possessor of a very unusual name, Studley seemingly had vanished into thin air. The return of Richard Malatzky to baseball research and the new tools made available by the Internet took us in a surprising direction and gave us a deeper appreciation of the reality that many missing players had disappeared to escape an unhappy life. Even more excitingly, it revealed just how easy it could be to turn an obscure player into a fleshed-out portrait.

Here's what we knew about Studley in the days before we could rely upon the Internet.

Seymour Studley was about 26 when he burst on the baseball scene in 1867 as part of the first major recruiting effort in baseball history (and for that matter in sports history). Two powerful Washingtonians and baseball enthusiasts, Colonel Frank Jones and future Senator Arthur Pue Gorman, were the driving forces behind a powerful club called the Nationals. After the war, they began aggressively recruiting players from New York to strengthen the club, using government clerkships in the Department of Treasury as inducements.

Before long, the lineup of the once-local Nationals featured New Yorkers at most positions, including Harry Berthrong, Dennis Coughlin, Frank Prescott Norton, Warren White, George Wright, George Fletcher and Seymour Studley. Future Hall of Famer Wright, although still a teenager, was the captain and by far the best player, and probably was paid simply for playing. The rest appear to have had actual clerkships and responsibilities that went along with them.

Nonetheless, these responsibilities were not onerous enough to prevent the players from embarking on a month-long tour in July of 1867. This historic tour marked the first time an eastern club had ventured west of the Allegheny mountain range and was the subject of a chapter in Albert G. Spalding's *America's National Game*. Seymour Studley was one of the starters on that team, and thus was a participant in some of the legendary games of early baseball, including the dramatic upset of the Nationals by a mere "country club" from Rockford, Illinois, and their 16-year-old pitcher, Spalding.

George Wright left for greener pastures the following year, while Gorman began devoting more time to his burgeoning political career. The Olympic Club of Washington began to lure away many of the remaining players, and the Nationals reverted to being primarily a club of local amateurs. Several New Yorkers, however, remained with the club, including Studley, who was a fixture in the outfield of the Nationals until the club disbanded after the 1870 season.

Baseball's first major league, the National Association, was formed in 1871, and prior to its second season the Nationals decided to reorganize. The experiment proved only that the game had passed them by, as the once-mighty club lost all eleven games that it played before withdrawing. These games did, however, allow the now 31-year-old Studley to have his name entered in the baseball encyclopedias, along with the (possibly spurious) nickname of "Warhorse." As far as we know, this brought an end to Seymour Studley's baseball career.

With such a distinctive name, Studley should have been easy to trace and initially this proved to be true. The Washington city directories listed him as a Treasury Department clerk from 1867 to 1873, first living with his brother Henry and then getting his own place after his marriage to a woman named Ernestine. Then in 1875 and several succeeding years, Ernestine's name appears instead, working as a clerk and often denoted as a widow. As confirmation, when the couple's infant daughter Josephine died, a death notice in a Washington newspaper referred to the father as "the late Seymour Studley."

It seemed obvious that Studley had died in the mid–1870s and the only question was exactly when and where. Yet a series of researchers tried to find a death certificate without success, leaving the search at a dead end.

There were a few stray clues that turned up as well. During his playing career, Studley told the *New York Clipper* that he had fought in the Civil War and there was a matching service record for a 100-day regiment. We were also able to trace family members in Rochester, New York, where Studley had lived before arriving in Washington.[2] Yet such clues seemed of little value since we were convinced that Studley died in the mid–1870s, probably in Washington, and needed only to find his death certificate to solve the case.

Everything changed when an intriguing e-mail arrived from Richard

Malatzky. He had been plugging the names of missing players into the growing number of searchable databases on the Internet and got some surprising hits when he entered Studley's name. "If we didn't know that Studley was dead by the mid–1870s," he mused, "you'd swear he was alive for years afterward." He pointed out in particular that a 1900 census listing in Nebraska looked for all the world like our missing ballplayer.

More digging turned up additional reasons to question the longstanding assumption that Seymour Studley had died young. Ernestine Studley was listed as a widow on the 1880 census, but by that time she had a three-year-old son named George whose father was listed as having been born in the state of New York. An 1878 article about the whereabouts of the old Nationals in the *Clipper* also indicated that Studley was alive.[3] A search of Rochester city directories turned up a listing for Seymour again living with his father in 1876 and then five more listings from 1879 to 1883. This man did not appear on the 1880 census, so it was still conceivable that this was a different relative by the same name, but it was looking more and more as though Seymour Studley was alive after his wife had begun listing herself as a widow.

The 1900 census listing in Nebraska led us to focus our attention there and compelling new evidence emerged. To begin with, there was an Omaha marriage listing for a 42-year-old Seymour L. Studley and Katie Clark on November 10, 1883, followed by several listings for Studley in the Lincoln city directory. This man next applied for a Civil War invalid pension on February 3, 1890, and two years later he was married for a third time, to a Mary Brennan of Lincoln. This was the same woman who was listed as his wife on the 1900 census listing and things got very interesting when she applied for a Civil War pension on September 15, 1901.

I sent a letter to the Nebraska State Historical Society to see if they had a record and received a copy of the burial card for one S.L. Studley, who had been born in 1841 in Bryan, New York, and had died on July 9, 1901, at the Nebraska Soldiers' and Sailors' Home in Grand Island. We knew that Seymour's father had been living in Bryan in the early 1840s, so there was now no doubt that the mystery had been solved. As added confirmation, a Rochester paper printed an obituary that described Studley as "a well-known baseball player, playing with the Charter Oaks and Stars, at the time when those teams and the Flour Citys, Live Oaks and Olympics were prominent in baseball circles. He afterward joined the National club, of Washington, together with Henry W. Berthrong and Dennis Coughlin of Rochester. Mr. Studley was a member of the Fifty-fourth Regiment and a member of 'Live Oak,' No. 3, situated on West Alexander street, in the days of the volunteer fire department."[4]

Once again, finding the missing player helped unravel a fascinating story. Invalid pensions were routinely granted to Civil War veterans, wounded or not, and it seemed unlikely that a young recruit like Studley who had served in a 100-day regiment and seen no battlefield combat had endured a debilitating injury. But when Bill Carle sent for Studley's pension records, we were in for a surprise.

After a day of loading horses onto a car, Seymour Studley had suffered such a severe case of sunstroke that he was unconscious for 20–30 minutes. Doctors warned him never again to go out in the sun, which would have ended his baseball career then and there if he had complied (since night baseball was still many decades in the future). Instead, only three years later, during the Nationals' celebrated 1867 tour, Studley played in at least one game in St. Louis where the temperature reached 100 degrees. Obviously his love for the national pastime was very great!

Studley's pension records and additional research also made it clear that his was a troubled life. He and his third wife both struggled with alcoholism, while his first marriage was troubled from the start — eleven months after their wedding, Studley was jailed for assaulting both his wife and a friend who came to her assistance.[5]

Did Seymour Studley's wartime case of sunstroke cause his later troubles? There was no way to be certain. But we did learn two important lessons from the surprising resolution of the long search for him. The first was what became known as the "Seymour Studley rule": never assume that finding a ballplayer's wife listed as a widow means that he is dead. The second was that missing ballplayers frequently were hard to trace precisely because of unhappiness in their lives. In fact, since any player still missing after all these years has frustrated generations of researchers, I now work on the assumption that some calamitous event is going to befall any missing player. When you start with a player and have an easy time finding his hometown and identifying his family, it's a virtual certainty that something is about to go horribly wrong. To use just a few examples of players who are still missing or who have been recently tracked down, the player in question will go to jail (Harry Decker, Pearce Chiles, Arthur Twineham, Jack Brennan); abscond with money (Joe Quest, Bob Leadley); leave his wife (Billy Magee, George Crable, Creed Bates); leave the country (Tom Letcher, Bob Leadley, Matthew Porter, William Pfann); go insane (Walker, Horace Phillips, Jake Knowdell); or have some other calamity befall him. Both of these rules of thumb would be consulted often in our later searches.

Chapter 3

Tom Carey

THE SEARCH FOR SEYMOUR STUDLEY had taught us not to put too much faith in a listing of a ballplayer's wife as a widow. The pursuit of Tom Carey made us realize that even a listing in the *Baseball Encyclopedia* could not always be trusted. Tom Carey, you see, was listed as having had a real name of J.J. Norton and as having been died in Los Angeles in 1899. This listing did correspond to an obituary in *Sporting Life* of a ballplayer named J.J. Norton who used Carey as a baseball alias, but there were a couple of problems. To begin with, the *Sporting Life* obituary gave the player's name as Jack Carey, rather than Tom Carey. That discrepancy might just have been an error, but there was a second discrepancy that could not be explained away: the death certificate of J.J. Norton showed that he was born in 1872, which was a full year after Tom Carey began his nine-year major league career.

More digging made it clear just how much faith was placed in encyclopedia data, whether justified or not. The clearly impossible J.J. Norton listing dated back to Hy Turkin and S.C. Thompson's pioneering *Official Encyclopedia of Baseball*, first published in 1951.[1] Turkin and Thompson's work was characterized by its great ambition, but that same ambition ensured that the project would be plagued by troubles. The resources needed to fill in dates of death with a high degree of accuracy did not yet exist and, with time also an issue, the published work included many identifications that do not survive scrutiny.

Subsequent researchers focused on filling in the gaps in the paradigm created by Turkin and Thompson, rather than questioning and re-examining their listings. The case of Tom Carey provided an extreme example of this tendency.

Away back in 1963, Baseball Hall of Fame historian Lee Allen wrote as follows to fellow researcher Tom Shea: "I believe all the deaths of 1876 players in the Encyclopedia are correct except for that of Thomas John Carey, who is shown as having expired on Feb. 13, 1899. The *Clipper Almanac* identifies the man who died on that date as John Carey, an infielder who died in Los Angeles. Turkin probably saw that and leaped to the conclusion it was Thomas John."[2]

Another researcher sent to California for J.J. Norton's death certificate and had noticed the obvious problem that Tom Carey was already playing in the major leagues when Norton was born. Yet instead of challenging the information, he simply noted the issue as a discrepancy and did not try to get a correction made.

Once the misinformation had at long last been removed from the encyclopedias, it was back to square one. There proved to be an abundance of notes that made it possible to fill in Carey's baseball career in considerable detail. An 1870 newspaper profile was especially helpful, showing that Carey played with the junior Amity Club of Brooklyn until 1867, then spent the 1869 season in San Francisco with the Eagle Club before returning east to play for the Marylands of Baltimore. An extended major league career followed, which included a season with the Fort Wayne Kekiongas, two in Baltimore, a year with the New York Mutuals, three seasons in Hartford, and one season apiece with Providence and Cleveland.

Among his career achievements was the distinction of recording the first two outs in major league history. On May 4, 1871, Carey started at second base for the Kekiongas against the Cleveland Forest Citys in the National Association's inaugural contest. After Cleveland leadoff hitter Deacon White slashed a double, the second batter, Gene Kimball, hit a sharp line drive to Carey, who then tagged out White to complete an unassisted double play.

Although he began his career as a second baseman, Carey's slight built and great speed made him better suited to shortstop. He was never a formidable hitter, but his slick fielding meant that his services were always in demand. "In the first days of the big league all the shortstops were little men," recalled ballplayer-turned-sportswriter Byron Clarke. "Carey, of Hartford, was a cracker jack of a short, wonderfully fast on his feet, and could run like a deer. His legs looked the spokes in a wheel when he was running to first base."[3] He led the National League in games played at shortstop in 1876, 1877, and 1878 — the league's first three seasons.

Tom Carey also served as captain of several major league teams, setting defensive alignments and handling other in-game strategy. But his fitness for this role was questioned during his final National League season, with the *Cleveland Plain Dealer* scolding: "It seems as if Captain Carey was ignorant of the fact that the other fielders depend upon him to call one of them to take a fly when three or four are in position to capture it."[4]

Perhaps the criticism had something to do with the decision Carey made next. He headed back to San Francisco after the 1878 season ended and spent as much of the winter as the climate permitted playing for the Eagles. When spring came, he chose to end his major league career and accepted the position of player-manager of another San Francisco club, the Athletics. The club must have been very well financed, for in March Tom Carey came east on a scouting trip and signed three well-known professional players: William J. Sweeney, Tom Dolan, and James "Pud" Galvin.[5] Yes, that James Galvin — the future Hall of Famer who had pitched a perfect game and a no-hitter on a single day at the 1876 tournament played in Walter Walker's hometown.

Unfortunately, the funding does not seem to have been enough, as Galvin soon got a better offer and returned east, with the others eventually following. Worse, Carey's bat collapsed completely and after compiling a .211 average in 32 games his playing days drew to an end. By 1882 Carey was back east again, umpiring in a newly formed major league, the American Association.[6] Alas, he was dismissed from the position after a controversial decision in which he called a base-runner out for delay of game because the runner had scampered home from second base on a foul ball.[7] So Carey made the long trip back to San Francisco, where he umpired local games for several more years. "The once noted Tom Cary [sic]," read an 1886 note, "is now umpiring in San Francisco."[8] And with that Tom Carey's name vanished from the sporting presses, an absence that led to the bizarre J.J. Norton listing.

Yet all the attention paid to Carey's on-field exploits was not matched by a corresponding wealth of notes about his life. One potentially valuable clue was a note that Carey, "it is stated, formerly belonged to the Presidio garrison of San Francisco, and in 1869 was a member of the Presidio and Eagle Clubs of that city."[9] Membership in the Presidio suggested that he might have been a Civil War veteran, but the wording was too vague to remove all doubts. In light of Carey's common name, his military service could not be established with certainty. Another promising clue was an 1879 note in the *New York Clipper* that Carey had become a father on April 28.[10] But the place of birth was not indicated and efforts to find a corresponding birth certificate or listing on the 1880 census were unsuccessful.

The end result was that there wasn't much hard information to base a search upon. We had a man with a fairly common name and a few stray clues that might prove helpful, but nothing that could be considered firm. The 1870 profile gave his age as 21, but baseball ages have always been unreliable and he might well have been several years older. Brooklyn seemed to be where he grew up, but he had a distressing tendency to flit about the county, even by the standards of an era of great mobility. Brooklyn, Baltimore, and San Francisco seemed to be his primary bases, but he had played in several other cities and there was no guarantee that those were the right places to look.

It was now clear that finding Tom Carey was not going to be a simple task. When searching for a man with a name as distinctive as Seymour Studley, it's not likely that you'll end up having to determine which of several men by that name was the ballplayer. Indeed, as we had learned, even when the name Seymour Studley pops up in as unlikely a place as Nebraska there's a very good chance that it will turn out to be the ballplayer. Walter Walker was not as unusual of a name, but it was far from common and when paired with the hometown of Ionia there was little likelihood of confusion. But here we had a man with a common name who was difficult to pin down. So we did the only thing possible and began making assumptions.

A few words about assumptions are in order. The most dangerous thing that any researcher can do is to make an assumption, as had been shown by the J.J. Norton listing. In that worst-case scenario, a ballplayer who had been mistakenly identified as the major leaguer, even though that man had not even been born when the real major leaguer's career began.

Yet, paradoxically, even though assumptions are extremely dangerous, good researchers make them all the time. When there is no alternative, they even make guesses. There is, of course, a crucial distinction between the faulty reasoning behind the J.J. Norton fiasco and the approach that meticulous researchers take. Careful research involves keeping track of every assumption or guess that was made and never confusing such leaps with actual facts. Any time such a leap of logic is made, the researcher must keep in mind that no subsequent conclusion can be relied upon until it has been validated by proof that establishes the correctness of each and every assumption.

Assumptions play an especially large role in genealogical research. Census listings and city directory listings are the primary way to trace a person, but it is always an assumption to conclude that the person found on the 1900 census is the same person as the one found on the 1910 census. In many cases, the assumption is a trivial one: if the man is at the same address on two consecutive censuses, with matching ages, birthplaces, occupations, and family members, then there is no reasonable doubt of it being the same man. But usually at least a few changes will occur in the course of a decade, and the larger the differences, the greater the possibility of error. Similarly, a man's listing in the city directory rarely remains identical over a long period of time and the directory provides fewer accompanying details, which makes assumptions unavoidable.

Along the way, some doubt inevitably creeps in, which is why sound genealogical research involves documenting any assumptions and, at the end of the process, finding the proof necessary to verify them. In the case of looking for "missing" ballplayers, the gold standard is an obituary that describes the man's baseball career. That is not, however, the only possibility. For example, the 1880 census listed John Curran as a "base ball player" living at 60 Tehama, San Francisco, with family members who included his brother Thomas and his widowed mother Ann. Curran proved very difficult to trace in subsequent years, but we eventually found a strong candidate who had died in Vallejo, California, in 1896. An obituary made no reference to baseball, but it did list survivors who included his mother Ann and his brother Thomas and stated that the funeral would be held at the home of a second brother at 62 Tehama in San Francisco. Obviously, we had the right man.

In the case of Tom Carey, since he last had been heard from in San Francisco, that was the logical place to begin the search. The 1890 California Great Register of Voters provided a promising candidate: a Thomas Joseph Carey, age 42, born in the state of New York, occupation laborer, living at 787 Folsom in San Francisco. There was a Thomas J. Carey, occupation laborer, at that address in the 1891 city directory, along with a Joseph Carey, who was also a laborer. The search seemed to be heating up.

Unfortunately, things got more difficult after that. There was no Thomas J. Carey at that address in subsequent years, though the 1892 and '93 city directories had a Thomas J. Carey, bartender, who looked like a possibility. A few articles in the *San Francisco Call* mentioned that this man was a bartender at a rather disreputable bar called the Wigwam, and that in December of 1893 he and the bar's owners were arrested and charged with several crimes, including serving alcohol to minors.[11] Perhaps that is why the only Thomas J. Carey listed in the next two city directories had a different occupation and address. Within a few years there was no man by that name in the directory, while Joseph Carey also disappeared.

The 1900 census was the next place to check but there were no good matches in San Francisco. When we looked further afield, however, we found an excellent candidate who was an "inmate" at a veterans' home in Napa County. Thomas J. Carey, according to the listing, was a widower who had been born in New York in March of 1846 to Irish immigrants. This was a good match to everything we knew about the ballplayer.

We wrote away for records of the veterans' home and received some intriguing information. The pensioner had enlisted in New York City on September 17, 1863, as a Private in Company C of the 17th New York Infantry. After seeing combat duty in Atlanta, Jonesboro, and Bentonville, he had been discharged in July of 1865. He had entered the home on May 1, 1896, suffering from "piles" (hemorrhoids), and reported that he was single, a laborer, had been born in New York in 1846, and had been living in California for thirty years. There were a few discrepancies, but all in all it was an excellent fit, and the date of admission explained why our best candidate had vanished from the San Francisco city directories.

But while everything seemed to point to this being our long-lost ballplayer, there was one huge problem. The records of the veterans' home also stated that Carey had left on October 11, 1905, and provided this explanation: "Discharged from the Vets. Home for noncompliance with pension rules and deserting with $6.50 of clothing." Tom Carey had eluded our pursuit once again and now it appeared that he was a fugitive with $6.50 worth of the veterans' home's clothing!

Worst of all, while we had a very strong circumstantial case that this was the ballplayer, we had made some assumptions along the way and still didn't have the proof needed to validate them. So even though there seemed to have been considerable progress in the search, we were still in the unhappy position of looking for an elusive man who might not even be the ballplayer.

Civil War pension records seemed the logical place to check, but every available pension request filed by dependents of a Thomas Carey was checked without finding a match. Of course that wasn't terribly surprising, since the veteran we had been tracing had reported himself as single in 1896. Death records were next and while there were several men of the right approximate age, one stood out: a Thomas Carey, age 61, who died in San Francisco on August 16, 1906. None of the available San Francisco newspapers had an obituary for this man but there was a brief notice in the *Call* that described him as a native of New York. So I wrote out a check to the State of California and waited patiently for his death certificate to arrive.

When the document arrived, it proved a mixed blessing. Tom Carey's death certificate left little doubt that that he was the Civil War veteran we'd been trying to trace, as he was buried at the National Cemetery at the Presidio. Other details also matched (his occupation of laborer, for instance), but there weren't enough of them to satisfy my curiosity. He had died at the City Hospital after a 24-day stay and it didn't seem that he had any relatives to provide information. He was listed as having been born in New York in 1845 but someone had placed question marks in the line where the day and month should have appeared. As a result, while it looked as though the mystery had been solved, there were still some genuine doubts. We had made several assumptions in the process and now that the search had ended, we hadn't come up with the "smoking gun" that would make it possible to conclude that those assumptions had been justified.

The one important new clue provided by the death certificate was the name of his parents: John Carey and the former Mary Burke, both of whom had been born in Ireland. This gave hope of finally identifying our ballplayer in the early censuses and finding positive proof that linked him to baseball. Yet even with this new information, efforts to find a census listing were unsuccessful.

In the meantime, the availability of Civil War pension records had been expanded and another check of them proved more fruitful. A record for Thomas Carey of the 17th New York Infantry, Company C, revealed that he had applied for a disability pension on September 3, 1896, and had died on August 16, 1906. It also informed us of additional service in other

Civil War regiments: the 2nd US Artillery, Companies F and M, and "Gen. Ser. USA" (presumably general service).

A check of a Civil War database turned up another lead that was worth investigating. Regiment records for the 17th Infantry gave this man's name as "Tom Casey" and showed that a "John Casey" and a "Martin Casey" enlisted in the same regiment within days. Was it possible that these were brothers and that all of their names had been mistranscribed? But research failed to resolve this question and other lines of inquiry yielded nothing new.

Having exhausted all vital records that were likely to help, it was time to take a step back and review our research. When we did so, two things became clear. The first was that we still did not have a "smoking gun" that proved the Tom Carey who died in San Francisco on August 16, 1906, was the former major leaguer. The second was that the circumstantial evidence pointing to that conclusion was overwhelming. The ballplayer was born in New York in the mid- to late 1840s; so was our candidate. The ballplayer first arrived in San Francisco in the late 1860s and spent most of the rest of his life there; that was also true, with a few minor discrepancies, of our candidate. Most important, the ballplayer had a connection to the San Francisco Presidio and so did our candidate. Even with a common name and some unresolved issues, it seemed hard to imagine that the two were not one and the same. On that basis, Bill Carle decided to accept the find of Tom Carey and the new death information took the place of J.J. Norton's information.

Yet the lack of closure continued to bother me and I kept my eyes open for additional information. Several years later, the elusive proof presented itself in the form of several previously undiscovered newspaper articles from 1906 and 1907. A 1907 compilation of recent baseball deaths in an Alabama newspaper included Tom Carey, described as a former major leaguer, who had died in San Francisco on August 21.[12] Better still, an August 28, 1906, article from a North Dakota paper reported: "Tom Carey, at one time a member of [Cap] Anson's Chicago team ... died in a San Francisco hospital a few days ago."[13]

Carey had never played for Chicago and the date of death was also a few days off. Also strange was the appearance of these articles in such far-flung newspapers, rather than ones in San Francisco or the many cities where he had actually played. Yet such quibbles mattered little, since we now had indisputable proof that the missing man had been found.

Particularly intriguing was a third article that was published in the *San Francisco Call* on May 24, 1906, three months before Carey's death and only five weeks after the devastating earthquake. Though littered with errors, the piece does fill in more gaps and provide insight into the elusive ballplayer's final days. "Tom Carey, the famous old-time short-stop," it announced, "is in the bread line at the park, down and out. Carey says his baseball days are over and cheerfully remarks that the sore-arm liniment, as he terms our fog, has put his 'wing on the bum.' The old fans will remember the days when Carey was regarded as the greatest shortstop in the baseball world. 'Them were 'appy days,' and old Tom Carey, one of the highest-priced ballplayers of his time, stands with the rest, in line, waiting for his daily handout."

We are told that Carey "can sit and talk by the hour about old-time ballplayers" and several anecdotes follow. Did he recall recording the first two putouts in major league history? Or reminisce about some of the star players he had played with during his stops in New York, Hartford, Cleveland, Providence and Fort Wayne? Nope—we are instead given a bizarre tale in which Carey "went on the field once to play the Knickerbockers in this city with a large revolver strapped around his belt. He was quickly seized and asked what he was going to do with the gun. Carey laughingly replied that he had heard that they shot a man out West for making an error and wanted to be prepared for any reception."

The article does close in poignant fashion: "'I've got a couple of glass arms now,' says Carey sadly; 'the bread line is my only chance.'"[14]

It was gratifying at last to have everything tied up neatly. Yet in the process of finding Tom Carey and expunging J.J. Norton from the baseball encyclopedias, another troubling issue had emerged. We were now aware that, in addition to searching for the players who were officially missing, it would also be necessary for us to keep an eye out for players whose date and place of death were supposedly known but who were in fact still missing.

There was a renowned doctor who liked to warn his medical students that 98 percent of what they would learn in medical school was true and the other 2 percent untrue and that there was no way for them to distinguish between the two during their student years. As a result, he counseled, once they began practicing medicine and started looking for the solutions to unsolved medical mysteries, they would also need to remain on the lookout for pieces of accepted medical wisdom that were untrue. We were learning that the same principle applied to the much less weighty matter of finding missing major league players.

Chapter 4

Eddie Kolb

Tom Carey had a solid major league career that included nine years as a big league regular and was highlighted by recording the first two putouts in major league history. By contrast, Eddie Kolb made an error in his only big league fielding chance and the circumstances that led up to that error would have embarrassed most people. But the Biographical Committee does not draw distinctions on the basis of the length or success of a player's career and Eddie Kolb was a ballplayer we desperately wanted to track down.

Plenty was known about the early years of Eddie Kolb's life. Born in Cincinnati on July 20, 1880, Edward William Kolb was one of five surviving children of Louis and Minnie Kolb.[1] By 1899, he was captaining the Norwood Base Ball Club and dreaming of a career in professional baseball.[2] There is no indication that he possessed major league talent, but he got his name in the encyclopedias anyhow because he seized a unique chance that presented itself.

The Cleveland Spiders had been one of the National League's strongest teams during the early to mid–1890s, boasting stars like Cy Young and Jesse Burkett and a fiery manager in Patsy Tebeau. But the club's owners, brothers Frank and M. Stanley Robison, became increasingly frustrated by the lackluster attendance at Spiders games and began to consider alternatives. When the team slid back into the middle of the pack, they made a drastic decision. Prior to the 1899 season, they purchased the St. Louis entry in the same league and assigned future Hall of Famers Young, Burkett and Bobby Wallace to their new club, along with manager Tebeau.

Cleveland was left with a team so hopelessly inept that it won only won only 20 games all season. By the second half of the season, scheduled home games were being played as road games whenever possible, which led the press to dub the club the "Exiles," the "Misfits," and the "Forsakens."

To make matters worse, the Robisons fell far behind on meeting the club's payroll.

On October 8, 1899, the vagabond team arrived in Cincinnati for the final series of the dismal season. Nineteen-year-old Eddie Kolb was working as a cigar boy at the Gibson House, the Cincinnati hotel where the team was staying, and he sensed an opportunity. Somehow he persuaded Cleveland player-manager Joe Quinn to let him pitch the second game of a Sunday doubleheader on October 15, the last day of the season. "Manager Quinn," reported the *Plain Dealer*, "sprung a local amateur named Kolb on the Reds in the second game."[3]

The results were predictable. Facing a lineup that included future Hall of Famers Sam Crawford, Jake Beckley and Bid McPhee, Kolb was "given a severe drubbing." He went the distance but was pounded for 19 runs and the damage could have been much worse if not for some sensational fielding behind him. According to the *Plain Dealer*, "The Cleveland outfielders did nothing but chase hits from the time the bell rang until the last man was retired.... [Suter] Sullivan and [Harry Lochhead] made wonderful one-handed catches of hot liners, while [Dick] Harley covered acres of ground in left."[4]

Kolb did at least collect a base hit and score a run, which left him with a career batting line identical to that of Walter Walker: four at bats, one run, one hit. But he also committed an error in his lone fielding chance. Adding to his indignities, the box score gave his name as "Holb."

The 19–3 defeat was the Spiders' 134th loss of the season, a major league record that has never been approached. It was also a historic game because of a couple of notable finales. The contest was the final game in the illustrious career of McPhee, who had spent his entire eighteen-year big league career in Cincinnati. In addition, it was the last National League game ever played by a Cleveland team (and thus also the last regular season game played between two Ohio teams until the advent of interleague play). "The season of 1899 is closed and no one is more pleased over this fact than the members of the Cleveland team," reported the *Plain Dealer* dryly. "After the double header today manager Quinn and his players gave three mighty cheers and hustled off the grounds."[5]

The game also marked the end of Eddie Kolb's major league career and such a farcical exhibition might have led many aspiring ballplayers to abandon the game for good. Instead Kolb retained his enthusiasm for baseball. Despite his youth, he was one of the two managers of an amateur team in Covington in 1900 and was at the helm of a traveling team known as the Cincinnati Tourists the following year.[6] In 1902 he managed a pennant-winner in the Ohio State League and in the following season he piloted the Huntington (West Virginia) club to the championship of the High River Valley League. Neither of these leagues were part of organized baseball, but Kolb had begun to make a name for himself.

In 1902, only a few months after celebrating his twenty-first birthday, Kolb was given a reception that was attended by more than fifty Cincinnati baseball enthusiasts. According to a write-up by Cincinnati sportswriter Ren Mulford, Jr., "Players of half a dozen leagues were represented, for among local amateurs and professionals few are better known than Kolb."[7] He managed and pitched for an amateur club in Urbana (Illinois) in 1903, where he was hailed as "a ball player of no mean pretensions ... [who] made a favorable impression with his appearance and manner."[8] By January of 1904, he was well enough known for *Sporting Life* to mention that he was heading to Palm Beach, Florida, to work for the Florida East Coast Railroad.[9] He was back in Cincinnati by the time the baseball season started and again managing the Norwoods in a Saturday semi-pro league.

Before the 1905 season, Kolb signed to play right field and manage the Vincennes (Indiana) entry in the Kentucky-Illinois-Tennessee ("Kitty") League.[10] His return to organized baseball prompted *Plain Dealer* sportswriter Henry P. Edwards to recall Kolb's very short stint as a major leaguer: "I ran across Eddie Kolb, a Cincinnati boy, who once wore a Cleveland uniform, at St. Augustine Sunday morning. Eddie used to run the cigar stand in the Gibson House at Cincinnati and 'Cy' Young, taking an interest in him, secured him a trial with some minor league team. It was in 1899 and in some manner, Eddie managed to hook on with Cleveland and played the last two games of the season with the Misfits. He is now manager of the Vincennes team in the K.I.T. league, but in the winter months enjoys life and draws a good salary by directing the movements of the Pullman car service at St. Augustine."[11]

He guided the Vincennes team, nicknamed the Alices, to the second-half title in 1905. "Eddie Kolb, who was a Clevelander for ten minutes in the 'Misfit' year," announced the *Plain Dealer*, "managed the Vincennes team, champions of the K.I.T. league, this year."[12] Kolb again led Vincennes to the league pennant in 1906, an accomplishment that earned the team a full-page photo in the 1907 *Spalding's Official Base Ball Guide.*

Kolb signed in 1907 to play the outfield and serve as captain of the Brockton team in the New England League.[13] He lasted long enough to play right field on Opening Day and be part of the day's impressive festivities, which saw players from both teams paraded around Brockton in five automobiles.[14] But his stay there must have ended soon afterward, as his name does not appear in team statistics.

This seems to have ended his playing career, but Eddie Kolb's reputation as a shrewd baseball man was continuing to grow. He was still spending each winter in Florida, and took advantage to run and organize a winter hotel league. Decades before it became common for clubs to hold spring training in Florida, Kolb became a leading advocate for baseball in the state during the months when it was impractical to play ball in the north.

By the winter following the 1907 season, he was managing a couple of Palm Beach teams in the Florida East Coast Hotel League. The teams represented two popular Palm Beach hotels, the Breakers and the Royal Ponciana, and major leaguers such as Howard Wakefield and Jim Delahanty were clamoring to spend their winters playing ball and keeping in shape at the "fashionable winter resorts."[15]

The following winter saw Ren Mulford insert this plea into his *Sporting Life* column: "Uncle Sam has been bringing me a lot of letters asking me for information about the managers of the Hotel League in Florida. Blessed if I know. I've fired all these communications at Eddy Kolb, who circulates between Palm Beach and St. Augustine when the oranges are sweetest in the Everglades State.... If there's anything about the Florida baseball situation Kolb doesn't know the news is not worth bothering about."[16]

Kolb responded with this description of the league:

> I have conducted this for some few years and will make another attempt this winter, but am afraid I will be unable to offer an encouragement to players whose character is not known to me. I am held responsible by the Florida East Coast Railway Company for the players' conduct on and off the field, and as you know about what class of patrons we have to attend the games on the East Coast Hotel System's grounds, I must select carefully. Might be a good idea, Ren, for you to insert a few lines in your weekly write-up to

"Sporting Life" regarding this winter base ball. I am in receipt of letters, every day in bunches from men all over the continent, inquiring of the possibilities to dodge the icicles up North. Some state their terms from ten dollars a month to five hundred a month while others express their desire to go South to see the country, and in some cases want to winter away from their homes so that they may be able to quit drinking and report in the spring in proper condition. Now my terms have been: All expenses to and from Florida and hotel. This includes sleeping car, meals en route, or, in fact, every cent incurred by a man to make the trip. Besides this I give twenty-five dollars a month, not as a salary, but more for spending money than anything else. We play from three to four games a week and when players are not playing they have privileges to all amusements provided by the hotels for their guests. In other words, these men have been extended the privileges that would cost the guests about two hundred dollars a month. To date I have had some three hundred applicants, but have selected but few, leaving the selection until December.[17]

Kolb was also acquiring a reputation for having an eagle eye for baseball talent. During his time in Vincennes, he had been credited with discovering such promising youngsters as Clyde Goodwin, Charlie French, and Hub Perdue, each of whom would spend time in the major leagues.[18] In the fall of 1908, he was described as a "veteran big league scout" who had made "about seven trips across the continent this summer" for the Reds and other teams. The list of his signees and recommendations who would eventually go on to the big leagues now included Pete Wilson, Marty O'Toole, Spec Harkness, Ham Hyatt, Bob Groom, and Tom Raftery.[19]

Eddie Kolb also seems to have been doing well financially, as he made an unsuccessful attempt to purchase the Montreal franchise in November of 1908.[20] At about the same time, he arranged several Florida dates for the Cincinnati Reds as the team made its way to Cuba for a tour.[21]

And then, having made a reputation throughout the baseball world, Eddie Kolb vanished. He was listed in Cincinnati on the 1910 census, but was still unmarried and was living with his parents. His name appeared in the Cincinnati directory up until 1910, but no hint of his whereabouts could be found after that. Newspaper accounts indicated that he was continuing to winter in St. Augustine, Florida, up until 1911, but he never appeared in that city's directory. As a result, Eddie Kolb's brief entry in the baseball encyclopedias contained no death information until more than a century after the lone major league appearance of the Gibson Hotel cigar boy.

The absence was not for a lack of digging by members of the Biographical Committee. Other members of his family were easy to trace, but they didn't lead us to Eddie. His father Louis died in Cincinnati in 1923, but no obituary could be found that included a mention of Eddie. When his sister Leona died nineteen years later, she was described as the "beloved sister of Edward and Clifford" but nothing more was said about Eddie. Clifford Kolb died in 1952 and there was no reference to Eddie in his obituary, suggesting that he had likely died between 1942 and 1952. But he was not buried with any of these family members, so exactly when and where he died remained a complete mystery.

Attempts to locate him on the 1920 and 1930 censuses also proved futile. An Edward Kolb who had died in Cincinnati in 1961 was investigated, but he turned out not to be the ballplayer. His name was entered into countless databases in hopes of a lucky hit, but one never came.

By this time, the story of a ballplayer disappearing without a trace was one that was familiar to me and my fellow biographical researchers, but in most cases there was a plausible explanation — marital woes, legal difficulties, or some such reason to pack up and start elsewhere. Eddie Kolb, by contrast, seemed to be an unusually enterprising young man who had established a network of business connections in both Ohio and Florida. Where could he have gone?

A book about the 1899 Spiders by baseball historian Tom Hetrick contained a potential clue. According to Hetrick, Kolb made some money in the restaurant business and bought the Calgary club of the Western Canada League in the early 1920s.[22] A move to Alberta would explain Kolb's absence from the 1920 and 1930 U.S. censuses. But a search for information on the Calgary team in the early 1920s uncovered no mention of Kolb and the team owner was a different man. Besides, would a man who had tried to lure northerners to Florida with promises that there would be no need to "dodge the icicles" really have settled in Canada?

At that point, we seemed to have exhausted all possibilities. A move to Canada still seemed a plausible scenario, but research there had special challenges, as I knew from my many conversations with Richard Topp. Most dauntingly, while the United States releases censuses to the public 72 years after they are taken, Canada waits a full century, meaning that there was no way to look for Kolb on the censuses on which he might have appeared. Other research angles in Canada were also pursued without success.

Leads in the United States were just as meager. We continued to check indexes, directories and other research sources in Ohio and Florida but his name never appeared. He was not married at the time of the 1910 census, so there was no wife or children to search for, and we had already traced his parents and siblings. His complete disappearance suggested an early death, yet his sister's 1942 obituary listed him as a survivor and thus seemed to rule out even that angle. Perhaps he had fallen in love with a far-flung part of the country or identified a great business opportunity during his "seven trips across the continent" in the summer of 1908 and moved there. But if so, where had he settled and why couldn't we find a census listing? The search for Kolb had reached a dead end and it remained there for several years.

Once again, the longstanding mystery began to unravel as a result of the combination of Richard Malatzky's return to baseball research and the availability of new Internet resources. Around 2004, the subscription website Ancestry.com began adding World War I registration cards, which were required documents for American males born between 1872 and 1900. Malatzky looked for a card for Kolb and found this:

Edward W. Kolb; date of birth, July 20, 1880; occupation, self-employed caterer; place of business: 8th Ave, Calgary, Alberta; nearest relative: Louis Kolb, Cincinnati; date of registration: September 26, 1918.

Obviously Hetrick's information had been correct in substance, if not in all particulars.

Now knowing where to look, I turned to the growing number of online records of burials and was able to locate a perfect match. Edward Kolb, the listing stated, had died in Calgary on October 1, 1949, and been cremated two days later. His age at death was given as 68 years, 2 months, and 11 days, which was within a day of the ballplayer's birth date of July 20, 1880.

By good fortune, my sister Joy lives in Alberta and she was able to find a lengthy obituary in the *Calgary Herald*. Under the headline "E.W. Kolb's Funeral Service Held Today," the six-paragraph obituary recounted his business and civic accomplishments after arriving in Calgary when it was still a "growing frontier town." There was also a paragraph devoted to his long-ago days on the baseball diamond. "Ed Kolb was once a professional baseball player with both the Baltimore Orioles and the Cincinnati Reds," it recorded. "He began his playing career as a pitcher, but later was transferred to the outfield when his heavy hitting was noticed."[23]

We had found our man at last!

The *Herald*'s obituary contained several factual errors and a bemusing exaggeration of the extent and success of his baseball career — being pounded around by the Reds in his one major league game had been transformed into a professional career with the Reds and Orioles, while the inevitable end of his pitching days had been reinvented as a shift "to the outfield when his heavy hitting was noticed." Yet at the same time, it was rather charming that the fleeting baseball career of a man who had experienced so much worldly success was still considered to be one of his most notable accomplishments.

The find of Eddie Kolb was especially satisfying because it made it possible to get an understanding of the man who had compiled that brief line in the baseball record books. Until his death information had been tracked down, little could be said about Kolb's life beyond a summary of his baseball career. In particular, nothing at all was known about the missing thirty-six years of his life. Now it was possible to reconstruct those missing years and get a fuller appreciation of the man who had once been only a cipher. With a lot of help from the *Calgary Herald*, which became available on the Google News Archive, a picture of the missing years emerged.

In 1911, Eddie Kolb left the United States for good to accept the position of superintendent of sleeping and dining car departments for the Canadian Pacific Railway. His obituary claimed that he spent time in Winnipeg, but if so, the stay was a very brief one as he was settled in Calgary by the spring of that year.[24]

It took him little time to become involved in his new city's baseball scene. In an article that appeared in the *Herald* after the conclusion of the 1911 season, Kolb was introduced as a "big league scout stationed in Calgary ... [who] represents the Detroit Americans, also the St. Louis Nationals, as scout for Western Canada.... Mr. Kolb has owned baseball franchises in the south and is known as one of the most famous baseball players who ever held an infield glove. He knows the game like a book and all the big moguls of the ... major leagues have the confidence to accept just what he sends him." After citing several examples of players whose careers he had furthered, including Jacques Fournier and David Skeels, the writer concluded by recommending Kolb for the presidency of the Western Canada League: "he is ... a good man ... who has owned franchises eight times the size of any one in this league, who knows nearly every player of baseball, knows the game, the night governorship, and is there with the goods."[25]

Nothing came of the recommendation and we can only speculate as to who was responsible for this exaggerated depiction of Kolb's credentials. But he remained in Calgary and there continued to be rumors that he was going to head a syndicate that would purchase the local Western Canada League franchise.[26]

Kolb married shortly after arriving in Calgary and he and his wife Gertrude McCaw soon began a family. In 1913, he resigned from the Canadian Pacific Railway and opened a restaurant and catering business near First Street. Kolb's Restaurant thrived from the start and he soon took on his brother-in-law, J. Allan McCaw, as a business partner. Before long the two men were planning to open a second restaurant on Eighth Avenue.[27]

The outbreak of the world war forced those plans to be delayed and it also made life very difficult for anyone with a German-sounding surname. After an angry mob tried to loot the restaurant in 1916, he and McCaw were forced to defend their patriotism: "E.W. Kolb and his partner, J.A. McCaw, state that they are entirely at a loss to know why any attack should be attempted on their premises. Mr. Kolb is a Canadian-American and was born in one of the southern states. Mr. McCaw is a Canadian. They state positively that no alien enemy is in their employ and that they would be the last in the country to employ such help."

The assertions were confirmed by the United States consul, who pointed out that Kolb and McCaw had made generous contributions to the war effort, including serving more than six thousand free meals to the families of Canadian soldiers. He added the intriguing claim that "Mr. Kolb comes from one of the oldest families in the southern states, his people being prominent in civic and state affairs of Florida prior to the American civil war, and later being established in Cincinnati, Ohio."[28]

The U.S. consul's statement offers a plausible explanation as to how Eddie Kolb became so involved in baseball in Florida. At the same time, we must be careful about accepting at face value an assertion made with the intention of protecting Kolb from a climate of virulent bigotry. Census records show that his father Louis had been born in Cincinnati in 1853, only four years after Louis's parents had arrived from Germany, which meant that any immediate family connection to Florida must have been brief.

Other Calgarians leapt to Kolb's defense after the near riot. F.H. Mitchell of the Big Brother Association of Calgary wrote to the *Herald* to cite examples of Kolb's benevolence and patriotism. "There has been no more loyal man to the 'cause' than Mr. E.W. Kolb," he declared, "and this loyalty has been shown by good, effective, expensive and cheerfully given work."[29] With Kolb and McCaw continuing to support the war effort and local charities, the hostility against them gradually subsided. Nonetheless, it cannot have been easy to know that so much hatred could be inspired by the possession of a German surname.

The 1918 armistice brought an end to wartime austerity and before long Calgary was booming again. The local baseball scene, largely inactive during the war, also sprang back to life. Eddie Kolb again played a major role, involving himself in the Calgary City League and even taking the pitching mound for the local Rotary Club. He also returned to scouting, signing formal papers that made him the official scout for the New York Yankees and Cincinnati Reds of "the talent between Winnipeg and the coast."[30]

The Western Canada League had returned to action in 1919 but with a reduced roster of four clubs, all in Manitoba and Saskatchewan. As the summer wore on, however, Kolb became part of efforts to bring organized baseball back to Calgary. By July, he was corresponding with interested parties in the states of Montana and Washington about the possibility of an international league.[31] At the season's end, he became the secretary of the Calgary Baseball and Recreation Company, sponsors of a bid to bring a Western Canada League franchise back to the city.[32] Presumably, an account of this effort was the source of the information in Hetrick's book.

Calgary did receive a Western Canada League franchise for the 1920 season, but it was in the hands of a different set of executives. Ed Kolb — by now old enough for the nickname of Eddie to fall by the wayside — still had plenty to keep him busy in the years that followed. In addition to overseeing his restaurant and catering businesses, he remained active in a wide variety of civic activities and helped Gertrude to raise their two young sons — Jack, born around 1915, and Robert, who arrived four years later.

Unbeknownst to the boys, their father was saving a pair of special treats to pass along when they were old enough to appreciate them: two carefully preserved sweaters from his baseball career.

The postwar return of prosperity at last enabled Kolb and his partner to expand their business. In 1928, the K. and M. Coffee Shop opened near the corner of Third Street and Eighth Avenue. "This lunch counter is one of the most modern in Canada and so constructed as to demand the patronage from the business ladies as well as the men," proclaimed the announcement. "The booths accommodate some persons, but some booths are so arranged as to take care of four. Messrs. Kolb and McCaw wish the public to know that it is only due to the kindly support given them at Kolb's Restaurant during the past sixteen years that has made possible the opening of this No. 2 location."[33] The original location also was expanded and the growth led to its division into Kolb's Café and Kolb's Blue Room, the latter featuring a dance floor and Victrola music.

Kolb's involvement with baseball gradually lessened, but his passion for the game never died out. As late as 1945, he was still doing scouting on at least an occasional basis.[34] He remained active in the Calgary Amateur Baseball League and in 1930 the *Herald* published a letter to Kolb from Connie Mack in which the venerable Philadelphia manager picked Buck Ewing as "the greatest catcher baseball ever knew." The *Herald*'s reporter went on to explain that Ewing (whose playing days actually ended in 1897) had been "on the team with Kolb, at Cincinnati. This was back in 1902-3-4-5."[35] Obviously, Eddie Kolb's willingness to exaggerate the extent of his playing career had also stood the test of time.

The Great Depression brought new challenges and another opportunity for Ed Kolb to display a strong social conscience. He played a key role in planning a commissary to feed the scores of homeless transients who passed through Alberta. Kolb's "long experience in the catering business," explained an account in the *Herald*, "had made him thoroughly familiar with purchasing of foodstuffs on a large scale and the preparation of menus on a basis of strictest economy. Mr. Kolb has worked out a series of charts covering almost every phase of operation of the kitchen."[36]

His involvement with these initiatives also led to his 1931 appointment as Supervisor of the Alberta Relief Commission. At first, this appears to have been a short-term, quite possibly unpaid, position, but it continued to expand as the hard times showed no signs of ending and the number of needy Albertans became overwhelming. It soon required all of Kolb's considerable energies and in 1935 he closed his restaurant business after more than two decades as a Calgary fixture.

One year later, however, Alberta Premier William Aberhardt announced that Kolb had been relieved of his duties.[37] The surprise decision was met with dismay by those who had worked closely with him. Colonel G.E. Sanders, a former member of the Commission, described Kolb as "the brains of the relief commission." He credited Kolb with having saved the province "hundreds of thousands of dollars" by implementing such measures as a successful monthly cost control system, a public works camp program with deferred pay program for single men, an efficient bed ticket system, a special home for the elderly and disabled, and many other innovations for providing food and clothing to the needy. Sanders also stressed that Kolb's keen eye for economy never came at the expense of those in need.[38]

Eddie Kolb remained involved in relief efforts during the next few years, but before long he was devoting most of his time to the province's newest industry. Oil first had been discovered in the oilfield that became known as Turner Valley around 1910, but the amount was small and the costs of transporting it too high for it to play more than a minor role in the local economy. Ed Kolb, however, was one of the first to sense that Turner Valley had much greater potential.

In 1914, he led a group of Calgary businessmen who made a trip to the Discovery and Herron-Elder wells. "While the Calgary public are somewhat forgetting the oil developments of the past," he reported, "it can not be said that the same thing prevails in the field. The development, at present, is greater than at any time since the field was discovered. The roads to and from the Dingman field, is [sic] simply lined with teams, carrying machinery and casing. The approach of the Black Diamond post office now brings no less than six derricks, all working both day and night."[39] By 1923 he was serving as a director of the Alberta-Illinois Oil Company and was making trips to oil centers all over North America to gain a better understanding of the industry.[40] Though the obstacles remained daunting, he expressed enthusiasm about the potential of oil to become a major part of the Alberta economy.[41]

When Kolb was suddenly dismissed as Supervisor of the Alberta Relief

Commission, the timing was perfect for him to revive this longtime interest. He accepted appointment as the first secretary of the Alberta Petroleum Association when it was formed in 1938, and began working closely with the provincial and federal government agencies responsible for petroleum. Later that same year the provincial government created the Alberta Energy Conservation Board and in 1939 British American Oil opened a refinery in Calgary. These two developments all but ensured Calgary's status as the administrative center of the now thriving industry.

Eventually the Alberta Petroleum Association grew into the Western Canada Petroleum Association and Kolb served as secretary and treasurer of the new group.[42] In 1947, a major oil strike in Leduc, Alberta, just south of Edmonton, transformed oil and gas into the province's biggest industry. By then Calgary was firmly established as the industry's administrative capital, so it was in that city that the oil companies that rushed to Alberta set up their headquarters. Kolb played a major role in making that possible.

His years as an oilman were not easy ones, however, because both of his sons served in the Canadian armed forces during World War II. In August of 1944, Ed and Gertrude Kolb received the dreaded news that their elder son Jack had been wounded in France.[43] Fortunately, Jack recovered from his injuries and he and his brother Robert returned safely home from the war.

In 1949, Ed Kolb died suddenly of a heart attack. His survivors included Gertrude, his two sons, three grandchildren, and his brother Clifford in Cincinnati. By then usually known as E.W. Kolb, he had come a long way from the day fifty years earlier when, as Eddie Kolb the cigar boy, he talked his way into a lone appearance on a major league baseball diamond. Nevertheless, as we have seen, his obituary in the *Calgary Herald* saw fit to devote considerable space to his baseball career amid his many business accomplishments.

That in turn reflects a passion for the game that never died. In later years, Kolb became an aficionado of boxing and golf and became somewhat disillusioned by Calgary's unwillingness to support professional baseball. In a 1938 interview, he predicted that baseball would continue to be dead in Calgary until the city featured a brand of ball similar to that played in the Western Canada League. He added with chagrin that golf had been the "death knell of baseball in Calgary."

Kolb's first-born son Jack became a prominent football player for the Calgary Bronks of the Western Interprovincial Football Union (one of the predecessors of the CFL), while his younger son Robert concentrated on skiing. This too was a source of dismay to their father, who told the same interviewer: "It seems peculiar that after so many years in baseball, I should finish off my sports career as a rugby football secretary."[44] Three years later, disgusted that his sons' "interest in baseball is as far from their dad's favorite pastime as palm trees are from the north pole," Kolb took the pair of major league baseball sweaters that he had been saving for them and threw them in the garbage.[45]

Despite his disenchantment, Ed Kolb's love of baseball became evident whenever he was invited to reminisce. "I missed many a meal to play ball when I was just a kid of 15," he revealed with pride. He went on to recall playing for a "supposedly" amateur team in Cincinnati alongside the likes of Miller Huggins, Nick Altrock, Doc White, George Rohe, Red Dooin, and Harry Steinfeldt, all destined for notable professional careers.

Turning to his major league debut, he recounted how he got his big break as a teenaged clerk at the Gibson House. After donning a Cleveland uniform, he had watched in awe when Sam Crawford knocked one of his pitches clear out of sight. "Batters in those days could really hit," he declared. "They used a deader ball than that of today, but those fellows could slam a ball farther than any of the present-day crop, including Babe Ruth and the other top-notchers."

Almost as evident as his enduring devotion to baseball was Kolb's willingness to stretch the truth in recounting his accomplishments. His account made no mention of the hapless state of the Spiders and in his version the visiting club is managed, not by Quinn, but by the immortal Cy Young, who offered the youngster the chance to pitch because "Kolb's playing ability had reached his ears." One season later, in Kolb's recollections, he joined the Cincinnati Reds, where: "Due to his ability to hit and run — he was a 10½ second man — he quit pitching and played in the outfield. He held this position until a knee injury slowed him up."[46] He concluded the account of his baseball accomplishments with the pennants won in Vincennes, but even here a touch of boastfulness slipped in and the two pennants became three.[47]

It is easy now to nitpick and point out the exaggerations — after all, we have the benefit of a baseball record book so exhaustive that even the date of death of a one-game player such as Eddie Kolb is documented. Yet perhaps it is better just to marvel that a man with so many accomplishments took such pride in his ballplaying skill that he felt the need to enhance it.

That was certainly the sense conveyed by a tribute written by *Calgary Herald* sports columnist Bob Mamini after Kolb's death. Mamini recited the usual exaggerated list of baseball accomplishments and even threw in a few new ones — Kolb was now said to have played for the Baltimore Orioles "in the days of John McGraw" and to have "been moved to the outfield when teams found they couldn't get along without his power hitting."

Once again, however, what is most conspicuous is Kolb's love of baseball. "He was a baseball student who absorbed every move of players out on the field," recalled Mamini. "When Ed Kolb sat in on a baseball game you couldn't talk about the weather, politics, or any other sport under the sun, for he was completely absorbed in what was happening out on the diamond."[48]

Reading accounts such as that is what makes it worth the effort needed to add the date of Eddie Kolb's death to the encyclopedias.

Chapter 5

Louis Phelan

EDDIE KOLB WAS A BALLPLAYER whose life only came into clear focus after his date of death had been discovered. By contrast, all of the interesting elements in Louis Phelan's life were known before he was "found." Even so, establishing a date of death did help to put that life into context.

Louis Phelan is not known to have played baseball at any level and his name appears is the encyclopedias as a result of what can only be described as nepotism. Chris Von der Ahe, a German-born St. Louis tavern owner, was involved in the 1882 founding of the American Association as a rival to the National League. The eccentric Von der Ahe also became the owner of the St. Louis Brown Stockings,[1] which emerged as the upstart league's dominant team, earning four straight pennants between 1885 and 1888.

His eccentricities were entertaining as long as his charges were winning, but the team fell on hard times after the 1892 merger with the National League and Von der Ahe's act soon grew stale. His finances and personal life were also in chaos as a result of chronic womanizing. A showman at heart, Von der Ahe tried to address his mounting debts by playing home games in a glorified amusement park, which featured such diversions as a "shoot-the-shoots" ride and a horse track.

Trying to distract spectators from his team's sorry performances was a clever idea, but it was doomed by a fatal flaw in Von der Ahe's approach. For all his marketing savvy, the man who became known as "Der Boss President" failed to understand that the press played an essential role in effective public relations. Instead, he developed a poisonous relationship with the St. Louis newspapermen, who lost no opportunity to savage the woeful team and its owner. Al Spink, founder of the St. Louis–based *Sporting News*, became a particularly bitter enemy who began referring to the beleaguered owner as "Von der Ha! Ha!" Instead of trying to smooth matters over, Von der Ahe foolishly responded to the criticism by disparaging his players and by hiring and firing a series of managers.

His sad-sack team became little more than a refuge for over-the-hill ballplayers, with the result that no competent manager wished to oversee it. Between 1895 and 1897, the downward spiral reached bottom when Von der Ahe used no fewer than four bench leaders each season. He alone, it seemed, was unable to recognize that the problem was not the skippers but his own misguided leadership. That was symbolized when the owner himself took several brief turns as manager, a course that prompted more howls from the press. After the end of one such stint, Spink wryly commented: "It appears that 'Der Boss' was only able to get along with himself for two days."[2]

The team was no better in 1898 but by then Von der Ahe was struggling to avoid bankruptcy and had lost interest, which enabled former umpire Tim Hurst to remain in charge for the entire season. As described in the previous chapter, the situation was resolved only in 1899 when Von der Ahe's business empire collapsed entirely and the franchise was bought at auction by the Robison brothers. They proceeded to transfer all of Cleveland's best players to St. Louis, making the 1899 Spiders an even bigger laughing stock than Von der Ahe's final St. Louis teams had been.

Yet as we also saw in the chapter about Eddie Kolb, even a joke of a major league franchise can represent a golden opportunity to a ballplayer longing for a shot at the big leagues, thereby creating memories that are treasured for a lifetime. The bedraggled teams of Von der Ahe's final seasons provided such an opportunity to many men who, on the basis of talent alone, had no business on a major league baseball diamond. In a later chapter, we will meet one such aspiring ballplayer, Joe Gannon. These forgettable years in the history of a city with a proud baseball tradition also enabled an unlikely man named Louis A. Phelan to get his name in the encyclopedias as a major league manager. Phelan's appointment in turn left the Biographical Committee with another mystery to solve.

In August of 1895, with the Browns possessing a 28–62 record that left them eleventh in the twelve-team National League, a "stormy interview" with Von der Ahe led player-manager Joe Quinn to resign as bench leader.[3] Does the name Joe Quinn ring a bell? He was the long-suffering man destined to manage the 1899 Cleveland Spiders and give Cincinnati cigar boy

Eddie Kolb his lone major league appearance. Quinn is now best known as the first Australian-born major leaguer, but he also deserves to be remembered as baseball's patron saint of lost causes.

After Quinn's resignation, Von der Ahe handed the managerial reins to a well-known local man named Louis Phelan. Even in a city accustomed to the owner's strange decisions and revolving-door approach to managers, it was a choice that raised eyebrows. One local reporter was tactful about the new manager's lack of credentials, writing that Phelan "is a clever fellow personally, but just where he got his experience as a base ball manager is a mystery to the local fans."[4] Sarcasm was a more common result, however, with another sportswriter reporting that, "Joe Quinn has given up his task as manager of the St. Louis Club and has been succeeded by a St. Louis saloon-keeper named Phelan. One of his principal qualifications is said to be that he knows less about the national game than Von der Ahe, and that is what Chris wants."[5]

Spink's *Sporting News* was especially caustic: "Fancy a National League team managed by a man who knows next to nothing about baseball! That is the state of affairs in St. Louis, since that honest player and competent general, Joe Quinn, resigned and Lou Phelan was appointed his successor. If Mr. Phelan were to go into the dressing room of any major or minor league club in the country, he would find himself a stranger. He knows nobody in the base ball world and nobody in the business knows him. Still he is placed at the head of the team which of all others needs a competent and experienced manager."

The article went on to point an accusing finger at one of the many disturbing aspects of Von der Ahe's mismanagement of the team. As usual, his personal life was in chaos and his latest paramour, a woman named Della Wells, had become notorious for using her influence to get jobs for her friends and relatives. Thus the hiring of Phelan was greeted with a stinging rebuke: "Phelan owes his appointment to nepotism. The 'Done Browns' are a family affair now. When it was suggested to Chris that he would do well to secure as manager a man with some ability and reputation in the base ball world, he looked on the plan with favor and promised to sleep on it. Upon his arrival at Sportsman's Park the next morning, Von der Ha! Ha! announced that 'the old woman wanted Lou and I got to give it to him, don't I?' That is the explanation generally accepted by the players and public."[6]

It was a telling jab, as we came to appreciate after we began our research on the "missing" manager. Louis Phelan, it turned out, was none other than the husband of Della Wells's sister Maud and thus was going to become Von der Ahe's brother-in-law once the irascible team's owner's divorce was finalized.

With that relationship established, the first thirty years of Phelan's life became easy to reconstruct and they contained much of interest.

Louis A. Phelan had been born in March of 1864 in St. Louis, the son of Richard Phelan, an Irish-born physician, and his wife Sarah. Theirs was a large family that was blighted often by sorrow. At least four of Louis's brothers died in childhood, while his only two sisters passed away in 1880 and 1887. His mother joined them in death in 1881, after which Dr. Richard Phelan remarried and started a new family. As a result, while Louis had a much younger brother and eventually had many stepbrothers and stepsisters young enough to be his own children, he shared an especially close bond with his brother Frank, who was three years his senior.

Neither of the brothers slipped easily into one of life's accustomed courses. Frank was said to have studied at Notre Dame, though the statement has not been confirmed.[7] Louis, then sixteen, was listed as a dry goods clerk on the 1880 census. Nine years later, his name appears in the St. Louis city directory as a student, living at the same address as his father, but on April 17 of that same year he was married in Chicago. According to the marriage license, Louis was a resident of Cook County, Illinois, while his bride, Maud Wells, was a resident of St. Louis.

Another gap in his whereabouts ensues, followed by Louis Phelan's reappearance in the St. Louis city directory in 1893 as a foreman. Then over the next few years, he began to make a name for himself in local circles. His rise to prominence occurred at about the same time that Von der Ahe became entangled with Maud Wells's sister, and this was probably no coincidence. Phelan became the manager of well-known boxer Dan Creedon, a New Zealand native who had relocated to St. Louis after claiming the Australian middleweight championship. He and Creedon also opened a saloon on Olive Street in St. Louis.[8]

While Louis Phelan was making effective use of his connection to Von der Ahe, Frank Phelan was figuring in national headlines. He had befriended Eugene V. Debs, organizer of the American Railway Union, and became one of the celebrated labor leader's key lieutenants during the Pullman Strike of 1894. Phelan was dispatched to Cincinnati to organize a work stoppage and succeeded in doing so despite an injunction signed by two circuit court judges.

Phelan was charged with contempt and went on trial on July 5 in front of one of the judges who had issued the injunction, none other than William Howard Taft. The night before his trial, Phelan gave a speech in which he defiantly declared, "Well, tomorrow I must go down and put on the gloves with Judge Taft."[9] Unamused, Taft ruled that "it was the purpose of Debs, Phelan and their associates to paralyze the interstate commerce of this country.... Therefore their combination was for an unlawful purpose and is a conspiracy."[10] He sentenced Phelan to six months in the Warren County jail.[11] Fourteen years later, during the presidential campaign of 1908, Taft's opponents would cite the case in an unsuccessful effort to portray him as unsympathetic to labor.[12]

Upon his release from jail, Frank Phelan was cheered by a large crowd of railroad workers. But by then Debs was serving his own sentence for contempt and, at loose ends, Frank returned to St. Louis and moved in with a prostitute named Kate Wadsworth. Soon he was operating a bookmaking establishment and becoming involved in a variety of shady enterprises.

Louis Phelan was also in transition. Dan Creedon had been exposed as more of a punching bag than a contender, forcing his manager to take on new projects. Della Wells used her influence to get him a job at Von der Ahe's ballpark-racetrack, where he became a familiar figure. So it was that in August of 1895 he was the eccentric owner's surprise choice to manage the ball club.

Phelan pledged to spend the off-season studying the game's finer points, but the promise only confirmed that he was out of his depth.[13] One reporter dubbed him "the ostensible manager of the Browns" and his players showed him little respect.[14] According to one observer, "The Browns all know he is manager, but sometimes forget it. In New York on the last trip [Pittsburgh manager Connie] Mack met [St. Louis pitcher] Red Ehret, [Joe] Quinn, [St. Louis catcher Heinie] Peitz, [St. Louis pitcher Ted] Breitenstein and one stranger in front of the Sturtevant House. After a half-hour's chat, during which the stranger didn't get in a word, Ehret suddenly exclaimed: 'Oh, I forgot, Mr. Mack. Let me introduce Manager Phelan, of the St. Louis Club.'"[15]

After the season, Ted Breitenstein related another telling anecdote about the novice manager's tenure: "Last season ... we had a smart Alec with the Browns named Lou Phelan, who was appointed manager by Chris. Phelan had a balloon head, and he prided himself on bluffing umpires. When [umpire] Tim Hurst walked on the field Phelan yelled from the bench: 'Say, Hurst, if any of those decisions are close make them in our favor, and if you don't you'll hear from it through [league president] Nick Young.' Tim trotted over to Phelan with that funny little pigeon-toed walk of his, and fanning his finger under Phelan's nose said: 'See here, you big stiff, if you make any more cracks like that I'll give you a punch in the nose.' Phelan turned white, and apologized, and afterward addressed Tim as Mr. Hurst."[16]

The Browns swept their first home series under Phelan's leadership, but the opponents were the downtrodden Louisville Colonels, the one team standing between St. Louis and the National League cellar. That series and an upset win in Baltimore over the eventual pennant-winners were the only highlights of his tenure, during which the team posted 11 victories and 30 defeats. The 1895 season ended with an embarrassing 18–2 home shellacking by the Pirates that marked the merciful end of Louis Phelan's association with baseball. In December, he was replaced as manager by Henry Diddlebock, whose appointment prompted Spink to sarcastically observe, "Mr. Diddlebock's mission will be to repair the damage Von der Ahe has done the game and the St. Louis Club."[17]

Meanwhile the downward cycle of Louis Phelan's brother Frank was reaching an alarming stage. In September of 1896, police closed the hotel he had been operating, and he and Kate Wadsworth moved to Chicago. Within a few months, he returned to St. Louis, where he and Louis operated a pool room at 703 Pine Street. But this too was shut down by the police in June, and by this time Wadsworth had left him.

A despondent Frank Phelan followed Kate Wadsworth back to Chicago. He spent a week fruitlessly searching the city's dives for her and made an unsuccessful attempt to kill himself by taking laudanum. On the evening of July 16, 1897, he finally found her at a saloon at the Grand Palace Hotel and a violent confrontation ensued. After attempting to cut the young woman's throat, Phelan shot her twice and then turned the gun on himself.

He left behind a note that left no doubt that the terrible act was premeditated. In it, Frank Phelan claimed, "I have sacrificed everything for three years trying to reform her, but to no purpose. Rather than see her further degrade herself I will kill her." The note provided instructions for disposing of her effects and concluded with directions to "notify Louis A. Phelan, in care of Chris Von der Ahe, St. Louis, Mo."[18]

Kate Wadsworth survived the attack, but Frank Phelan did not. His body was brought back to St. Louis and, at the family's request, he was buried in a ceremony attended only by a few immediate family members.

Louis Phelan's life also entered a downward cycle in the aftermath of his brother's death. Von der Ahe had at last married Della Wells and Phelan briefly returned to work as a bookmaker at the horsetrack/ballpark. But soon the mercurial owner's new marriage was on the rocks and bankruptcy was staring him in the face. He responded by removing his estranged wife's friends and relatives from the payroll, Phelan among them.

Within the next year or two, Louis Phelan left St. Louis and vanished. His wife remained and was listed as being married on the 1900 census, but there was no trace of her husband. The family burial plot, which already contained the remains of so many of Louis's siblings, became the final resting place of more family members, but their obituaries made no mention of him. The onetime manager of the Browns seemed to have vanished without a trace.

That was the mystery that we pursued doggedly for many years before arriving at a solution. Our most memorable searches involve an unexpected twist and an "Aha!" moment of discovery. Much more common is the far less dramatic process that led to the discovery of Louis Phelan: identifying a prime suspect by means of censuses and city directories and then painstakingly putting together the evidence to prove that he is in fact our man.

In Phelan's case, there was a strong candidate in Los Angeles on the 1930 census. According to his listing, "Louis A. Phalan" was 60 years old, had been born in Missouri to an Irish-born father and an Illinois-born mother, and was first married at age 30. Living with him was his Wisconsin-born wife Angelina (42) and their children Camille (24) and Louis (17), both born in Montana.

The parents of our missing manager had indeed been born in Ireland and Illinois respectively, making this a promising candidate. Yet it was far from being a perfect match. To begin with, the spelling of his surname was off, though this is not uncommon. Louis's age was a full six years off and while census ages are also unreliable, a discrepancy of that magnitude raises serious doubts. His year of marriage was even farther off, differing by a full eleven years from the actual date. It was possible that the year had been altered to match the fabricated age, but even then it was very far off.

All in all, however, it seemed more likely than not that this was the right man. His name was not a common one and it seemed especially unlikely that there would be another man by that name with a perfect match of birthplace and birthplaces of both parents. Another encouraging sign was that the age at first marriage for Angelina did not correspond to his, which suggested that Louis had a previous marriage. Of course the ages in the listing were already off, making it unwise to put too much stock in any inference based upon them, but still it was an encouraging sign.

Yet there were still several questions to answer. What happened to this man after 1930? If this were indeed the long-lost manager, where had he been in the more than three decades since leaving St. Louis? Most of all, even if we did find this man, would we be able to prove that he had once been Chris Von der Ahe's implausible choice to manage the Browns?

As had been the case with Tom Carey and other searches, the only thing to do was to proceed with the search for our prime candidate and then work backward in hopes of finding the necessary proof. Los Angeles city directories were our first stop and they narrowed the pursuit down: Louis A. Phelan was listed with the same family members as had appeared in the 1930 census from 1931 through 1933, first at 5632 DeLompere Avenue and then at 8071/2 North June. No listing at all could be found in 1934, and then his wife was listed as "Mrs. Angelina Phelan" in the 1935 directory, now living at 1222 Gordon with her daughter Camille.

This pointed to a death between 1933 and 1935, which led us to a promising entry in the California death index: a Louis A. Phelan who had died in Los Angeles County on January 2, 1933, age 66. A successful end of the search now seemed to be in sight, since the age was very close to being a match for our missing man and even the spelling of the surname was correct. Alas, when Los Angeles SABR member Bob Timmermann agreed to check for an obituary, he reported back that none appeared in either the *Los Angeles Times* or the *Los Angeles Examiner* between January 3 and 9.

Timmermann is a librarian with extensive experience in the special challenges with doing research in Los Angeles, so he shared the most likely explanations for the lack of an obituary. The first was that Phelan had been indigent, perhaps as a result of the Great Depression, and was buried in the local equivalent of Potter's Field, which was located near Evergreen Cemetery. The second was that he lived in an outlying part of the county, such as one of the South Bay Beach Cities or out in the High Desert. This was very helpful advice, but it was most certainly not what we wanted to hear, as either scenario would make our search very difficult.

Forced to backpedal, we eventually discovered a crucial typo in the death index — instead of January 2, 1933, his death had occurred on *November* 2, 1933. This in turn led us to a death notice in the *Times* that listed the survivors as his wife Angelina, son Louis and daughter Camille. We had now tracked down our prime suspect, but the death notice contained no details about Louis Phelan's life, which meant that we still lacked the proof needed to close this cold case.

The next step was to fill in his missing years, and since both of his children had been born in Montana, that was the obvious place to look. The 1920 census found our family in Butte, but the information that appeared beside Louis's name was disturbing. He was a Missouri-born hotel proprietor whose age was difficult to read but appeared to be either 54 or 59. So far, so good, but his father was reported to be of Canadian birth and his mother a native of Minnesota. This was very odd and made us eager to check earlier censuses in hopes of clearing up the discrepancy.

The 1910 census proved much more in line with what we knew about the missing manager. Louis Jr. had not yet been born, but the rest of the family was in Butte and Louis Sr. was listed as age 43, living on his own income, with a birthplace of Missouri and parents' birthplaces of Ireland and Illinois. So it seemed obvious that the 1920 census just had some mistakes. Better still, the 1910 listing indicated that Louis and Angelina had been married six years and that this was Louis's second marriage.

All of the pieces of a very strong circumstantial case were now in place, but we researchers hate the word circumstantial and so we continued to search for incontrovertible evidence. A 1900 census listing in particular was high on our wish list, but all efforts to find one were unsuccessful.

At last researcher Bruce Allardice discovered the elusive proof by tracking down an August 10, 1903, marriage record in Butte. According to the record, Louis A. Phelan was 37 and a native of St. Louis, who was the son of Richard A. Phelan and Sarah M.L. Phelan (nee Doyle). His wife, Angelina Arbeck, was 16, and had been born in Iron Rod, Wisconsin, the daughter of John Arbeck and the former Bridget Nolan. The record ended with the notation that "Both parties are legally divorced from their former marriages."

Things are rarely perfect in genealogical records, and the marriage record had a significant discrepancy — Sarah Phelan's maiden name was in fact Bradley, not Doyle. But everything else fit so nicely, right down to Sarah Phelan's middle initials, that there could now be no reasonable doubt about the identification.

To top things off, Bruce Allardice also tracked down the elusive 1900 census records for Louis Phelan and his estranged wife. After much digging in the census index, he found a "Louis Blin" in a rooming house in Butte. When he checked the actual handwritten record, he determined that the name was in fact Louis A. "Palin" and that it was a near-perfect match. "Palin," the record informed us, was a traveling salesman who had been married for twelve years but whose wife was not living with him. He had been born in Missouri, his parents in Ireland and Illinois respectively, and even his birth information was correct: March of 1864. That compared favorably to the 1900 census listing for Louis's wife Maud, who was living alone in St. Louis but reported to have been married for eleven years.

As we've seen in previous chapters, the most gratifying searches are the ones in which a long trek through vital records enables us to get a picture of the man behind the record in the baseball encyclopedias. The search for Louis Phelan did not provide a lot of insight into his character, but it did give us a general understanding of his missing years.

After his brother's death and Von der Ahe's bankruptcy, Louis Phelan and his first wife also separated. With little left to keep him in St. Louis, Phelan found work as a traveling salesman. By 1900, he had relocated to Butte, Montana, where a divorce from Maud and remarriage to the teenaged Angelina Arbeck soon followed. Louis Phelan quit the road after the birth of their two children and eventually operated a hotel in Butte. At some point during the 1920s, the family headed west to Los Angeles, where Phelan died on November 2, 1933.

It's not an illuminating sketch, and there is much about Phelan's life that will likely never be known. Nonetheless tracking down his death did enable an unusual and eventful life to come into clearer perspective.

Chapter 6

Abbie Johnson

A BBIE JOHNSON WAS ONE OF the few Canadians to have a lengthy career
in professional baseball that began prior to 1900. He eventually spent
two full decades on minor league diamonds all over North America, with
the result that clues about his identity were abundant. Nonetheless, the
search for him lasted nearly as long as his career and took as many unexpected twists and turns as any I have ever been associated with.

The first matter of business was to sort out Abbie Johnson's playing
career. This is never easy with a player with a common surname and it
turned out that Turkin and Thompson had made some rather far-fetched
identifications of several contemporary players named Johnson in their encyclopedia. Abbie Johnson was a second baseman and several notes indicated
that his real name was Albert, yet somehow an 1893 one-game Chicago
pitcher had been given the name of Abraham Johnson and a Louisville second baseman had been pegged as Albert Johnson. Adding to the confusion,
a subsequent researcher had identified Albert Johnson as a Swedish-born
man who had died in Chicago. Abraham Johnson was officially the missing
player and was said to be from London, Ontario, but everything about the
listing looked fishy. Was the Swedish-born man in fact the 1897 player? Or
was he the 1893 player? Could he be both? Or was it possible that he was
neither? Before we could look for our missing player in earnest we needed
to answer these questions.

Committee member Reed Howard specializes in minor league records
and with his help an overview of Albert "Abbie" Johnson's career emerged.
Johnson first began to attract attention in 1893 while playing for a London
club called the Alerts. This earned him the chance to finish the season with
the city's Canadian League team and an 1894 contract to play for Buffalo
of the Eastern League. He next headed to a New England League team in
Augusta, Maine, where he spent most of the next two seasons.[1] By August

53

of 1896, Johnson was team captain and was batting over .300, which earned him a shot at the big leagues with Louisville. He made his National League debut on September 1, 1896, and played second base for the Colonels in all 25 of their remaining contests.

Johnson's work was not outstanding by statistical measurements, but he seems to have brought stability as the last-place Colonels went 11–14 after his arrival, easily their best month of the season. As a result, he returned to Louisville in 1897 and saw regular duty for a team that surprised the National League with a fast start. The club turned out to be over its head and gradually sank back into the second division, but this was still a huge improvement over the last-place finish of the previous season. Better still, a talented nucleus was being assembled that included left-handed pitcher Rube Waddell and player-manager Fred Clarke, both future Hall of Famers.

Abbie Johnson was nobody's idea of a rising star — he was now 26 and better known for his glove work than his bat — but he was earning a reputation for steady play at a difficult position to fill and it was easy to imagine him remaining a starter on a team that looked like it might be on its way to pennant contention. Then at the end of June, the Colonels made a fateful trip to Chicago. The team was already crippled with injuries and in the second game of the series pitcher "Chick" Fraser was pummeled for 14 runs before leaving with an injury. With few healthy pitchers and the game hopelessly out of reach, Clarke handed the ball to an untested rookie named James Jones.

Jones turned out to be "as wild as an Oklahoma forest Johnny-jumpup, and his curves either tried to kill a man on the bleachers or else hunted the bat."[2] The Chicago batters had a field day, scalding line drives all over the park in a record-breaking 36–7 rout that saw several more members of Clarke's beat-up team hobble off with injuries. The most serious injury was sustained by Abbie Johnson, who was struck in the right eye by a bad-hop liner off Cap Anson's bat and rushed to the county hospital.

There were initial fears that Johnson would lose his eye but fortunately the injury was not that severe. Nonetheless it was a huge blow that effectively spelled the end of his major league career. After being released from the hospital, Johnson returned to Louisville and played a few more games but was not his old self. There was no disabled list in those days and little compassion for injured players. In mid–July the club acquired a youngster named

Honus Wagner from Paterson, New Jersey, of the Atlantic League. A few weeks later, Johnson was shipped to Paterson.

So was Abbie Johnson traded for the greatest shortstop who ever lived? The evidence suggests that that was indeed the case. Player trades were a new and highly controversial subject, with players understandably resenting the idea that owners could exchange their contracts as though they were pieces of property. To mollify them, trades were often presented as coincidental sales of contracts, especially when one party was a minor league team and the other a major league team.

That is exactly what happened to Johnson. After his injury and a broken leg suffered by Louisville third baseman Charlie Dexter, team president Harry Pulliam began furious negotiations to obtain Wagner. According to an account in *Sporting Life*, "President Pulliam left town during the week without telling any one of his mission, as is his custom. It is said he has gone to complete the deal for Hans Wagner, of the Paterson, N.J., team, and for whom he has been dickering for the past couple of months. Hock [Irv Hach] and Johnson, it is said, will be given for him, and a bonus of $1800 thrown in. This is a very high price for a minor leaguer, but report has it that Wagner is worth the money, as he has been tried and will fill the bill. He will play at third base until [Billy] Clingman gets entirely well, and after that the programme does not seem clear."[3]

Paterson co-owner Ed Barrow was a shrewd baseball man who would later build the first Yankees dynasty, so when he sensed Pulliam's desperation the price for Wagner went up. The two men settled on a cash figure of $2,100, an extraordinary amount considering that Barrow and his partner had paid only $800 for the entire franchise.[4] The details of trades were never announced but most reports indicated that Johnson and Hach remained part of the deal. Hach was a Louisville amateur who had been signed out of desperation by the injury-riddled team, so was essentially a throw-in. He reported to Paterson immediately to fill the void left by Wagner but batted below .200 for Paterson and several other minor-league teams before slipping out of organized baseball. Johnson, by contrast, remained with Louisville for several weeks after Wagner's arrival, suggesting that the trade had been conditional on Wagner showing himself worthy of the hefty price. Once the future Hall of Famer proved to be as good as advertised, his contract was officially assigned to Louisville and Johnson became Paterson property.[5]

Johnson himself would later write that he had "been traded to Paterson."[6] So it seems fair to say that Honus Wagner was acquired for Johnson and a very substantial amount of money, along with a throw-in.[7] The conditional nature of the trade, however, meant that not only was Johnson traded for this immortal but that he was also able to boast about having been Wagner's teammate.

While the details of the trade are difficult to untangle, there can be no doubt that it signaled a stunning reversal of fortunes. Wagner mostly played center field after joining Louisville, but he was also giving an extended look at second base to see if he could take over for Johnson. By the end of the 1900 season, his versatility had allowed him to spend long periods at first base, second base, third base, center field and right field, while occasionally seeing action in left field and even pitching one game. In 1901 Wagner was finally given a chance at shortstop and settled in there immediately, going on to become one of the greatest players in baseball history. For Abbie Johnson, meanwhile, the deal marked the end of his days as a big leaguer.

Johnson's professional career, however, was just getting started. He spent the entire 1898 season with Paterson and then played four full seasons for Montreal. In 1903 he jumped to Oakland of the outlaw Coast League but contracted malaria and returned east in June.[8] He finished the season with Rochester, serving briefly as player-manager. He signed with Utica in 1904 and was named captain, only to sustain a broken collarbone after colliding with another player.[9] After working hard to expedite his recovery, he returned to action after a one month's absence, only to be released almost immediately.[10]

It was another tough blow for Abbie Johnson and, now well past thirty, seemed likely to spell the end of his career. Instead, he showed his resilience yet again, surfacing with Troy in 1905.[11] Johnson once more was released in mid-season that year and his stops thereafter become increasingly difficult to trace. He reportedly had brief stints in 1907 with Portsmouth of the Virginia League and Lancaster of the Tri-State League.[12] His whereabouts for the next three seasons are a mystery, but he seems to have been playing in London and Strathroy, Ontario, perhaps in a semipro league. Then in 1911 he signed on to manage Guelph of the Canadian League and, when that didn't work out, joined the league's umpiring staff.[13] Even at that advanced age, he was not willing to hang up his spikes and applied to play for Peterborough of the Canadian League in 1912.[14]

Putting together this overview of Abbie Johnson's career left no doubt that he was indeed the man who played second base for Louisville in 1896 and 1897 but was not the one-game 1893 pitcher. The next question was whether the Swedish-born man whose 1924 death was listed in the encyclopedia. It seemed unlikely, to say the least, and unlikely turned to impossible when a 1935 letter written by Abbie Johnson's son was discovered in his Hall of Fame file. In the letter, Albert Johnson, Jr., described his father as having "played second base for Louisvill [sic] alongside of Hans Wagner in the nineties for several years" and added that his father was now "in very poor circumstances financially."[15]

Further digging established that the Swedish-born man was not a ballplayer at all, leaving us with a new missing player. There was at least no shortage of clues. Notes about the ballplayer showed that he had been born around 1872 and grew up in London. He was generally referred to as Abbie, Ebbie, Abby or Abie, but since his son signed his letter "Albert Johnson Jr." it seemed logical to believe that that was Abbie's real name. In addition, we knew that he had moved around quite a bit during his playing days — several references put him in London, but others had him living in Chicago, Buffalo, and the Ontario towns of Strathroy and Petrolea. Finally, we knew that he was still alive in 1935, possibly in Sandwich, Ontario, a town on the outskirts of Windsor that was given as the son's address.

Ontario seemed the logical place to begin the search, which gave me the opportunity for a visit to my home province. Windsor was my first stop, but a thorough check of deaths in the area did not turn up a match. I headed next to the London library, where a search of local cemetery records also proved unproductive. Widening my focus, I began going through the clipping files in the local history collection, hoping to find new information about Abbie Johnson.

Imagine my surprise when I happened upon a photocopy described as coming from the "memory box of Joseph John McInnis and Margaret Ann Feeney-McInnis." The photocopy included four newspaper clipping about Abbie Johnson's baseball career, the last of which was an obituary! Under the headline of "Ex-City Ball Player 'Abie' Johnson Dies," it read in its entirety: "Albert 'Abie' Johnson of Detroit and formerly of London died Monday in Detroit. He was 85. Mr. Johnson was a well-known ball player and manager in Western Ontario. He played and managed for London and

Guelph ball teams. He was also a playing-manager at Louisville in the United States."

Mystery solved, right? Wrong! Based on the typeface and layout, it was quite clear that the clipping had been torn from the *London Free Press*, but no date was included. It seemed that this would be a detail that would be easy to fill in, but that was not the case.

The next step was to try to obtain a death certificate from the Michigan Secretary of State. But this was not as easy as it sounds — I needed the death certificate so I could learn the date of death, but in order to obtain a death certificate I had to provide a date of death! Wheels within wheels...

The Michigan Secretary of State does allow searches of a three-year period so I forked over $13 and made an educated guess of 1956–1958 based upon the age of death. The search came back as a "no find," so I paid another $13 to search from 1959 to 1961. This search produced the death certificate for someone who matched very few of the details I had provided. When I asked the clerk for clarification, the response was that that was the closest match they could find, and that they would be happy to give me another "no find" form instead. Twenty-six dollars poorer, but not a bit wiser, I returned home.

Upon reexamining the clipping, I came up with another idea. Because the clipping had been torn from the newspaper, parts of the adjoining articles could be seen and maybe they could narrow down the date. To the right of the obituary was an advertisement that was of no help. To the left was an article about nuclear disarmament that told me that the article was likely from the Cold War era, but was of no help in pinpointing a date. Above the obituary, however, was part of another obituary that had the potential to be of help. Most of the name of the deceased person was torn off, but it did appear that his first name was James and that his middle name was something beginning with "Ed." The fragment also indicated that services had been held at the James M. Carrothers and Son funeral home. The names of the pallbearers and several other details could also be deciphered, leaving hope that the person might be identified.

On my next trip to London, I stopped by the James M. Carrothers and Son funeral home and explained my research. The man who greeted me was very helpful and if he found my request odd, as he surely must have done, he made no sign of it. He told me that detailed records had been kept during those years and that I would be welcome to look through them for my James Ed–something something. After twenty minutes or so of digging, I hit paydirt: a man named James Edgar Bedggood had died on November 27, 1960, and fit perfectly. Since one of our mystery man's pallbearers bore the surname of Bedggood, there could be no doubt of the match.

It was now time to return to the London Public Library and search for the actual obituary in the *London Free Press*. After cranking the microfilm reader for a few minutes, the November 30th issue yielded the same article that had appeared in the photocopy. I looked for several more days in hopes of finding more coverage of Johnson's death, but there was none to be found.

Upon returning to Michigan, I mulled over my options. I could always pay the Secretary of State another $13 and hope that they would locate the right record this time, but that approach seemed unlikely to pay off. So I began by looking for an obituary in the Detroit papers. When that failed, I made a trip to the Detroit Public Library to look through an index of deaths from the city of Detroit. Once again, however, the search was in vain, as no Albert Johnson was listed as having died in or around that date.

The inability to obtain a death certificate was extremely frustrating, but it was not unprecedented in my dealings with the state's records. We still had a very specific obituary that detailed the player's baseball career, so all indications were that he had died in Detroit and that his death certificate was for some reason unobtainable. I sent all the information on my quest to Bill Carle and he agreed that it was good enough to list. Since a 1905 article in the *Free Press* stated that "Johnson was born in Chicago, came to London as a boy," we recorded Chicago as his place of birth.[16] The obituary stated that his death had occurred on a Monday, which would be the 27th, so the amended record of the Louisville infielder read: Albert J. Johnson, b. 1872 Chicago, d. November 27, 1960, Detroit.

Once again, the search seemed to have come to an end, but nothing could be further from the truth. I passed the information about Johnson along to my old colleagues at the Canadian Baseball Hall of Fame, explaining that he had spent most of his life in Canada even though his birth and death seemed to have occurred in the United States. A few years later, I received an email from Bill Humber, one of the directors of the Canadian Baseball Hall of Fame and the author of the definitive book on the history of Canadian baseball. Humber told me that he had been contacted by a granddaughter of Abbie Johnson and wondered if I would like to be put in touch with her. This was great news, especially since there were still some confusing issues that might at last be resolved. I had no idea of how far we still were from pinning those details down.

I began a long correspondence with Ann Tonge, the granddaughter of Abbie Johnson. I was able to fill in many details about his baseball career, while she supplied new information about the family. Piece by piece, a clearer picture started to come into focus.

His birth, for example, turned out not to have taken place in Chicago. Ann was able to locate the family on both the 1901 and 1911 Canadian censuses, both of which designated Ontario as Albert's place of birth. At least one note in the sporting presses gave London his birthplace, while the only thing pointing to an American birth was that lone note in the *London Free Press*.

So what was the source of the erroneous reference to Johnson being born in Chicago? Chances are that it was Johnson himself. Prior to the 1894 season, *Sporting Life*'s London correspondent reported: "The alien labor law has prevented Abbie Johnson, of this city, who was the leading second baseman in the Canadian League last year, from going to Buffalo, and consequently that city loses a gentlemanly and thorough ball player."[17] In the end, Johnson was allowed to play for Buffalo that season, but after that close call it is easy to see why he might have subsequently tried to avoid such hassles by claiming an American birthplace. With the evidence now pointing to a London birthplace, his listing was once again revised and Abbie Johnson again became a Canadian-born major leaguer.

Ann Tonge continued her painstaking search for family research and kept me apprised of her progress. Family records had his wife's maiden name being Churnie, but no such marriage record could be found. When their daughter Marion was born in 1909, the birth record provided these details: Father: Abbie Johnson; Occupation: Baseball player; Full Name of Mother: Annie Costigan; Where were the parents married: Montreal; When were the parents married: October 31, 1900. After two years of trying to locate a marriage record in Montreal, Ann Tonge learned that they had in fact been married in Chicago. When she at last tracked down the marriage record, it matched none of these details. Albert Johnson, the actual record stated, had married Annie O'Connor in Chicago on February 6, 1900. As she told me in amazement, "Well, at least the year was right!"

The confusion over Abbie Johnson's marriage paled in comparison to the chaos surrounding his birth and true name. At one point Ann reported to me via email, "I've never given up trying to find Abbie's birth info, but it has been hard. It is like he popped out of a cabbage patch."

It is difficult enough to track down correct birth information when you know the correct name, but Abbie Johnson's name kept changing. It had been Albert on the 1891 and 1901 Canadian censuses and his 1900 marriage record, but each new vital record that Ann Tonge tracked down only served to muddy the situation. Eventually she created this summary: Ebenezer (1871); Ebenieser (1881); Ebbie, Abbie, and Abba (1891); Albert (1901); Abner (1908); Albert J. (1911); Albert Tremagne/Abbie (1912); then after his career was over he went back to Ebenezer (1940). Worse, the son who had signed his name "Albert Johnson Jr." turned out to be named "Albert Richard Johnson." To top matters off, several documents gave the family name as Johnston instead of Johnson.

The alien labor law offered a likely explanation for the confusion surrounding Abbie Johnson's birthplace. But what could possibly be gained by all of these different names unless the elusive ballplayer was intent on driving family genealogists and baseball researchers crazy?

His place of birth proved just as murky. While we now knew that he had been born in Ontario, the evidence pointing to London was less than overwhelming and family tradition had his birth taking place in a small town, either Blenheim or Portland. Further complicating matters, an 1871 census listing in the township surrounding Portland seems to be the family except for two problems: the three-month-old baby who apparently was Abbie was listed as "Ealloner Johnston" and as being female. Even by Abbie Johnson's standards, this was quite a stretch!

All of the issues were finally settled when the indefatigable Ann Tonge tracked down a certified birth record. According to the document, Ebenezer Tremayne Johnson was born in Portland, Ontario, on January 19, 1871. There's no accounting for all of the misinformation in the years that followed, but at last his actual birth information had been uncovered. This in turn led at long last to a death certificate, which revealed that he died in Detroit on November 24, 1960, three days earlier than I had inferred from the obituary. No wonder my efforts to find a death certificate had been unsuccessful.

It would be nice to be able to report that all of this research brought a wealth of new insight into Abbie Johnson's character, but that was not the case. We do, however, know significantly more about the outline of his life.

We know, for example, that Johnson was born in Portland in 1871, was living in Blenheim by 1881 and then moved to London, where he "learned the great game of baseball ... on Tecumseh Park."[18] We know, at least for most of the time, his whereabouts during his twenty years as a professional ballplayer. We know that he married in Chicago in February of 1900, probably out of necessity, since his first child — Albert Jr. — was born six months later. We know that his life after baseball included many struggles as he and his wife tried to raise a large family in the years that included two world wars and the Great Depression. We know that the family moved to Sandwich and then, around 1940, crossed the border and settled in Detroit. And we know that Abbie Johnson and his wife celebrated their sixtieth wedding anniversary shortly before their respective deaths. Time may yet bring more new information to light.

We have also gained a few glimpses into his personality. Perhaps most importantly, we know that he told his children of his baseball career and remained fiercely proud of having been "one of the few Canadian ball players to make the grade to Major League Ball." As his son explained, "My father will be only too glad to supply you with details regarding his Big League career in the old days."[19]

Chapter 7

Bert Miller

ABBIE JOHNSON WAS NOT the only missing member of the 1897 Louisville team and my search for one of his teammates turned out to have almost as many unpredictable twists and turns. The pursuit even ended up involving a house just down the road from mine, making it especially memorable.

Readers may recall from the previous chapter that Louisville had gotten off to a surprisingly strong start in 1897. But by July, injuries had taken their toll and the fast-sinking team was on its way to an eleventh-place finish. A host of replacements were brought in, including the immortal Honus Wagner, who made his major league debut on July 19. But the search for new talent is an inexact science and four days earlier another rookie debuted for Louisville whose career and life could scarcely have been more different.

While Wagner had been such a hot commodity as to force Harry Pulliam to surrender $2100 and two players, Bert Miller arrived in Louisville with little fanfare. The young pitcher had started the 1897 season pitching for Kalamazoo of the Michigan State League, where one of the local papers dubbed him "Little Miller." By June, the entire league was on the verge of collapse and at the end of the month word came that Kalamazoo was going to fold and that Miller would join Louisville. Then new ownership emerged and the players reassembled, only to learn that the club now was slated to move to Flint. Miller decided he wanted no part of the new arrangement and headed to Louisville.[1]

Exactly who had recommended Miller to Louisville president Harry Pulliam is not clear. The jump from the Class D Michigan State League to the National League was a big one and the new acquisition looked to have been made out of desperation, since it came when the injury-riddled Louisville team was described as being "in such a bad way for pitchers that President Pulliam is ready to give nearly anybody a trial on the pitcher's slab." The experiments included James Jones, the novice who had absorbed the 36–7 beating in Chicago that had such a calamitous effect on Abbie Johnson's career, and Roy Evans, who was signed after being released by a minor league team and was described by an underwhelmed sportswriter as "another twirler who is being carried about the country by the Louisville club."[2]

Under the circumstances, the arrival of another little-known pitcher could not have been expected to elicit much enthusiasm. To make matters worse, Pulliam had been feuding with the local press corps and responded to their highly critical coverage by keeping them in the dark about the new acquisitions. One scribe responded by caustically suggesting that the club president buy "a blackboard and write 'No deals on, none likely to be made in the near future. If anything turns up we will let you know. Nothing for publication at present. Call again.' and hang it on the office door. Players have taken their positions on the club, practiced with the club and been signed before the press knew who they were."[3]

Through no fault of his own, Bert Miller brought the sportswriters' frustrations to a head by trotting out to start a game against the New York Giants and superstar pitcher Amos Rusie on July 15. One reporter fumed that Pulliam's "action in ringing in a new pitcher without saying anything about it was not relished. Pitcher Miller, who is said to have played with the club at Kalamazoo, Mich., and a practical unknown, appeared in the box pitted against Rusie in the first New York game. No one knew he was in town, or had ever heard of him, and it was a scoop on all of the papers. If Harry thinks that is fair treatment his sense of right don't agree with a good many others."[4]

Not surprisingly, Miller's performance was described in dismissive terms. The same writer added, "In the game Rusie pitched the boys gave it up before it started and put in Miller from Kalamazoo to oppose him. That's hardly treating the public fair. They ought at least to have a run for their money. A good many thought [Bill] Hill, [Bert] Cunningham or some of the experienced pitchers should have been pitched."[5]

As those comments suggest, Bert Miller's major league debut was inauspicious. Facing future Hall of Famer Amos Rusie, a flame-throwing 26-year-old who was already the winner of over 200 major league games, the rookie lost, 10–0. Despite the lopsided score, Miller's performance was quite creditable. Six or seven errors were made behind him, depending on which box score is to be believed, which made eight of the ten New York runs unearned. Miller allowed 13 hits and walked nobody in nine innings, and even collected a single off Rusie.

Nevertheless, it was his only major league start. Louisville's injured pitchers returned to action and in three relief appearances Miller was hit hard. In August he was released to New Castle (Pennsylvania) of the Class B Interstate League.

From then on, the young pitcher's descent was rapid. He started the 1898 season with New Castle and finished it with the Youngstown (Ohio) entry in the same league, but was plagued by arm troubles. He pitched for two more Interstate League teams in 1899 but ended the season in the Class D Canadian League. By the next year Miller was out of organized baseball for good. His career had attracted so little attention that he left behind not a shred of biographical information. When I began to research his career, his vital information in the encyclopedias read in its entirety: Burt Miller, b. Kalamazoo, Michigan, Deceased. The birthplace looked to be just a filler based on his previous minor league team, while his first name also seemed to be a guess. Everything else was blank — his height and weight, his middle initial, even the hand with which he batted and pitched in four National League games.

Since I was essentially starting from scratch, the first step was to try to recreate his career. Efforts to trace his post-major league career soon reached a dead end. After the 1899 season, he was reported to have made a few appearances in 1900 for a semipro club in Clarksville, Michigan, and that was it. Coverage of his three-week stint with Louisville was just as sparse. The reporters for three local dailies, no doubt still angry over Pulliam's failure to notify them of Miller's acquisition, had little to say beyond that he was "nearly 21."

My search for information about the early stages of his career proved a bit more productive. After spending a lot of time in the microfilm collection of the State Library, I was able to trace his career backward for several years. Miller had signed to play for Kalamazoo in 1897 only after an agreement to play for New Castle had fallen through.[6] Before that, he had spent part of two seasons playing for a semipro club in Hastings, Michigan.[7] He had also pitched five games for Kalamazoo's Michigan State League entry in 1895, but that seemed to be as far back as his minor league career went.

Prior to that, Miller had done his pitching for town teams in the western Michigan communities of Kalamazoo, Hastings, Nashville, and Woodland.

It was in this last town that Miller's baseball career seemed to have been launched in the spring of 1894. Game accounts of his exploits in the newspapers of the surrounding area that year provided many intriguing descriptions of the young pitcher. "Kid" Miller turned out to have been particularly renowned for his habit of allowing several runners to reach base, then smirking and either striking out the side or dispatching the base-runners by means of a lethal and controversial pickoff move. If his pitching prowess was not enough to win the game, he would deliver a game-winning hit.

Woodland put together a long string of victories over larger towns that summer, which brought many offers for Miller's services. He eventually joined the club in Nashville and was borrowed by teams representing Hastings and Kalamazoo for important games, including two memorable contests against the Page Fence Giants, the celebrated African American touring team. In June of 1895, he moved to Hastings to stay and spent the next year pitching for the local town team.

While these accounts added some colorful details, there was still very little that could be used to identify Bert Miller. The only note that suggested a hometown was an intriguing claim in August of 1897 that "Miller, whose career with the Louisville team was short, but not particularly sweet, is a Saginaw boy and pitched for the Lumbermen last season."[8] This note filled in a mysterious gap in Miller's playing career, as the young pitcher had left Hastings without explanation in July of 1896.[9] But the claim that Miller was from Saginaw seemed unlikely, and my attempts to find a candidate there were unsuccessful.

So I was left with an extremely common surname, an approximate age, multiple potential hometowns, and the first name of Burt or Bert, which in turn could be short for Gilbert, Norbert, Herbert, Hubert, or even for such common names as Albert or Robert. It was not much to go on.

Since Woodland was the first town team that Bert Miller had played for, that seemed like the best place to start. Unfortunately, the 1880 census turned up no Miller family in the farming community of Woodland and no promising candidates in the county. It was the same story in Nashville and Hastings. Miller had had two stints in Kalamazoo, so that was where I checked next and I soon found a Burt Miller of perfect age who had been the victim of a notorious 1905 murder.

There was nothing to connect this man to baseball, but he fit well enough to merit further investigation. For more than a year I gathered details about Burt Miller's life and tried to determine whether he could be the missing ballplayer. At first, it looked promising, but as time went by it felt more and more like trying to fit the proverbial square peg into a round hole. Nothing screamed out that this Burt Miller couldn't possibly be the major leaguer, but it had begun to seem very unlikely.

So it was more sifting through the evidence until I found an 1899 note that placed Miller in Woodland.[10] This led me to an 1894 state census that included a Herbert Miller, age 18, in Woodland Centre, the small village at the heart of the rural community. Once again I had a legitimate candidate to research—but even if I found him, would it be possible to prove that he was the ballplayer?

Piece by piece, this new story of the contender's life began to emerge. The second son of Alexander Herbert Miller and the former Susan Brudell Coheon, Herbert Alexander Miller was born on either the 26th or 28th of October, 1875, on a farm in rural Riley, Michigan. This was getting quite close to home for me—Riley is located near DeWitt, a northern suburb of Lansing, the metropolitan area which has been my home since I moved to Michigan to pursue graduate studies. Little did I suspect that the pursuit would soon come even closer to home.

Alexander Miller was a farmer at the time of Herbert's birth, but shortly after the 1880 census he moved the family to Woodland, where he became a minister. The earliest reference to Bert that I was able to find in an area newspaper came in the summer of 1893, when he and another lad from Woodland were the first two people to be charged with riding their horses too fast down the main street of the neighboring town of Lake Odessa. For the offense, Otto Gipe and Bert Miller were fined two dollars apiece, plus court costs.[11] While I got a chuckle out of this note, it was also valuable to my search because it proved that Herbert Miller was known as Bert.

Reverend Alexander Miller died a few months after his son's minor brush with the law. Bert's older brother William was already married and supporting a young family of his own, so Bert found work as a typesetter. It was the next year that "Kid" Miller began to pitch for the Woodland town team and everything at last seemed to be fitting into place. While references to the Woodland player never mentioned his first name, there was only one Miller family listed in Woodland on the 1894 state census. Putting that together with the knowledge that Herbert was known as Bert and the fact that his age was perfect, I became convinced that I had at last identified the missing major leaguer.

But as we've already seen, finding a missing player can still be very hard, and it can prove just as difficult to establish that a strong candidate is in fact the major leaguer. In the case of Bert Miller, there were to be many more twists and turns before the solution to the mystery emerged.

The next break came when I located a good match on the 1920 census. According to the listing, Herbert Miller, now in his mid–40s, was living in St. Johns, a town just north of DeWitt, and working as an interior decorator. Living with him was his wife Rose and her children from a previous marriage. The census record enabled me to find a 1917 marriage record from Lansing that provided parent's names, thereby proving that this Herbert Miller was the man I had been pursuing. The marriage record also informed me that at the time both were living in the town of Mason, just south of Lansing, and that the marriage was Herbert's second and Rose's third.

Bert and Rose Miller proved difficult to trace, but eventually I located a death record for Rose in the early 1930s. I next looked up Rose's obituary, expecting to find a reference to Herbert, but to my surprise there was no mention of him. He could of course already have been dead, but even then one would expect to find his name somewhere in the obituary. Instead, her children were all mentioned but Bert Miller's name was pointedly omitted. Nor was Bert buried with her. What could have happened to him?

Running short of options, I decided to take advantage of my proximity by tracking down a descendant. I managed to locate one of Rose's grandsons, still in the area and now retired. To my surprise, he told me that he had lived with Bert Miller around 1931 when he was a child. "Where was that?" I inquired. To my amazement, he informed me that the house was on Shepard Street in Lansing, which was the street where I then lived!

Yet while it was thrilling to know that the man I was seeking had once lived within a few blocks of me, the rest of the conversation was discouraging. Rose's grandson was under the impression that Bert had left Rose around that time and that her family never heard from him again. This account explained the omission of Bert's name from her obituary, but it meant that the most promising avenue of exploration had turned into a dead end.

Worse, my informant had no knowledge of Bert having played baseball. This was hardly a shock since he was very young at the time and was not a blood relative, but in concert with the other news it was disheartening. For all the progress that had been made, I still seemed a long way from either finding my prime suspect or proving that he was the missing major leaguer. Where to turn next?

Since the marriage record of Bert and Rose Miller indicated previous marriages for both, I decided to work on that angle next. I was soon rewarded with a 1900 marriage record for Herbert Miller and Alice Cattell in Lake Odessa, the town where Bert Miller had once been fined for riding his horse too speedily. Herbert's listed information matched my candidate in all particulars and, best of all, his occupation was listed as "base ball player." Checking the local newspaper for more details, I found a brief front-page article in which the groom was described as "Bert Miller, the ball player, of Woodland."[12]

"Pitcher Miller" the "practical unknown" whom nobody "had ever heard of" at last had a full name and a date of place of birth. I sent the new information to Bill Carle and it was a proud day for me when the listing for "Burt Miller" was changed to include his actual name and birth information. Even so, there was still much work to do.

The 1900 marriage to Alice Cattell presented some new research opportunities and I explored them next. A 1900 census listing in Lake Odessa showed Alice Miller living with her mother and stepfather, but Bert was nowhere to be found. Even more intriguing, Alice was the mother of a one-month-old baby girl.

This opened up a world of new possibilities but the results were discouraging. Alice and Bert Miller were divorced in 1904; she remarried in 1910, but her second marriage was even shorter in duration. Alice's mother also obtained a divorce, making her impossible to trace. As for Alice and Bert's daughter, she seemed to have been living in a nearby town when the 1910 census was taken, but efforts to trace her after that were also in vain.

A follow-up article about the wedding in the Lake Odessa paper mentioned that Bert Miller had played for the Woodland town team in 1899 and intended to play for the nearby town of Portland in 1900. Was it possible that he had been able to revive his baseball career at that point? I duly checked out that lead but it too led nowhere. Once again, the search was at a standstill.

Since both of Bert Miller's marriages had been unsuccessful, the only real option remaining was to try to research his older brother William and hope that a descendant might be able to help. Researching someone with a name as common as William Miller looked like a daunting task, but in fact his side of the family turned out to have been very stable. In no time I located a granddaughter who was the family genealogist and knew everything there was to know about the family. Everything, that was, except what became of Bert Miller — he had lost touch with the family in the 1930s and nobody knew what had become of him.

Nevertheless we had a nice chat and she provided me with a great deal of information about the family. Bert Miller, it turned out, had lived with his brother's family in the Lansing suburb of Grand Ledge after his first divorce and later had moved in with one of his nephews after his second divorce. She gave me the names and phone numbers of two children of that nephew, both now retired, and suggested that I call them.

I soon found myself once again talking to people who could actually remember meeting Bert Miller. Bert's grandnephew was too young at the time to remember much about him, but Bert's grandniece was a few years older and a fascinating tale unfolded. She described Bert as "a bit of a drifter" who had lived with her parents one summer, most likely 1932. It was the height of the Great Depression but Bert somehow convinced her father to buy an automobile so that the two men could sell fish door-to-door. The business failed and the automobile was repossessed or sold, at which point Bert left for parts unknown. As far as she knew, he had never contacted the family again.

While it was a great tale, it left me wondering if Bert Miller would ever be found. Over the next few years, I researched a few longshots and even drove out to Woodland, which is as small and picturesque today as it was when "Kid" Miller first unleashed his deadly pickoff move. But no new leads turned up and it looked more and more as though it was going to take a lucky break to ever solve the mystery. Nevertheless, I didn't forget Bert Miller — how could I when he was brought back to mind whenever I drove past the house where he had once lived?

Several years after my pursuit of Bert Miller had reached a dead end, I finally got my lucky break. In the course of some other research, I happened upon a death index listing for a Herbert Miller, age 61, who had died in Flint on June 14, 1937.

There were a limited number of men by that name and of that age in Michigan, so this seemed promising. Yet Bert Miller had no known connection to Flint, other than that his brief major-league career had been made possible forty years earlier when he refused to report to Flint and instead headed to Louisville. What would have brought him back to Flint all these years later?

More discouragingly, the only way to determine whether this was the missing ballplayer was to pay the Secretary of State $13 for a death certificate search. Even assuming that they located the record, no certainty, it could easily turn out to be a different man. Even worse, the death certificate might have so little information that I could never be sure — after all, by 1937 Bert Miller had lost contact with all of his known relatives. Americans often didn't carry identification in that era and it was all too common for the death certificate of a person without family to be filled with blank spaces. The more I thought about it, the more it seemed like a waste of money to pay for a death certificate.

Needless to say, this didn't stop me. And I was thrilled when I examined the death certificate and read that Herbert Miller had been born on October 26, 1875, in DeWitt, the birthplace that I had already established for the missing ballplayer. As I had feared, many fields on the death certificate were not filled out — the word "unknown" appeared next to spouse's name, father's name, mother's name and many other fields. So where had the all-important birth data come from? It had been provided by the Flint Transient Bureau.

Bert Miller, it appeared, had arrived in Flint in the summer of 1936 and had either been homeless or moved around frequently during the last year of his life. His death certificate is not very specific about the circumstances of his death, but it appears that he had already been dead for some time when his body arrived at Flint's Hurley Hospital, where he formally was pronounced dead. He was buried at the Flint City Cemetery in an unmarked grave.

Searches for missing ballplayers are most rewarding when they provide a window in the once-great athlete's life. In the case of Bert Miller, that life does not appear to have been a happy or successful one. Nonetheless, it was rewarding to have been able to fill in the missing details after so many years of searching. Best of all, when I am back in my old neighborhood, I no longer have to wonder whatever happened to the former major leaguer who once lived down the street from me.

Chapter 8

Arthur Sunday

T HE UNMARKED GRAVE IN WHICH Bert Miller is buried is a common fate among missing ballplayers, since having fallen into obscurity after their baseball careers is one of their defining traits. Imagine my surprise when the search for a forgotten player named Arthur Sunday ended with finding him memorialized in a monument unrelated to baseball.

The early parts of the search for Arthur Sunday were fairly routine. We pieced together an eight-year professional playing career that included these stops: St. Joseph, Wichita and Kansas City of the Western League; Fort Worth, Houston and Dallas of either the Texas or Texas-Southern League; Toledo of the International League; Tacoma of the Pacific Northwestern League; Birmingham of the Southern Association; and Los Angeles, Stockton and Sacramento of the California League. The highlight came in 1890 when Sunday spent twenty-four games as a major leaguer with Brooklyn of the Players' League.

Sunday has also been credited with a role in coining a familiar term. According to an oft-reprinted explanation that seems to have originated in the *Cincinnati Times-Star*, Sunday and two Houston teammates, Bill Joyce and Emmett Rogers, were sold from the Texas League to Toledo in the middle of the 1889 season. In their first game in the International League, each of the three newcomers plunked a base hit that fell in between the infield and outfield, with the result that such balls became forever known as "Texas Leaguers."

Arthur Sunday's only major league stint came in 1890, a season in which the existence of three warring big leagues gave some less-than-qualified players the right to call themselves major leaguers. Yet Sunday was by no means undeserving of a chance to play in the big show. An outfielder noted for his work with the bat, he amassed a team-best .419 on-base percentage during his time with Brooklyn. His performance in strong minor leagues confirmed his ability to hit any pitcher in the land.

So why didn't Arthur Sunday get a longer look at the major league level? Several factors appear to have contributed. For one thing, his glove work never earned the praise earned by his skill at handling the bat. In addition, Sunday's muscular build was often mentioned during the early years of his career, but as he approached thirty the notes instead began to hint that he would do well to shed some weight. Concerns about his conditioning were aggravated by hints that heavy drinking was a problem. Finally, luck often played a considerable role in reaching the big leagues — with scouting still in its infancy, one recommendation or unfavorable review might spell the difference between a major and a minor league contract.

Sunday's many professional stops provided plenty of clues that might help in identifying him, but question marks surrounded most of these clues. At some point, a birth date of January 21, 1862, and a birthplace of Springfield, Ohio, had made their way into the encyclopedias. It seemed likely that the source was a newspaper profile of Sunday, but the original could not be located. Doubts about its accuracy grew when another sketch was found that gave Springfield, Massachusetts, as the ballplayer's birthplace.[1] Since he had no known connection to Ohio, save for spending part of one season with Toledo, one possibility was that the city name might be correct but the state name in error.

Adding to the confusion, several notes connected him to towns in southern Illinois. Jack Brennan, another mysterious player who wrote a column for *Sporting News*, listed Sunday's hometown as Pana.[2] Notes after both the 1887 and 1889 seasons indicated that Sunday was going to spend the winter in the town of Oconee.[3] Pana and Oconee are less than ten miles apart, so this gave us a narrow region in which to focus our pursuit. In addition, both towns are within sixty miles of Springfield, Illinois, so perhaps that was where Sunday was born.

There were plenty of red herrings as well. A caption in a history of the Texas League described Sunday as the brother of Billy Sunday, the Iowa-born outfielder who became a famous evangelist.[4] It seemed inconceivable that a missing player could really be the brother of such a major figure, but we had to investigate anyhow. Naturally, it didn't take long to prove that the claim was untrue.

An especially intriguing clue was that Sunday's encyclopedia listing stated that his real name was August Wacher. Unlike the birth information, we were able to track down a pair of notes that seemed to have been the source of this information. In 1889, *Sporting Life* printed a peculiar note that read, in its entirety: "The right name of Arthur Sunday for Toledo is said to be August Wacher."[5] It was hard to know whether or not to take that seriously and the second note was even more puzzling. Published one month later in the *National Police Gazette*, it read as follows: "August Wacher has been reading novels, and it don't seem fair for him to come into the baseball arena and fool us by saying his name was Arthur Sunday. It is well enough to give them that in a little country town like Toledo, but it seems a trifle chilly to spring it on the rest of the fraternity."[6]

The *National Police Gazette* offered some of the most engaging material of any nineteenth-century sporting publication, but it was hardly known for offering sober journalism. So we now were looking for a man whose name might be either Arthur Sunday or August Wacher and who might have been born in the Springfield located in Ohio or the one in Massachusetts or the one in Illinois. Or perhaps none of the above information was correct. Clearly, this was going to be an interesting search!

Sunday played for Sacramento in both 1891 and 1893 and several notes placed him there during the off-season, including one at the end of the 1892 season reporting that he would return to his "home in Sacramento and hunt and fish this winter."[7] That gave us yet another lead to explore, especially since the 1893 season was Sunday's last full year in professional baseball. But research in Sacramento soon reached a dead end. In October of 1893, the Sacramento correspondent for *Sporting News* reported that Sunday had been running a coffee house there but had left town a month earlier.[8] City directory listings for a bartender named Arthur Sunday also ended around then.

There were also a few stray notes that might come in handy if we ever identified a candidate. *Sporting News* reported in 1889 that Sunday was a boilermaker by trade and was living in St. Louis. An earlier researcher had concluded that Sunday was married but this information could not be confirmed.

While the clues were confusing and many of them seemed unreliable, there was enough data to raise hopes that a good candidate might be located on the 1870 and 1880 censuses, perhaps in Pana, Oconee or Springfield. Alas, there was no appropriate Sunday or Wacher family in any of these towns, nor did wider searches of these two censuses turn up an Arthur Sunday or an August Wacher of the right age anywhere in the United States. Hoping that Wacher might be a misspelling, we tried numerous "wild-card searches"[9] of the census, but still came up with nothing. We also checked cemetery records from Pana and Oconee and had no more luck.

With the 1870 and 1880 censuses having turned up nothing, and the 1890 census having been destroyed by fire, the only remaining course was to try to locate him on a census taken after his career ended. Discouragingly, the 1900 census failed to turn up any reasonable candidate under either possible name. But then the 1910 and 1920 censuses yielded a decent candidate living in Nevada. Arthur Sunday was living in Carson City, Nevada, in 1910 and working as a market fisherman. He was single, 48, born in Illinois, his father had been born in Pennsylvania and his mother in Kentucky. Ten years later, the same man was living at 514 Spear in Carson City and working as a trapper in the hills.

Things were now looking up. We had no proof that this was the ballplayer, but his name and age were perfect and the Illinois birthplace matched our working theory. The Nevada man's occupation even corresponded to the note about the ballplayer spending the winter hunting and fishing, although of course that was hardly a distinguishing trait.

Our prime candidate could not be found on the 1930 census, so we next looked for a death record in the 1920s and were able to locate one. When I checked the Carson City newspaper for an obituary, I was stunned to find that Sunday's death was front-page news. It turned out that a giant forest fire had started in at the base of Clear Creek Canyon and threatened to destroy the entire state capital. Sunday, a park ranger, had been one of several volunteer firefighters who had been gravely injured when heavy winds caused an unexpected change in the fire's path.

Arthur Sunday was still alive when rescued and was flown to a hospital in Reno, where he died of his injuries several days later, on October 2, 1926. By then the city of Carson City was out of danger, but the blaze had claimed the lives of five firefighters. A bleak headline in the *Carson City Daily Appeal* informed readers "Brave Men Die," while Nevada governor James G. Scrugham was moved to issue this statement: "The death of Arthur Sunday completes the toll taken by the fire and closes a chapter of heroism in which Sunday's name stands out brightly. With no thought of himself he urged

Bryant Whitmore to save himself and now both are sacrificed to their daring and devotion. Sunday was a hardy pioneer character whose death is in keeping with his life of service, courage and unselfishness. The names of Arthur Sunday, George Brown, Bryant Whitmore, J.E. Mitchell and Ralph Morse must not be forgotten and I will urge a suitable memorial tablet be erected at the capital for them."[10]

The promise was finally kept in 1993 when the Nevada Firefighters Memorial was erected at Mills Park in Carson City, about a mile and a half from the capitol. There are forty-five plaques honoring a Nevada firefighter who died in the line of duty, one of which belongs to Arthur Sunday.

Doubts about whether this man was the missing major leaguer were resolved when one of the articles about the tragedy described Sunday as having been "a big league baseball player in his younger days." But obituaries provided few other details about his life, which meant that there were still many puzzling questions. Was Sunday in fact his real name? Where was he born and where did he grow up? Why were we unable to find him on the 1870 and 1880 censuses?

These questions proved very tricky to resolve. The only listed survivor was a sister named Mary E. Harris of San Diego, who was reported to have collapsed upon receiving the news of Sunday's death and been unable to attend the funeral. We obtained a death certificate, but it added nothing to what we already knew. Sunday's cemetery plot was purchased by a man named Frank Meder, but research determined that this was a close friend, not a relative.

So Mary E. Harris seemed the only way to solve the mystery and the fact that she had married someone with such a common surname meant that it would not be easy. Eventually, however, we found a 1931 California death that looked promising. Researcher Gary Fink tracked down her obituary and learned that Mary Harris and her husband had died together in a car accident. There were several survivors on his side of the family, but her only listed survivor was John Hawker of Pana, Illinois.

The reference to Pana was very exciting and we eagerly began to research this new surname. Sure enough, there was a Hawker family in Pana in 1870 that included Mary E., age 12, John Jr., age 9, and Arthur, age 8. It was a similar picture in 1880, by which time Arthur was working as a laborer. Moving back to the 1860 census, we found the same family in

Springfield, though of course Arthur had not yet been born. Any possible doubt that Arthur Hawker was our major league were removed when we found an 1884 article that referred to a ballplayer named A. Hawker from Pana. Obviously Arthur Hawker had changed his name to Arthur Sunday around 1885 and it was under the assumed name that he had won baseball glory and earned a plaque near the Nevada state capitol.

This solved the main mysteries surrounding Arthur Sunday, but several questions remain unresolved to this day. Where was he, for example, between leaving Sacramento in 1893 and first appearing on the Nevada census in 1910? More perplexingly, why did he change his name from Hawker to Sunday? Alas, vital records usually provide the answers to when and where questions if we're willing to do enough digging, but questions about the underlying reasons are often impossible to answer.

Chapter 9

Wally Goldsmith

WALLY GOLDSMITH WAS ANOTHER mystery ballplayer whose actions frequently led us to ask "why" questions. Questions such as "Why is Wally Goldsmith making my life a living hell?" Okay, it wasn't quite that bad, but the search for Goldsmith did end up being unusually lively and frustrating.

Wally Goldsmith played for four clubs in the National Association, baseball's first major league, between 1871 and 1875. Several notes indicated that he was from Baltimore and Marshall Wright's *The National Association of Base Ball Players, 1857–1870* provided additional information: Goldsmith played nine games at second base for the amateur Enterprise Club of Baltimore in 1868, then joined the Marylands of Baltimore and was a fixture through the end of the 1870 season, playing second base, shortstop and catcher.[1] An 1870 profile confirmed that he was from Baltimore and gave his age as 21. It added that he began playing baseball with a junior club called the Monumentals in 1863, then played with the Excelsiors until joining the Marylands in 1868 (where he played alongside Tom Carey). William Ridgely Griffith's history of early baseball in Baltimore listed "Walley Goldsmith" as one of the pioneer players.[2]

There was just one problem — no Wallace or Walter Goldsmith appeared in the Baltimore city directories during these years, nor could a good candidate be found on any census. The sporting presses that provided so many helpful clues in later years had only started to develop, so that didn't leave us many options. There was an early twentieth-century cartoonist named Wallace Goldsmith who often did sports-related work, but he was checked out and eliminated. An 1890 note in *Sporting News* had Goldsmith working as a hotel clerk in Peoria.[3] That city's directories had a William M. Goldsmith, hotel clerk, listed from 1885 to 1887, which made us wonder: could Wally be just a nickname that didn't stand for one of the names usually associated with it? But we couldn't find a William Goldsmith in Baltimore during the years that the ballplayer should have been there and, worse, couldn't trace William M. Goldsmith. We also considered the possibility that Goldsmith was a "baseball name" and investigated a Peoria hotel clerk named Wallace Morrow, but nothing tied him to baseball or to Baltimore. Another lead was a 1901 article that cited "'Wally' Goldsmith and 'Natt' Hicks, players of 'ye olden days'" as authorities on the origins of the bunt. This told us that the elusive ballplayer was still alive at the century, but since no clues were given as to where he was living it was not of much help.[4]

With that, the search for Wally Goldsmith ground to a halt and it remained stalled until a most unusual clue surfaced. James Bready's 1998 history of baseball in Baltimore included a photo of a gilded 1870 trophy baseball won by the Marylands of Baltimore that had been loaned to the Babe Ruth Museum by Lloyd Kirkley, a descendant of Wally Goldsmith.[5] That's right, a descendant of a missing player who we'd been unable to identify!

The obvious next step was to contact Lloyd Kirkley for more information, but we were unable to speak to him. So we did the next best thing and tried to find a Kirkley family that connected to a Goldsmith family. Richard Malatzky tracked down this family in Baltimore's 20th Ward: Lewis Goldsmith, 65, laborer; Mary A. Goldsmith, 48, keeping home; Warren Goldsmith, 21, no listed occupation; Emma V. Goldsmith, 17; R.A. Perkley (female), 23; Charles Perkley, 25, merchant; Lloyd Perkley, 2; William Perkley, 3 months old. All of them were born in Maryland.

Could the name "Perkley" be a mistake and the actual name "Kirkley"? If so, could Warren Goldsmith be our missing "Wally" Goldsmith?

More digging located the family in Baltimore in the 1850 and 1860 censuses, which helped to clarify the relationships. Warren Goldsmith's information was very consistent; the only issue was that his given name was difficult to read on the 1860 census and had been indexed as Marion, but close examination of the handwriting suggested that it was in fact Warren. Warren had a sister named Rachel on both censuses and since her age matched the "R.A. Perkley" from the 1870 census, it would make sense for this to be the same person. The 1850 census listed a different woman as Lewis Goldsmith's wife, so it appeared that Warren's mother had died during the 1850s and he had been raised by his stepmother. Warren also had three much older siblings on the 1850 census who had either moved out or died by the time of the 1860 census.

All of this was useful to know, but it didn't get us much closer to determining whether Warren Goldsmith was our ballplayer. We turned next to the Baltimore city directories, which showed Lewis Goldsmith working in a variety of professions, including as hostler of the Swan Tavern. In 1870 he was an oyster dealer and was living at the same address with Warren M. Goldsmith, who had no listed occupation, and Charles P. Kirkley, a hardware dealer.

We now had a very strong circumstantial case that Warren Goldsmith was our missing ballplayer. The man we were seeking had relatives named Kirkley and Warren Goldsmith's sister had married a man with that surname. Our missing ballplayer was said to have been born in Maryland around 1849 and grown up in Baltimore; that fit Warren Goldsmith to a tee. Since he was the only male member of the family whose age was remotely plausible, he had to be our missing ballplayer. Getting "Wally" from Warren is a bit odd, but nicknames often defy logic. Now all we had to do was trace his later movements in the census and discover what became of him, which proved anything but easy.

In earlier chapters, I have referred to looking someone up on the census as though the process is as easy as looking a name up in a phone book or city directory. In fact, the process can be much more complex and in the pre–Internet days it was downright cumbersome. Census research has changed so drastically in the past twenty years that any attempt to describe the changes has the whiff of one of those "when I was your age we had to walk eighteen miles through the snow to get to school" lectures.

Until censuses became available on the Internet, there were two primary ways to search for someone on the census. One was to plunge directly into the census, but with so many names this was very time-consuming if you happened to know exactly where the person lived and all but impossible if you didn't. The more efficient way was to first consult the Soundex, an index of the census based upon the first three consonants of the person's surname and the person's first initial. The researcher then located a likely candidate, jotted down the page number, retrieved the appropriate reel of microfilm and checked to see if it was the correct person; if not, the whole procedure was repeated until successful. This was almost always a slow process and there was no guarantee of success, since one was dependent on the census-taker to have transcribed the name accurately and on the indexer to have correctly deciphered the census-taker's handwriting. Both of those pre-supposed that the census-taker was given the information by someone who knew how to spell the person's name, which was far from certain in an era when illiteracy was still high and with neighbors sometimes supplying the information. Not all censuses even had a Soundex index and some of the ones that did only included the head of household, with the remaining family members unindexed. All of these variables meant that one could spend much of the day at the library looking unsuccessfully for a single census listing and leave with the nagging suspicion that the search had been thwarted by a spelling or transcription error.

Even if one is lucky enough to find a census listing, its value may prove limited. We are still dependent on the person who supplied the information to be both knowledgeable and truthful and upon the census-taker to transcribe the information accurately and legibly. As should be clear from the examples in earlier chapters, the result is that accuracy is the exception rather than the rule. Ages, in particular, are notoriously likely to be fudged, while the spelling of names is erratic at best. If one is fortunate enough to have the information provided by a family member who is both literate and painstaking and to have it taken down by a conscientious census-taker, then there's a good bet that it will be highly accurate. But there's the rub — the identity of the person who provided the data is never known, so everything has to be taken with a grain of salt.

Thus while the censuses are an incredibly powerful tool for tracking a person over time, it is rare that they provide as complete a picture as desired. The fire that destroyed the 1890 census is another huge encumbrance, while changes in the recorded information pose another obstacle. Prior to 1850, the names of family members other than the head of household weren't given, making these censuses of little value. Relationships only started to be listed on the census in 1880, so one has to make suppositions about that crucial information when consulting earlier censuses. Other pieces of data, such as year of immigration, number of children, length of marriage and number of marriages, were not collected in all censuses.

Our research on Goldsmith began in the pre–Internet days when no search was routine and when we still believed that his given name was either

Wallace or Walter. Not surprisingly, we failed to locate the ballplayer on the Maryland censuses of 1850, 1860 and 1870. Determining that his given name was actually Warren had enabled us to locate those listings and offered hope that we could now find him on later censuses. Alas, we tried again and failed again.

With the whole Goldsmith family seemingly having left Baltimore, it made sense to check neighboring states for them. Once again, it was a search for the name Lloyd Kirkley that got us back on track. The 1890 city directory for Washington, D.C., showed Lloyd S. Kirkley living at the same address with Mary A. Goldsmith, who was listed as the widow of Louis, and a man named Viraldo J. Matchett. Just as genealogical researchers dread having to find a person with a name like Smith or Jones, they dream of looking for someone with a name as unique as Viraldo Matchett. We soon established that the man with this fortuitous name had married Warren Goldsmith's younger sister Emma and then settled in Washington.

When we located Viraldo and Emma Matchett on the 1910 census, there was an added bonus. Living with them in Washington were a son, a widowed daughter, a granddaughter, a niece, and a man named William Goldsmith who was described as the brother-in-law of the head of household, Viraldo Matchett. Could William Goldsmith be our long-lost ballplayer? It seemed possible, especially since when we'd followed up the note about the ballplayer being a hotel clerk in Peoria that clue had led us to a William Goldsmith.

The more we looked, the more inescapable that conclusion appeared. William Goldsmith was listed as being 57, born in Maryland, and the manager of a hotel. He was reported to be married but his wife was not part of the household. While a few years had been shaved off his age, our missing ballplayer was the only one of Emma Matchett's brothers that this could possibly be and even his occupation was perfect.

But there were still plenty of mysteries, most obviously why a man whose name seemed to be Warren Goldsmith and was known as Wally Goldsmith was now being listed as William Goldsmith. It would be convenient to view it as just another census-takers' error, but the name William also appeared in the Peoria city directory.

The confusion mounted when we found the Matchetts on the 1900 census. Once again their household included a brother-in-law who was working as a hotel clerk and had to be our missing player — this time, even his birth date was dead-on. Yet his name had changed once again and now read Warren W. Goldsmith. It was beginning to seem as though our man had a revolving series of first names that he rotated on a regular basis.

That suspicion became stronger when we checked the Washington city directory. In 1902 Warren M. Goldsmith was listed as a clerk, living at 1531 M Avenue, while William M. Goldsmith was a hotel clerk at the Howard House. Which one of these was our man?

Subsequent directories suggested that both of them were. In 1903 Warren M. Goldsmith was a clerk living at 638 Q Avenue Northwest and William M. Goldsmith was a hotel clerk living at the same address. Only Warren M. Goldsmith, hotel clerk, appeared in 1904 and 1905 but the bizarre entries resumed in 1906 when two consecutive directories contained listings for both "Wallace M. Goldsmith, salesman" and "Warren M. Goldsmith, salesman" at the same address. After that, Warren's name appeared up until 1912 when his sister Emma died.

Our man's name disappeared from the city directories at that point, so we began the search for an obituary or death notice. Eventually we found identical notices in the *Washington Post* and *Evening Star*: "suddenly on Thursday, Sept. 16, 1915 at the residence of V.J. Matchett, 1113 P St. NE, Warren M. Goldsmith. Services from Wright's Chapel, 1337 10th NE, Saturday, Sept. 18, 4 PM (Chicago papers please copy)." A death certificate confirmed that this was our man and gave his name as Warren M. Goldsmith but added nothing new.

Some searches for missing ballplayers resolve all of the major questions while other searches raise new ones that seem unanswerable. Our pursuit of Goldsmith was certainly one of the latter. As best we could tell, he had been known to friends as Wally for most if not all of his life but his real name was listed as Warren M. during his early years in Baltimore, as William M. while in Peoria, Illinois, as Warren W. on the 1900 census, as William on the 1910 census, and by all three names in the Washington city directories, with double listings in several years.

One would almost imagine that he had a twin except that the census listings make it very clear that he didn't. Dizzy Dean was in the habit of responding to reporters' questions about his real name with different answers, then explaining that he wanted each of them to have a scoop. It sounded as though Goldsmith had a similar desire, but even this made no sense because how would he know that future researchers would pursue him? It was a vexatious mystery.

In hopes of resolving it, we delved into the missing years before he turned up in Washington. The 1900 census indicated that he had been married around 1884 and that led us to an 1883 marriage record in Keokuk, Iowa. The record had Wallace M. Goldsmith marrying Clara E.N. Seidlitz, the daughter of a local doctor.

More digging filled in a few more gaps. In 1890, "W.M. Goldsmith" and "C.E. Goldsmith" were living in nearby Fort Madison, Iowa, where he was listed as proprietor of the Hotel Metropolitan. By 1893 he had moved to Chicago, where "W.M. Goldsmith" or "Wallace M. Goldsmith" was listed as either manager or clerk of the Saratoga Hotel for several years. He was described as the hotel's day clerk in an October 1896 newspaper article but left town soon afterward.[6]

It appears that it was during his time in Chicago that Goldsmith's marriage fell apart. In the 1898 Chicago city directory, he is nowhere to be found but there is a listing for a Mrs. Clara Goldsmith. After "Wally" had relocated to Washington, there were a couple of listings for a Clara Goldsmith in that city's directory as well, so it's possible that they made an attempt at reconciliation. But if so, the effort failed — Clara Goldsmith obtained a divorce and then remarried in Chicago in 1907.

The census, once such a labyrinth for researchers, has been made steadily easier to access in recent years. A couple of websites, the subscription ancestry.com site and the free familysearch.org site, make it possible to use wild card searches to find listings that had previously been elusive. I took advantage to find Goldsmith in Keokuk on the 1880 census, with his occupation being given as salesman. Once again, the record gave testimony to the difficulty of tracking people by means of the census: his name was listed only as "W.M. Goldsmith" and his age was a few years off, which is why we had never been able to locate the record.

In the end, with considerable help from these new resources, we were able to find Wally Goldsmith's listing on every census that was taken during his lifetime (with the exception, of course, of the 1890 census, which was destroyed by fire). We were also able to find city directory listings for him in Baltimore, Fort Madison, Peoria, Chicago, and Washington, thus establishing his whereabouts for almost the entirety of his life. We managed in addition to determine that he died in Washington on September 16, 1915, and that he was born in Baltimore, most likely in October of 1848.

The one remaining mystery was the issue of his name and that will probably never be resolved with a high degree of certainty. I do, however, have a theory that seems to make sense of his baffling array of names. As I see it, Warren M. Goldsmith was his name at birth, but he was nicknamed Wally as a child. He probably never much cared for the name of Warren, so continued to answer to Wally as an adult and to sign his name as W.M. Goldsmith. The former practice led some to incorrectly assume that his real name was Wallace and the latter habit caused others to conclude that it was William. Meanwhile, Goldsmith raised no objections to such mistakes, perhaps even encouraged them. That at least is my current theory, but I have to admit that I have had many other hypotheses over the years, only to have to abandon them. If you ask me in five years, it's very possible that new information will have come to light and that I'll have a new theory.

All of these census and city directory listings and vital records only do so much to bring Wally Goldsmith's life into clear focus. We now know where he was living at pretty much any time in his life, but the reasons for his moves are unclear. We know that his life after baseball saw him work mostly as a hotel clerk or manager, with occasional stints as a salesman, and that it included a failed marriage. But what we know about the man himself remains limited.

It is at least clear that he retained some of his affection for baseball, as was shown when he weighed in on the origins of the bunt in 1901. There was also a far more impressive piece of evidence to Wally Goldsmith's continuing attachment to baseball: the 1870 trophy ball that was eventually loaned to Baltimore's Babe Ruth Museum. Had he not chosen to preserve it, we might still be asking, "What ever happened to Wally Goldsmith?"

Chapter 10

Al Nichols

T HE MAJOR LEAGUE CAREER OF Al Nichols ended in dramatic fashion when he was one of four Louisville players banned from the National League for life as a result of the league's first game-fixing scandal. He then vanished and left only a few tantalizing clues, with the result that it took an extraordinarily lucky break to unravel a longstanding mystery.

The National League had opened for business in 1876 with a season that was short on drama. The Chicago White Stockings were the heavy favorites after having purchased the services of Boston's "Big Four"—pitcher A.G. Spalding, catcher Jim "Deacon" White, second baseman Ross Barnes, and jack-of-all-trades Cal McVey. The Hartford and St. Louis clubs proved surprisingly strong, but in the end neither could match Chicago's star power. With each member of "Big Four" having a terrific season, the White Stockings cruised to a relatively easily pennant.

It was a very different story in 1877 as Chicago's "Big Four" contributed next to nothing: "Deacon" White returned to Boston, Spalding gave up pitching, Barnes missed most of the season with a serious illness, and McVey was pressed into action behind the plate, where he was found sorely lacking. The White Stockings were never a factor in the National League's second pennant race, which allowed a dark-horse contender to emerge.

The Louisville Grays had finished in fifth place in 1876 and there seemed to be little reason to anticipate improvement. Over the winter, the team had signed veterans Bill Craver and George Hall, but neither was in first youth. Craver in particular was well past 30 and had made his mark as a bare-handed catcher, but was now being expected to play shortstop. The holdovers in the lineup were also an unimpressive lot, with the possible exception of hard-throwing young pitcher Jim Devlin, let go by Chicago after the signing of Spalding. But nobody imagined he could carry the team by himself, so few expected Louisville to be a factor in the 1877 pennant race.

To everyone's surprise, Louisville started strong and by mid–August boasted a 27–13 record and a four-game lead. Devlin had emerged as the unquestioned star, but he was getting plenty of help from dependable catcher "Pop" Snyder and a steady supporting cast. Craver had made an effortless transition to shortstop and was teaming with slick-fielding second baseman Joe Gerhardt and center fielder Bill Crowley to provide the proverbial strength up the middle. Crowley was flanked by Hall and another newcomer named George Shafer, who was known as "Orator" for his endless flow of conversation and who will be featured in a later chapter. First baseman "Jumbo" Latham and third baseman Bill Hague filled out the lineup.

Perhaps the team's greatest strength was reliability. Five of Grays manager Jack Chapman's nine regulars appeared in all 61 games played by the team that year, while none of them missed more than four games. This enabled team management to do without paid substitutes for much of the season, instead using a local amateur on the very rare occasions when the need arose. Eventually, however, the team signed a backup named Al Nichols who had the important recommendation of being able to play all four infield positions.

Louisville held a four-game lead on the morning of August 17, 1877, but that margin was far from secure. Boston had the most formidable lineup as a result of the signing of White, who would end up leading the National League in batting average, runs batted in, and a host of other categories. The team had been inconsistent for much of the season, handicapped by a schedule that had called for two lengthy road trips. Yet the pennant was still within reach and a golden opportunity now awaited. Boston was scheduled to host Louisville and cellar-dwelling Cincinnati and to play all twenty-one remaining games on its home grounds, while the first-place Grays were playing a long series of games in the east.

Boston took full advantage, winning ten straight on its home grounds while Louisville was suddenly unable to beat anyone, even losing several exhibition games during a disastrous skid. By the end of the first week of September, Boston had seized a five-game lead and the race was over. Louisville returned home and the team's winning ways returned, but Boston had suddenly become unbeatable and captured the pennant by seven games.

To many observers, Louisville's late-season slide was unremarkable. Boston had always been the more talented team and had taken advantage of the long season-ending home stand to win 20 of 21 games, thereby snatching the pennant away from a team that had never been expected to be a contender. But in Louisville, the mood was different and the public and team owners demanded answers. Several players had received suspicious telegrams during the trip and rumors began to fly. "The Louisville Grays, alleged baseball players, have returned from their triumphal tour," wrote one reporter snidely, "and will play the Amateurs on the Louisville grounds this afternoon. It will scarcely be profitable to throw the game to the Amateurs, as the pennant does not depend on it."[1]

An investigation established that several Louisville players had been in contact with gamblers about game-fixing. Devlin, Hall, and Nichols all confessed to at least some degree of guilty knowledge and the trio was banned from baseball along with Craver. Their teammates were cleared of involvement and the National League did its best to move on from its first major scandal.

While there is no question that several of these players had discussions with gamblers, the extent and exact nature of the four players' involvement is a secret that each man took to his grave. Craver always maintained his innocence, while even the three who admitted awareness of a game-fixing plot gave very different versions of events. Other details remain even murkier. It seems very likely that some of the exhibition games during the fateful road trip were fixed, but were league games and the pennant itself also thrown? That's a question that historians continue to debate and a definitive answer may never be reached.[2]

I set myself a more straightforward question to explore: what became of Nichols? There were plenty of clues about him but no death information next to his listing in the encyclopedias and it soon became clear why that was the case.

The other three banned players were stars and Nichols was only a reserve, so some have claimed that he didn't really belong in the major leagues in the first place. His .171 batting average in parts of three major league seasons seem to confirm that point of view. In fact, a review of his career shows that his services were always in demand, suggesting that his slick fielding offset his struggles at the plate.

Nichols had played for several amateur clubs in the metropolis and was described as "a very fine young fielder of local reputation" when he signed to play for the fabled Atlantics of Brooklyn in 1875.[3] A sportswriter who must have had plenty of opportunity to observe the young infielder offered this assessment: "Nichols, a really promising young player from the Arlington Club of New York, is billeted for third base, but he can't play the position. At short-stop he is really brilliant, but is altogether too slow in touching a base-runner to admit of his playing the third bag. With the bat he promises much, having always been considered one of the best batsmen among our amateurs. Upon two or three occasions while playing against the Mutuals last season, he hit [star pitcher Bobby] Mathews with more freedom than any other amateur has yet done."[4]

Defying this forecast, Nichols didn't hit much during his rookie season but made quite an impression with his fine fielding at third base. In one early season contest he turned "the best double play of the season," showing "coolness and judgment" that stamped him as "one of the most promising of the 'pony' players of the season."[5] His talents were especially valuable during a season in which it proved very difficult to find fielders capable of filling the position that was soon to become known as the "hot corner." As one sportswriter put it, "The great need of next season will be third basemen. There are but few up to the requisite mark, and these are [Ezra] Sutton, [Bob] Ferguson, Warren [White], ["Chick"] Fulmer, Nichols and [Joe] Gerhardt, both the latter having been showing up in fine form recently."[6]

As a result, Nichols signed to play for the New York Mutuals in 1876. He played third base for the team in every inning of the season, once again having little success with the bat but showing excellent defensive skills. Fatefully, the young third baseman turned in one of his best performances in a game played at Louisville on July 10. "Nichols had by far the most difficult fielding to do, and a glance [at the box score] will show how well he attended to it," wrote a Louisville sportswriter. "A majority of his stops were really wonderful, especially some difficult and hard ones from the bats of Devlin, Hague and [Ed] Somerville."[7]

Al Nichols began the 1877 season with the Alleghenys of the rival International Association but became available at the end of June. He was promptly snapped up by Louisville, where local fans were reminded that the team's new "first-class infielder" was the "gentleman who played so well at third base for New York here last year."[8]

Nichols had exclusively played third base since joining the professional ranks, but Louisville manager Jack Chapman used him as a utility infielder. He saw duty in only six games during the next two months — three at second base and one apiece at the other three infield positions. He did flawless work at shortstop, third base, and first base, but struggled at second base. Even so, both his fielding and batting average in those six games exceeded his previous career bests.

The real concern was the flurry of telegrams that he received during the east-coast road trip and the losses that ensued. Nichols did not return to Louisville with the team for its final home stand and soon found himself at the center of the flurry of game-fixing accusations. Nichols admitted playing a role and was expelled by Louisville, earning him a spot on baseball's blacklist along with Devlin, Hall, and Craver.

The subsequent lives of the four banished Louisville players took very different courses. Jim Devlin unsuccessfully begged National League president William Hulbert for another chance, maintaining that he had no other way to support his wife and young children. Eventually he moved back to his native Philadelphia and became a policeman, only to contract tuberculosis and die in 1883. The defiant Bill Craver also returned home, in his case to Troy, where support for the local hero was unwavering. After playing briefly for Troy's entry in the rival International/National Association, he too became a policeman and patrolled the streets of Troy until his death. George Hall alone accepted his banishment without a murmur, quietly living out his life as a brass engraver.

Long after Devlin, Craver, and Hall had resigned themselves to their fates, Al Nichols remained unwilling to give up baseball. In 1884, a full seven years after his banishment from professional baseball, he was reported to be playing for the semipro Franklin Club of Brooklyn under an assumed name.[9] He attempted to join a club representing Bedford in the Long Island Amateur Association one year later, but protests ensued and he had to be replaced.[10] He was also reported to be playing at the Rauff Grounds in Queens County for a club calling itself the "Artics," which led to complaints from the better-known Arctic Club.[11]

He spent the rest of the 1885 season playing Sunday games for a Long Island nine known as the Skelly Club, but even in that out-of-the-way spot his presence stirred up controversy. Under the terms of Nichols's expulsion, clubs in organized baseball could not play even an exhibition game in which he participated. As a result, when the Eastern League team in Trenton agreed to a Sunday game against the Skelly Club, it was with an explicit stipulation that Nichols would not take part. Trenton manager Pat Powers was thus surprised when he arrived at Skelly Park and "the first man I met there was Mr. Nichols himself. He requested me to allow him to play. I told him it was impossible, as it was against our rules. He then claimed that he had a right to play with any club he wished, claiming that his expulsion did not cover Sundays. I told him he might do what he pleased regarding other clubs, but he could not play with or against the Trentons.... It was the first time I ever met Mr. Nichols, and I was very sorry that I was compelled to speak the way I did, for he seemed very much distressed over the matter. I afterwards learned that it was not through any money interest, but love for the game that he wished to play a game now and then. It is reported that he has a good position in New York."[12]

Despite the formidable obstacles being placed in his way, Nichols showed no signs of losing that love for the game. A false rumor before the 1886 season had him signing with Jersey City of the Eastern League.[13] He resurfaced with a club in Bergen Point in 1887, only to again lose his spot when a tempest again ensued, and then played for the Monroe and Lee clubs of Brooklyn and an unidentified independent club in New Jersey.[14] As late as 1891, he was playing for a club called the Allertons and still being described by the *New York Herald* as "the best third baseman in this vicinity."[15] At the close of the next season, after a full fifteen years in exile, Al Nichols was still an active participant in Sunday leagues in and around New York City.[16] Even that does not seem to have marked the end of his involvement with baseball, as a 1901 article reported that he had remained active on the local semipro circuit until "only a few years ago."[17]

Throughout those years, Nichols made no excuses for his involvement in the scandal and repeatedly expressed his heartfelt repentance.[18] His obvious love of baseball and the remorseful tone of his annual petitions for reinstatement led many to believe that the National League ought to forgive and forget. "Nichols' petition, that the cloud over his life be lifted so that the sunshine of contentment could once more be his, would have brought sympathy from most men," remarked reporter George E. Stackhouse. "[I]t does seem to humane people as if Nichols had been made to suffer enough. Nichols' fate can, of course, be held up before the eyes of other players, and it may have the desired effect. I have talked with him frequently, and if ever a man repented of wrong-doing he surely does."[19] "It seems hard that a brilliant player like Al Nichols," declared another sportswriter, "should be shut out for ever and hounded if he attempts to play with amateur clubs, all on account of his doing wrong some eleven years ago when there are men now flourishing in baseball circles ten times worse than he ever dared be."[20]

Yet the National League refused to remove him from its blacklist, in large part because of the opposition of venerable sportswriter Henry Chadwick. In Chadwick's view, "The most impudent of the crooks was Al 'Nichols,' the go-between of the pool gamblers in the Louisville Club fraud, who, the very next year after his conviction, came on the old Union grounds to practice with the Mutuals, as if he had done a smart thing. This fellow has tried again and again to be reinstated by the League, he claiming that he was injured in his business, while he well knows that his name is not Nichols, that being an alias, and therefore could not have injured him in that way. The National League never did a wiser thing than to resolve that any player once convicted, after trial, of crooked play, should never again be allowed to play on a professional club nine, and they never will."[21] Chadwick prevailed, and around the turn of the century Nichols abandoned his annual pleas for reinstatement and faded into the obscurity that led him to become one of our "cold cases."

On the surface, this should have been an easy case to solve. We knew that he had been gainfully employed in the New York City area until at least 1901 and that he had connections to Brooklyn, Long Island, and New Jersey. He was believed to have been born around 1855, though one note stated he was a teenager at the time of the scandal, which would suggest a slightly later date. His name was usually given as Alfred H. Nichols, though at least one note had Albert as his first name.

It would have been enough to identify a candidate except for one daunting problem: we didn't know his real name. Nichols had used the alias of Williams in some of his subsequent efforts to continue his career, but all indications were that Nichols wasn't his real name either. Henry Chadwick was especially adamant, placing the name Nichols in quotation marks in one article and declaring in another, "This fellow has tried again and again to be reinstated by the league, he claiming that he was injured in his business, while he well knows that his name is not Nichols, that being an alias, and therefore could not have injured him in that way."[22]

How do you look for a man when you don't know his surname? It's next to impossible. Even the indefatigable Lee Allen, the Baseball Hall of Fame's historian during the 1960s, became discouraged. "Of all the men we are trying to trace," Allen wrote in a 1967 letter, "my hunch is we will never get Al Nichols unless we find out his real name. Possibly the [Brooklyn] *Eagle* may have an obit buried away but I doubt it. I have never seen his real name."[23] It was the only occasion I've found when Allen seemed to despair of ever finding a missing player.

The Louisville scandal remained a fresh memory for several years and was rehashed in the sports pages from time to time. Unfortunately, none of the principal figures were willing to discuss it, so the coverage contained little that was new and often added plenty of misinformation. A 1913 article, for example, reported that Craver and Nichols became freight handlers, that Devlin became a policeman in New York, and that Hall got a government job.[24] Soon even unhelpful articles disappeared and the National League's scandal was relegated to the dustbin of history.

We also explored censuses and city directories in our search for Nichols and identified one possibility: an Alfred Nicholls from Staten Island of about the right age. When this man died in 1934, an obituary noted his prowess at ice skating and yachting.[25] Under other circumstances he would have been a strong candidate, but in light of Chadwick's insistence that Nichols was a pseudonym it seemed unlikely that he was our man. So the search reached a dead end and there was no reason to feel optimistic about our chances of ever identifying Al Nichols.

Then in 2005 the first book devoted entirely to the Louisville scandal was published. I purchased a copy, hoping among other things that author William A. Cook might have unearthed some new information about the mysterious Nichols. To my amazement, the author reported that Nichols had died in Steubenville, Ohio, in 1937. Alas, my excitement turned to dismay when I checked his source and discovered that Cook had sloppily taken the date of death of a different (and unrelated) major leaguer named Sammy Nicholl and assigned it to Al Nichols.[26]

Soon after this experience, I happened to be at a convention attended by my friend Gary Mitchem, an editor for the publisher of both this book and the one written by Cook. I mentioned the flagrant error and was stunned when he responded by sighing and saying, "Yes, we heard about that mistake from a descendant of the ballplayer as well." Afraid that I might have misunderstood, I asked whether he meant a descendant of Al Nichols or of Sammy Nicholl and was thrilled when he indicated that the letter was from a great-great-granddaughter of Al Nichols. I hastened to explain our long, fruitless search and to ask whether it would be possible to put me in contact with her. He agreed to check with her, and before long I was corresponding with a descendant of a missing ballplayer and reading a copy of one of the plaintive letters he wrote asking for reinstatement!

Of course the big obstacle had always been that Nichols had begun using the name Williams after his banishment and we were unsure of what his real name was. It turned out to be none other than Williams.

Our elusive ballplayer had been born Alfred Henry Williams in Worcester, England, on February 14, 1852, the son of William Williams and the former Emma Nicholls. Emma Williams immigrated to the New York City area on the ship *Belle Wood* on July 13, 1861. She was accompanied on the journey by her 12-year-old daughter Annie and her son Alfred but not by her husband, about whom little is known.[27] It is possible that he had died by then, but the fact she soon began using her maiden name suggests that the marriage was a troubled one.

After arriving in America, Al Williams/Nichols was raised in Jersey City and Brooklyn. His baseball career blossomed in the early 1870s, only to end suddenly with his blacklisting after the 1877 season. So Williams went to work as a shipping clerk and rented a room in the home of William and Mary Luther.

Intriguingly, when the Luther household was enumerated for the census on June 9, 1880, Williams was listed as their roomer. In fact, he was by then the Luthers' son-in-law, having married their 21-year-old daughter Mary on February 14, 1880, his twentieth-eighth birthday. Does that mean the marriage was kept a secret from Mary's parents? That's certainly a possibility, especially since her surname is still listed as Luther on the census. But, as should be all too apparent by now, census listings are incorrect with enough frequency that that appearance could just have been the result of miscommunication between the census-taker and the person providing the information.

After his marriage, the former ballplayer — now exclusively using the name of Williams — worked first as a shipping clerk and later as a gas company inspector. He and his wife welcomed three children but only one, a daughter named Edna May who was born in 1885, survived childhood.[28] Family tradition confirms that he was deeply remorseful about his role in the scandal and a copy of one of his letters asking for reinstatement was passed down from one generation to the next. In it, Williams offered to retire immediately if reinstated. The National League's refusal to grant his pleas caused him great sorrow.

Al and Mary Williams were still in Brooklyn in 1906 when they gave Edna May away in marriage. By then Al's mother was in her eighties and had outlived her second husband, John Baron. Emma Baron continued to live by herself in a farmhouse on Clinton Avenue in Glendale, a rural community on the outskirts of Queens. Her daughter's family lived nearby and her son-in-law and four grandsons were glad to help out in times of need, such as when Emma Baron discovered a family of seven possums living under her barn.[29] But when her son-in-law died and her grandsons began to move away to start families of their own, it became difficult for the plucky old lady to cope on her own. So in 1911, Al and Mary Williams came to live with her in Glendale.

Now almost sixty, Al appears to have taken this occasion to retire from his work as a gas company inspector. But his life in Glendale was far from leisurely, as his new home needed a great deal of attention. So Al set about having "the old homestead renovated, installing modern improvements and filling in the surrounding grounds" in order to make "the old place look more up-to-date."[30] The three family members who had crossed the Atlantic on the *Belle Wood* fifty years earlier were again living in close proximity for the first time since Annie's marriage in 1869, so there must have been many shared family moments.

Annie Hughes's eldest son Charles became one of the country's best-known cartoonists, creating a comic strip called "Hughes' Zoo" in the early 1920s and also drawing cartoons for the burgeoning motion picture industry. Several decades later, Charles Hughes published several reminiscent articles about the Glendale of his childhood, "a sparsely settled hamlet, populated by truck farmers, dairymen, and commuters to business in Brooklyn and New York."[31] Myrtle Avenue in Glendale, Hughes recalled, "was used by farmers as a one-way thoroughfare. On Fridays a steady stream of loaded farm trucks from many points on Long Island headed for Wallabout Market, Brooklyn. Next day, with empty trucks and full purses, the drivers dozed in their seats while the teams, with slackened reins, lazily wended their way homeward."[32]

The picturesque setting meant that great pleasure could be derived from simple entertainments, such as "A jolly straw-ride, a barn dance in a real barn, or a surprise party at a farm house!" As he recalled, "Despite almost primitive living conditions, our childhood was a happy and contented one. We had ample playgrounds, ballfields, and two swimming holes."[33]

One of Hughes's reminiscences featured the exploits of the local ball club, the Glendale Indians, and the Hanovers, their "bitter rivals for local baseball supremacy." Important games were preceded by a series of quaint rituals: a recitation of "Casey at the Bat" by "Mr. Bennett, shoemaker and Shakespearean poet"; the singing of "Sweet Adeline" by the village quartet, led by "Harry Affourtit, warbling station-master (also postmaster and candy store proprietor)"; a first pitch thrown by Constable Ed Eldert, depicted by Hughes in an accompanying cartoon with spurs, stirrups, and a handle-bar mustache.[34] Another piece described an excursion taken by Charles and two of his brothers, under the supervision of their mother and their "Grandma Baron," all of whom are depicted in a sketch based upon an old photograph.[35]

No mention of Charles Hughes's uncle, the former major leaguer, is to be found in any of these articles. The omission may not mean much, since all of the events he recounts predate Al Williams's 1911 move to Glendale. Yet Hughes was born in 1874, so was old enough to have had vivid memories of his uncle playing for the Skelly Club and other Long Island clubs of the mid to late '80s. As a result, the absence of any mention of an uncle who had once made a national name for himself on the baseball diamond adds to the sense that Al's banishment from professional baseball cast a lasting pall.

That may be why little is known about the later years of Al Williams. He and his wife lived with Al's mother Emma until her death on April 21, 1915, at the age of 91. Their daughter Edna had four children, so time spent with their grandchildren must have brought joy to their later years. Al Williams died in Richmond Hills, Queens, on June 18, 1936.

Filling in that piece of information ended the search for the man who'd played ball as Al Nichols but I've continued to keep in touch with his great-great-granddaughter and even got to meet her on the way home from a trip to Cooperstown. In 2008, she sent me an announcement of the birth of her first child — the great-great-great-granddaughter of a man who once had seemed to have disappeared without a trace!

Chapter 11

Patrick Murphy

E VERY SEARCH FOR A MISSING PLAYER begins with the hope that finding the player will also help to unearth an interesting story. In the vast majority of cases, success at determining a date of death isn't accompanied by much of a tale. The quest to find Patrick Murphy, however, brought to light such a fascinating story that it resulted in a book.

With each new "missing player" investigation, I became increasingly aware that an absence of information is the biographical researcher's most daunting obstacle. Even the most optimistic researchers do not hold out much hope for identifying a chap named Jones—first name unknown— who played four games for Washington in 1884 and apparently never played professional baseball again. By contrast, a player listed as Lawrence Patrick Murphy seemed much more findable. Murphy had played in the major leagues only in 1891, but spent almost that entire season with Washington of the American Association. He even served as a pallbearer at teammate Ed Daily's funeral that October. Better still, our missing player was known to have spent four seasons with Minneapolis and St. Paul of the Western Association prior to joining Washington, and was believed to have had stints with minor league clubs in Buffalo, New Haven, Indianapolis, Birmingham and Nashville.

We also had the benefit of having three names, quite a bounty considering that only one name of many missing players is known. This was a bit of a mixed blessing, however, since there was conflicting information as to whether the player's name was Patrick Lawrence Murphy or Lawrence Patrick Murphy. The source of the existing listing appears to have been a note from the Washington correspondent of *Sporting Life*, who in 1891 referred to "Lawrence Patrick Murphy, our left fielder, who played in St. Paul last year."[1] The 1890 St. Paul city directory seemingly confirmed this by listing Lawrence P. Murphy, occupation ball player, as a roomer at the International Hotel.

But just as much evidence seemed to point the other way, including a source that referred to him as "P.L. Murphy" and an 1890 note in *Sporting News* reporting that the previously ailing "P. Lawrence Murphy is himself once more."[2]

Despite all of this potentially useful information, none of these leads gave any indication of Murphy's hometown, which made the search for a player with such a common surname a bit like looking for a needle in a haystack. His four-year stay in the Twin Cities suggested that as a possibility, but nobody hailing from either city seemed to match — besides, why would a local stay at the International Hotel? We also checked out a Lawrence Murphy who managed Newark in 1887, but that turned out to be a different man. With no firm leads on where to start looking for him, the pursuit of Murphy reached an impasse.

Then a single clue got the search back on track. Minor league expert Reed Howard sent me a note suggesting that Murphy was from Indianapolis, which in turn led to the discovery of this listing in the 1893 Indianapolis city directory: Patrick L. Murphy, ball player. Murphy was residing at 49 Johnson Avenue. Also listed at that address was a printer named Edward F. Nelson.

The next step was to try to trace this man through the directories. That yielded the following listings:

1882 Patrick Murphy, fireman, 134 Meek
1883 Patrick Murphy, laborer, 134 Meek
1884 Patrick L. Murphy, fireman, 146 Meek
1885 Patrick Murphy, fireman, 134 Meek

Then he disappeared for several years, until the 1890 directory showed a single listing of a Patrick L. Murphy, no occupation, at 500 East Georgia. Another two-year gap occurred and then there was the 1893 listing already mentioned. Patrick L. Murphy was once again missing from the 1894 directory but he returned in 1895 as a city fireman, continuing to be listed as such through 1911.

The logical supposition was that this fireman was our missing ballplayer. He was in the Indianapolis directory as a fireman both before and after the baseball career of the man we were seeking, left the city directory for most of the period when our man was playing baseball, and then returned shortly after the ballplayer's career ended. Even the listing of him as a ballplayer in the 1893 was an especially promising sign, as our missing player joined the Indianapolis club during the 1892 season and city directory listings typically were gathered during the preceding autumn.

Unfortunately, there was still no concrete proof that the fireman was the missing ballplayer. The 49 Johnson Avenue address given for the one listing of the ballplayer in 1893 did not correspond to any of the addresses given for the fireman, so it was still conceivable that they could be different men. It didn't seem likely, mind you, but it was conceivable, especially since we were dealing with a very common name. The only thing to do was to investigate the fireman as thoroughly as possible and hope to find evidence showing that he was our baseball player.

The first step was to find out what happened to the fireman and that didn't take long. Richard Malatzky checked the listings of Indianapolis's Crown Hill Cemetery and found a Patrick L. Murphy who was buried in Section 35, Lot 132, on October 9, 1911. I located two obituaries for this man that established that he was indeed the fireman. The *Indianapolis Morning Star* published a short front-page article on the death of Patrick Murphy, who had succumbed to a sudden heart attack while on duty at city fire station number 11. It reported that he had been a city fireman for eighteen years, spending the last decade at the station where he had died. The only listed survivor was a daughter, Mrs. Bessie Houppert of 41 S. Bradley. The deceased was also described as being 54 years old and a member of the Red Men's Order, but baseball was not mentioned. Two brief death notices in the *Indianapolis News* contributed no new information.[3]

Since there was still room for doubt, it was necessary to continue piecing together the lives of the ballplayer and the fireman to see if they were the same person. Researcher Bob Tholkes did some digging in the Twin Cities and discovered a striking woodcut of the ballplayer that was accompanied by this profile: "Patrick Lawrence Murphy, the popular center fielder, lives in Indianapolis. He is of Irish parentage, and first sprang into prominence in 1885, while playing in Birmingham and Nashville. He played with Minneapolis in 1886, his fine work attracting the attention of the St. Paul management, and he was signed for the season of 1887. He is a fine left-handed batsman, a first-class base runner, and is sure of any hit that comes in the vicinity of the middle garden. Murphy is twenty-eight years old, five feet seven and three-fourths inches, and weighs 170 pounds."[4] This once again suggested that we were on the right track, yet did not provide the elusive proof that the fireman and the ballplayer were the same man.

Another intriguing discovery was a 1912 column by old-time baseball man T.P. "Ted" Sullivan. In it, Ted Sullivan recalled that while managing Chattanooga in 1892 he had signed a player named Pat Murphy. According to Sullivan, Murphy previously had been a well-known slugger in the Western League with St. Paul, Columbus, Minneapolis and Indianapolis. All of these cities except Columbus were indeed places where the missing player had spent time.

Sullivan went on to claim that he could tell after Murphy's first game in a Chattanooga uniform that the veteran had lost his batting eye and could no longer play. Murphy, however, was not willing to acknowledge this reality and made a different excuse after going hitless in each of his first four games. His excuse after the fourth game was so implausible that his teammates burst out laughing, forcing Murphy to finally admit that his career was over. Sullivan ended the column by stating that Murphy "is now a rich contractor in railroad work near Indianapolis."[5]

It was hard to know what to make of this anecdote. There could be no doubt that Ted Sullivan was describing the missing ballplayer, but his comments were a mixed bag. The indication that Murphy had returned to Indianapolis pointed to my prime candidate, but his profession didn't match. Moreover, Sullivan was notorious for telling colorful stories that included many exaggerations and embellishments. So the digging continued.

The fireman's Meek Street addresses corresponded to a large family of Murphys and the censuses provided this overview:

1870 census, Indianapolis
Morris Murphy 40, born Ireland, tar roofer
wife Bridget 35 Ireland, keeps house
daughter Mary 18 Ireland, at home
son Patrick 16 Canada, telephone dispatch boy
son John 14 Canada
daughter Johanna 12 Canada
son Morris 10 Canada
son Thomas 7 Canada
daughter Bridget 4 Indiana
son Michael 1 Indiana

1880 census, 136 Meek Street, Indianapolis
Morris Murphy 60 born Ireland, laborer
Bridget 60 Ireland
Patrick 26 Canada, laborer
Morris 18 Canada, laborer
Thomas 16 Canada, laborer
Bridget 13 Indiana
Michael 11 Indiana

These listings gave us some potentially useful information but they were also cause for concern. Census ages are often incorrect and there are indeed discrepancies in the ages of several members of the Murphy family. Patrick's age, however, was consistent and it was very troubling. If indeed he had been born in 1854, as reported on both census listings, then he would have been at least 36 when he made his major league debut. This was certainly not inconceivable but it was highly unusual and doubt began to creep in to my mind.

The complete list of family members renewed hope that we'd be able to tie one of them to the Johnson Avenue address listed for the ballplayer. Alas, none of them ever appeared at that address. I also investigated the possibility that Edward F. Nelson, the man listed as living at that address with Murphy, might turn out to be a relative, but no connection of any kind could be found.

Additional research turned up more troubling information. Coverage of the ballplayer in the local press left no doubt that he was a very well known figure in Indianapolis. The Indianapolis correspondent to *Sporting Life*, for example, reported in 1889 that "Pat Murphy of the St. Pauls" was one of the local players who was preparing for the season.[6] When Murphy had joined Indianapolis in 1892, another local sportswriter observed: "The Indianapolis team will play Patrick Murphy, a well-known outfielder, in right field from this afternoon on.... Murphy is one of the family of ball players living here, five brothers being employed on the diamond."[7] This was very perplexing. Given his local renown, was it possible that he could have died less than two decades later and be the subject of an obituary that made no mention of baseball? The statement that the ballplayer was one of five brothers was more encouraging, but it too raised a troubling question. If all five of them were ball players, why were none of the others ever listed as such in the city directory?

So doubts continued until the long-sought link between the fireman and the ballplayer finally turned up. In late February of 1889 one of the sporting presses published this sad note: "Center fielder Murphy of St. Paul lost his wife at Indianapolis a week ago. Murphy was taking her to Colorado, but she had been too ill to go further than Indianapolis."[8] Buried alongside fireman Patrick L. Murphy in Indianapolis's Crown Hill Cemetery was Mary M. Murphy, who had been interred on February 22, 1889.

There could now be no doubt that the firefighter was our elusive ballplayer and subsequent research turned up more confirmation. Remember Bessie Houppert, the daughter who was the only survivor listed in the fireman's obituary? She had been living with a cousin named William McBride on the 1910 census and a check of Indianapolis wedding records uncovered a July 9, 1883, marriage between Mary McBride and Patrick Murphy.

This ended the search proper, but there was one puzzling loose end: the statement in the Indianapolis newspaper that Patrick Murphy was one of five brothers who were "employed on the diamond." The census listings had provided the names of his four brothers, so it would seem a simple matter to trace their playing records. I again enlisted the help of Reed Howard, who was able to establish that John Murphy had had a brief minor league career but was unable to find any record for the other three — Morris, Michael, and Thomas Murphy. Had the sportswriter's claim been a complete fabrication?

The solution to the mystery proved to be deceptively simple. Patrick Murphy, so obscure that no biographical information about him appeared in the encyclopedias, was a member of baseball's first great groundskeeping family. Two of Patrick's brothers — John and Thomas Murphy — had reshaped and reconfigured the game in countless ways and had been responsible for many celebrated innovations. And yet, precisely because their contributions were so obvious, they had remained hidden in plain sight.

The more digging I did, the more fascinated I became. It turned out that the careers of John and Tom Murphy had intersected with so many major baseball figures that they are frequently referred to in baseball's extensive literature. Of particular note was the close connection that both brothers had to the legendary John McGraw.

During the 1890s, McGraw starred as the feisty third baseman of the Baltimore Orioles, a team that earned three straight pennants by finding new ways to win ball games. As their groundskeeper, Tom Murphy played a role in several of these tactics, making the ground in front of home plate rock-hard so that the Orioles could beat out what became known as "Baltimore chops" and slanting the baselines so that their bunts would stay fair. It was even said that the long grass in the outfield was another ploy — extra baseballs were reportedly hidden in strategic places, allowing Baltimore outfielders to retrieve them instead of chasing down the actual baseball.

When McGraw moved on to New York to begin a three-decade stint as Giants manager, he hired Tom Murphy's older brother John to tend the Polo Grounds. John Murphy had a very different type of challenge as groundskeeper of the Polo Grounds, a ballpark situated on an oddly shaped mud flat that had once been part of the Hudson River. His brother had enjoyed the luxury of trying to build a home-field advantage for the Orioles, but it often took all of John's energies to prevent the Polo Grounds from becoming a lake. He was forced "to keep a rowboat and on days when the Harlem swelled and the Polo Grounds was covered with surface water, Murphy would get out his oars, paddle around in the outfield and find the manholes which answered for a drainage system."[9]

Yet John Murphy overcame all of the impediments and became known as the "greatest genius in his line" for his supervision of a playing field that was a perfect blend of aesthetics and function. When the great infielder Napoleon Lajoie played at the Polo Grounds for the first time, he declared, "I'd like to play here all the time. If a fellow doesn't get the ball it is his fault. The old pill comes true as a die every clip."[10]

Despite their renown, Patrick Murphy's two groundskeeping brothers were the subject of widespread confusion. John McGraw, in particular, has been the subject of many books, none of which do justice to the Murphys. McGraw himself didn't mention either of the brothers in the closest thing he wrote to an autobiography (a series of syndicated columns that were collected under the title *My Thirty Years in Baseball*). Being overlooked, however, was probably a better fate than the misconceptions fostered by other works.

McGraw's widow Blanche misidentified Tom Murphy as the groundskeeper of the Polo Grounds in her 1953 memoir, *The Real McGraw*. She went on to compound the mistake with a description that jumbles the two brothers into one and adds several spurious details.[11] Even worse were the comments of Hall of Famer Hugh Jennings, who had worked closely with Tom Murphy as both an Oriole player and as manager of the Tigers. Nonetheless Jennings would write, "Tom Murphy, fresh from Ireland and speaking with a distinct brogue, was our groundkeeper and was just getting wise to the ways of base ball."[12] This of a man who was born in Canada and grew up in Indianapolis with two older brothers who played professional baseball! Not surprisingly, recent scholars have added to the confusion.

The lack of respect made me indignant and spurred me to do more research, which only increased my amazement at the extent of their accomplishments. Soon I knew that I had to do something about it and the result was *Level Playing Fields*, a book about the Murphy brothers that was published by the University of Nebraska Press in 2007.

During my research, I also discovered an interesting tidbit. In 1913, a *Sporting News* obituary of John Murphy mentioned that "Murphy's brother, Patrick, who died suddenly in Indianapolis not long ago, was a member of the Washington League Club in 1886 and 1887."[13] The details were a bit off, but there was no doubt that this was a direct clue to the identity of the missing ballplayer. In retrospect, it's a bit surprising that no researcher ever noticed the reference and made the connection. If that had happened, however, *Level Playing Fields* would never have been written, so I have no complaints.

Chapter 12

Harvey Watkins

E VERY MISSING MAJOR LEAGUER featured in this book has a story that included surprising twists and turns, some of them very unpredictable. I don't believe, however, that any of those searches had more implausible elements than the Harvey Watkins saga. To begin with, there was the odd way in which Watkins, a circus man with no prior affiliation with baseball, earned a line in the baseball encyclopedias. That was topped by the truly extraordinary manner in which the mystery of his disappearance was solved.

Born in Seneca Falls, New York, on June 14, 1869, Harvey Lennox Watkins was the only child of Harvey Watkins, a brickmaker, and the former Barbara Lennox. Little is known about his childhood, but in the early 1880s the family relocated to New York City, where the elder Harvey Watkins found work as a machinist and his son continued his education.

After completing his studies, Harvey Watkins was hired as the private secretary of James Anthony Bailey, co-founder of Barnum & Bailey's Circus. Bailey was an orphan who had worked his way to the top and Watkins earned his trust by demonstrating similar initiative. According to a retrospective account, "No man in ... Bailey's employ was ever closer to him than Harvey Watkins, his confidential agent, commissioner and assistant manager of the show."[1] A contemporary portrayal of Bailey had this to say: "At his right hand his private secretary and invaluable aid is Mr. Harvey L. Watkins, a young man of bright eyes, alert step and genial spirit. Like the various heads of departments outside, Mr. Watkins is imbued with all the enthusiasm of his chief, and attacks the details of the winter's work as if he had a large monetary interest in the next season's receipts."[2]

There was no shortage of work and Watkins continued to add to his responsibilities. Circus promoter Louis E. Cooke later recalled that "Harvey Watkins was for years private secretary to J.A. Bailey, which made him a valuable assistant, and as he was apt and well informed on everything in connection with the operation of the show, I finally persuaded Mr. Bailey to shift him over to the advance department in charge of the newspaper advertising, knowing that he would make good, and I was never disappointed in this respect."[3]

By 1890 Watkins had also assumed the important duty of helping to compile the circus's annual route book.[4] One year later, he became solely responsible for the route book. In the preface of the 1891 edition, Watkins remarked, "Now there have been route books, so called, but it is gravely to be doubted if any of them attained their objective. They had, however, the merit of perpetuating many pleasant events, and, in a measure, served as partial stories of many a successful and unsuccessful venture in the tented field. As such, those little books proved souvenirs to all the parties immediately connected with those enterprises, but as faithful records of either the principal events happening or the various facts of value to the circus world, they may be said to be utterly useless...." Circus historians have not agreed with this assessment. The writer of a 1960 article marveled, "How modest Mr. Watkins is and how amazed he would be to learn how his compilation of facts is treasured today by the circus fan along with other books of equal merit as an accurate and excellent source of circus history."[5]

Watkins again served as publisher and author of the circus's route book in 1893 and it appears to have been around this time that he also assumed the title of general manager. His had been an extraordinary success story for a man still in his mid-twenties, but he was starting to explore a career change. It appears that he had wearied of the ceaseless travel and was ready to settle down — after two short-lived youthful marriages, Watkins had married a young Englishwoman named Edith in 1894.[6]

Whatever the reason, the young man accepted a position as the financial secretary of New York Giants owner Andrew Freedman. The mercurial Freedman had strong ideas about how to run a baseball team and little willingness to defer to those with first-hand knowledge of the game. During the 1894 season, he exasperated Giants player-manager Johnny Ward by using the team's bench as a sort of V.I.P. seating area. The players often had to compete for seats with as many as a dozen non-players, including team directors, police officers, three batboys, an African American Broadway show mascot, and someone described cryptically as "the big man with the blue suit and the straw hat."[7]

This was no way to run a ball club and few were surprised when Ward retired after the 1894 season. Another Hall of Famer, infielder George Davis, was named to replace Ward as captain and Harvey Watkins also was promoted. Reports differ as to his title — the *Chicago Tribune* reported that he was the team's "Assistant Manager" while the *New York World* described him as the "Assistant Treasurer" — but it seems clear that his only duty was to "look after the team's finances" and that Davis would handle baseball matters.[8]

This was a very sensible arrangement, since it was asking for trouble to expect an active ballplayer to choose the playing lineup, make travel arrangements, and handle the team's finances. Few players had enough business experience to be competent at such chores and, even if a team's player-manager did have all of the necessary skills, it still was preferable to divide up the roles. Attempting to perform so many duties was sure to stretch a man too thin and, perhaps worse, to strain his relations with his teammates and the owner.

Despite the tumult that sometimes swirled around the team, the Giants had compiled an 88–44 record in 1894 and finished a close second in the pennant race. So hopes were high in New York that the new leadership team would bring better results in 1895. Instead the Giants hovered around the .500 mark for the first month and a half of the season. Andrew Freedman grew increasingly dissatisfied with Davis's leadership and the last straw came on June 1 when the visiting St. Louis Browns routed the Giants, 23–2. A few days later, with the team sporting a mediocre 16–17 record, first baseman Jack Doyle was named to succeed Davis as captain.

With Doyle at the helm, the Giants completed their home stand in strong fashion, only to collapse and lose seven straight contests when they first took to the road. A brief resurgence at home was followed by more road struggles that again dragged the team's record down to near the .500 mark. Disturbing whispers about a lack of discipline began to be heard.

Those whispers grew much louder when outfielder Eddie Burke spent an evening enjoying Baltimore's night life and showed up for the next day's game in no condition to play. Burke was only a fringe player whose services could easily be dispensed with, but the same was not true of his best friend and invariable companion, ace pitcher Amos Rusie. Convinced that the two men had been together, Doyle fined them $100 apiece. Rusie was understandably disgruntled and appealed to Freedman, who told the star pitcher that he would remit the fine if his play improved.[9] It was a reasonable decision on the surface, but Doyle's authority had been fatally undermined. It soon came to be "generally known that he could not control some of the players."[10]

The team's erratic play continued until the tensions reached a boiling point in mid–August. *New York Advertiser* sportswriter Sam Crane, a former major leaguer, wrote a stinging critique of Freedman's leadership. The Giants owner was on vacation in Nova Scotia at the time, but upon learning of Crane's comments he sent a telegraph ordering that the sportswriter be barred from the Polo Grounds. When Crane showed up for a game on August 16, his season pass was taken and he was even prevented from purchasing a ticket.[11]

Crane's colleagues were understandably outraged. In one particularly hyperbolic article, Freedman's decision was described as "the sharpest blow that has ever been struck at the free press of America and the right of holding views and expressing themselves." According to its author, "Crane reported the last game from a knot-hole in the fence, and will probably utilize a balloon in the future."[12]

With the team owner off in Nova Scotia and a respected reporter banished from the Polo Grounds, where was the team's player-manager? Nowhere to be found, it turned out. Nursing an ankle injury and no doubt angry about various slights, Doyle was conspicuously missing from the team's bench during several games. "If Doyle is manager, he should act as manager," chided one reporter. "His place is on the bench, whether he be in uniform, citizen's dress or pajamas."[13] When word of Doyle's absence reached Freedman in Nova Scotia, he concluded that he had no choice but to fire him. On August 21, 1895, the *New York Herald* broke the news that Harvey Watkins was the team's new manager.

According to a later account, the many people who were taken by surprise by the *Herald*'s scoop included the new Giants manager himself. "Without consulting Mr. Watkins," a reporter revealed in 1906, "Freedman deposed Doyle as manager and gave the post to Mr. Watkins. Now, Andy Freedman was peculiar, as most baseball fans who remember his connection with the game will recall. And in making Mr. Watkins manager of the team he gave the news to the baseball reporters under pledge of secrecy until he should learn whether Mr. Watkins would accept the post or not. Then Andy forgot all about Watkins and never consulted him at all. One of the newspaper men, becoming fearful, violated his pledge and published the story of the deposition of Doyle and the elevation of Watkins. That made the other newspaper men howl. It was also the first that Mr. Watkins had heard of being made manager and he was as much surprised as anybody else. He wired Freedman for particulars and received a reply that the statement was correct."[14]

After receiving the news of his new job in this roundabout fashion, Watkins was by no means sure that he should accept. He first consulted with Doyle, who told him that the firing was a "relief" and that he "was only too anxious to give up the thankless task. Manager Watkins asked him to retain the captaincy of the nine, but 'Jack' begged hard to be allowed to return to the ranks, promising that as soon as his ankle grew strong he would get into the game again with his whole heart and soul. Mr. Watkins accordingly agreed to grant the request, provided George Davis would accept the captaincy once more. After much persuasion Davis took the appointment and will act in that capacity for the rest of the season. Mr. Watkins knows little about the technical points of the game, and that part he will turn over to Davis. But he has business executive capacity, and will look well to the members of the team who have been breaking the rules of discipline. If any one of them does not, from this day to the end of the season, do his duty to the club he will suffer for it, if the new manager's word is good."[15]

Not everyone was convinced that it was a good idea to hire a manager who lacked familiarity with the finer points of baseball. In particular, members of the local press who were already outraged over Freedman's treatment of Sam Crane were quick to take advantage of a golden opportunity to take shots at the belligerent owner. The next day's *World* summarized Watkins's experience with the Greatest Show on Earth, then added that the new manager shared his boss's ignorance about baseball. The *Sun* and *Herald* also contrasted Watkins's knowledge of the world of the circus with his lack of experience in baseball.

Freedman was the real target of these gibes, however, and comments about the new manager were sympathetic. "Watkins is popular with the patrons of the Polo Ground [sic] and with the players of the team," wrote one reporter. "The appointment certainly bears general approval, and better results from the Giants may be confidently expected."[16]

After taking the reins of the Giants, Watkins seems to have adhered to his stated intention of minding the club's affairs but letting Davis make the baseball decisions. The team won ten of its next twelve games and the new manager earned his share of accolades. "Manager Harvey Watkins certainly is a diplomat," one sportswriter remarked, "and he deserves much praise for the able and successful manner in which he has taken up the task of getting the players in line. He has succeeded in harmonizing the team, and as a result the men are playing a great game. Harvey's elevation to the management has not changed him one bit, and he is the same affable Harvey Watkins."[17]

Then the team's problems began to resurface. The initial success under the new manager had come at the Polo Grounds and another road trip brought back the losing ways. Rusie had earned five straight victories after the switch but he too began to struggle. By the time the Giants returned home for a season-ending four-game series against the pennant-winning Orioles, they needed one more victory to ensure a winning season. Rusie did indeed win the first game of the series, but then two losses followed. On the last day of the season, Rusie was handed the ball again — a decision that would have enormous repercussions. He was hit hard and the Giants lost again, thereby ending the season with a disappointing 66–65 record and a ninth-place finish in the twelve-team league.

The loss to the Orioles was also the finale for reluctant manager Harvey Watkins, who had compiled a record of 18 victories and 17 losses. After the season, experienced baseball man and former player Arthur Irwin was named to succeed him as manager of the Giants. The initial plans were for Watkins to continue to handle the club's business affairs and travel arrangements. As one reporter noted, "By making Watkins financial manager of the club, President Freedman displayed rare judgment, as Watkins is a man of experience in handling just such work. His traveling experience with the big circus made him a most desirable man for the position he now holds in the New York Club."[18]

In December, Watkins traveled to Jacksonville, Florida, to complete the team's arrangements for spring training.[19] He also kept busy while in New York making plans for the upcoming baseball season.[20] But then in January, Watkins announced his resignation from the team and returned to Barnum & Bailey.

The move gave the press an irresistible opportunity to compare Freedman's chaotic management team with an actual circus. "Harvey Watkins is going to swap circuses," declared one sportswriter. "In a few days he will leave the New York Club to return to the Barnum & Bailey show."[21]

Another local reporter expanded on the theme:

> One need not go to Central Africa to meet with thrilling adventures and to encounter the terrors of the animal kingdom. The circus and baseball sometimes furnish all that. Harvey Watkins has had a marvellous experience in both lines of business. Two years ago he was associated with "The Greatest Show on Earth," and it was his misfortune to be the first man to enter the menagerie tent one day after Chico broke from his cage. That nerve straining experience caused Harvey to long for a less exciting business. Therefore — Last year he left the "show" and engaged to conduct the business part of the New York Baseball Club. Out of the frying pan into the fire. It was Mr. Watkins' misfortune again to be the first man on the scene when the chief gorilla from the Giants' menagerie broke out of his cage at Jacksonville. Then he realized that poor Chico had not been the most vicious animal in captivity. Now he has returned to the lesser danger; he has left the baseball club and gone back to the circus. Chico is dead, but Johanna lives. So does the What-Is-It of the New York team.[22]

While Harvey Watkins's tenure with the Giants was over, the events surrounding his final game as manager would continue to haunt the team. Andrew Freedman had promised Amos Rusie that he would remit Jack Doyle's earlier $100 fine if the star pitcher returned to form and stayed out of trouble. Rusie seemed to have lived up to his end of the bargain, but his performance on the last day of the season changed Freedman's mind and he insisted on withholding that sum from the pitcher's final paycheck. According to some versions of events, another $100 fine for poor play was also added on.

Rusie was furious when he received the check and appealed the fine to the game's board of arbitration. At the hearing, the great pitcher was represented by former Giants manager John Ward, now a lawyer, who declared that Freedman's failure to honor the contract made Rusie a free agent. When Freedman was upheld, Rusie announced his intention to sit out the 1896 season.

Suddenly stripped of their ace, the Giants staggered out of the starting gate, losing ten of their first eleven games. On August 7, a 16–1 trouncing in Baltimore dropped the team to 17 games below .500 and Irwin was fired.

New player-manager Bill Joyce was able to guide the Giants to a strong finish, but by then most of the city had ceased to care.

Talk around New York in the summer of 1896 instead focused on whether the standoff between Rusie and Freedman would ever be resolved. John Ward was now preparing to challenge the legality of Freedman's actions in the courts. Freedman continued to maintain that he was in the right, but his fellow owners were not so sure and they dreaded the possibility of a landmark ruling that might make Rusie a free agent and bring an end to baseball's reserve clause.

Since Harvey Watkins had been the team's manager at the time, his views on the subject were eagerly solicited. At first, he expressed solidarity for his boss and declined to testify on Rusie's behalf before the arbitration board. When tracked down by a reporter, Watkins commented, "I believe the club will win its case before the Board by a unanimous vote. I can't see how Rusie can hope for any other outcome. In one capacity or another I have been connected with the show business for some years, and thereby have come in contact with all manner of men; yet I tell you frankly that I never had as much trouble and worry over any of them as I had over Rusie. As a player, owing certain obedience to the club, he was wholly unreliable, and was constantly keeping the management guessing."[23]

In September, however, he told a very different story that shed considerable light on Freedman's decision-making process. According to *Sporting Life*, Watkins provided the following statement:

> At the time Doyle was the manager of the club something came up between Doyle and the New York president and the latter decided to depose Mr. Doyle. He telegraphed to me that he would like to have me take hold of the club and manage it. I came on and took charge and had splendid success with the club to the end of the season. The trouble with Rusie came up, as you may remember, in the last game of the season, when we were playing with Baltimore. I had been working Rusie pretty hard and it was not his turn to pitch, but when the president asked me who was to be in the box and I told him, he said: "No, I want Rusie to pitch this game." I said "All right," and told Rusie, who said he would pitch. Well, he went in and the Orioles pounded him pretty hard for four innings, scoring several runs, which eventually lost us the game. This made the president angry, and he said he would fine Rusie $100 for playing indifferent ball. I, of course, had to inform him of the fine, and several of the New York papers came out in the morning roasting Rusie and said he should have been fined.

At the time I thought Rusie pitched the best ball he knew how, and think so yet, and if the papers had not made such a rumpus I am inclined to believe that the president would not have let the fine go, but he is a very determined man, and after the talk had been made would not do anything but let the matter stand. At the end of the season Rusie did not come up for his check, but took the next train for Indianapolis. I mailed him his check there, less the $100 fine, and on the receipt of the check he immediately entered a protest, which was settled by the Board adversely to Rusie, as almost any matter of that kind would be decided against the player and for the magnate.

I sincerely believe that the fine was an injustice, but think that for the best interest of the game the Board was right in sustaining the New York president. The underlying cause of the trouble was the first fine that was charged against Rusie, when the club was playing in Baltimore. Burke, who is the most intimate friend of Rusie on the team, went out one night before one of the games, and the next day was not in condition to play, and Manager Doyle fined him $100. Doyle was convinced that Rusie had been with Burke, and also fined him. The president had promised Rusie that if he played satisfactory ball for the rest of the season he would refund him $100. Rusie went to the president just before the end and asked him for the money, but the official said he thought he hadn't earned it, but, if he did all right, that at the end of next season he would give it to him. I did not hear just what occurred in the president's office, but Rusie came out very angry, and when I asked him what was the matter he said the president wouldn't give him the $100 he promised him.[24]

When Freedman learned of the comments, he maintained that Watkins had assured him he was misquoted. It was not a very convincing claim, however, and there could be no doubt that Watkins's version of events was very damaging.[25]

The Giants owner remained as stubborn as ever, but his fellow owners had been reduced to a state of panic. Believing that their entire investments would be in jeopardy if the reserve clause were overturned, they offered to reimburse the amount in dispute, to pay Rusie his entire salary for the season he had sat out, and to pay him *to pitch against their clubs in 1897*. It was an extraordinary offer and Rusie agreed to accept it and drop the lawsuit.

In the meantime, Harvey Watkins had returned to working on the circus route books and was busily making preparations to send the Greatest Show on Earth on an extended tour of Europe. When the 1897 American outdoor season ended, three shiploads of circus personnel set sail for London.

Watkins supervised the final group, which left American shores on November 12, 1897.[26]

The plan was for Watkins to remain behind in New York while the circus was performing indoors at the Olympia in London, then join them in the spring when the tour began. But in a surprise twist, Watkins agreed in January 1898 to return to his previous job as business manager of the Giants.[27] This was soon followed by word that "Harvey Watkins will not enter the employ of the New York Club after all. It seems that the Barnum and Bailey people are not willing to let him go."[28]

This odd series of events proved to be Watkins's final dalliance with baseball. He accompanied the Greatest Show on Earth for the next two years as it toured Great Britain on sixty-seven specially built railroad cars. In 1899, the show moved to the continent and performed extended engagements in Germany and Austria-Hungary before concluding in France in 1902.

Watkins published a history of the tour entitled *Four Years in Europe: The Barnum & Bailey Greatest Show on Earth in the Old World*, which included maps showing the routes, photographs of performers, and a complete list of the personnel for the tour. The book does not include the 1902 season, suggesting that Watkins was not involved in that part of the tour.

A likely reason is that by then he was involved in another ambitious venture. James A. Bailey had acquired control of the Buffalo Bill Wild West show and decided to send it to Europe in 1903. While the extent of Watkins's involvement in this project is not known, he must have played a major role since in 1904 he was reported to have returned from Europe after a three-year absence.[29]

After both European tours had concluded, Harvey Watkins returned to New York and returned to working as contracting press agent for the circus.[30] When James Bailey died in 1906, Watkins became the assistant to circus manager Charles Hutchinson. He was soon as busy as ever, helping to arrange a cross-country town in the fall of 1907. A profile in a trade publication observed that Watkins, though still a relatively young man, "has behind him a record of twenty years' continuous service — with one exception, i.e., one season spent as manager of the New York baseball team. In the course of these two decades he has filled almost every executive position with the mammoth enterprise, always exhibiting an indefatigable energy, untiring loyalty and devotion. Persona grata in the editorial rooms of America and Europe, his enthusiasm in the cause he represented threw open the columns of the most conservative newspapers during the years when he was press agent both with and ahead of the show. On the two occasions when Barnum & Bailey visited Europe, Harvey Watkins worked day and night side by side with the late James A. Bailey carrying out the details directed by that great and lamented showman. For many years his figure has been a familiar one at the New York docks, where he has met and assisted through the customs many a strange freak of nature and a multitude of foreign troupes.... An infinity of detail incident to the opening performance each season has always rested upon his shoulders, and on rehearsal night his nervous activity has soothed out the rough places."[31]

By then, however, Watkins apparently had tired of circus life. In 1908, he joined the firm of Keith & Proctor and began working as a booking agent for various New York theatres. He remained in that line of work into the 1920s but slowly faded out of the spotlight. Trade publications such as *Billboard* and *Variety* mentioned his name from time to time, but generally only in passing. His marriage to his English-born wife endured but produced no children and at some point during the 1920s he seems to have retired. His name continued to be listed in the New York city directories until 1933, at which time he vanished and left an enduring mystery.

The timing of Watkins's disappearance made his an especially difficult "cold case" to solve. Due to privacy concerns, U.S. censuses are not released to the public for 72 years, meaning that until 2012 the 1930 census was the most recent one available. The Social Security Death Index is an invaluable tool for people who died after 1963, but it has very few records prior to that year. The result is that research on people who died between 1930 and 1963 is almost entirely dependent on local resources.

There is an excellent death index for all five boroughs of New York City that goes up to 1948, but neither Harvey Watkins nor his wife appeared in it. I corresponded with several members of the Circus Historical Society and added to my limited knowledge of this fascinating subject, but was unable to advance the search for Watkins past 1933. So research hit a dead end, leaving plenty of questions and no answers. Did Harvey Watkins and his wife retire to the countryside? Did they move to another state or perhaps even head back to Europe? Had they both lived to old age in New York City, dying after the end of the city's death index but prior to 1963?

With all of these possibilities viable, there was no way to narrow the search down. The next best thing in such cases is to trace family members, but this provided little helpful information. Harvey Watkins had no children and no siblings. His father died in Manhattan in 1911 and his mother passed away at a ripe old age in 1929, but their brief obituaries didn't add any information of use.

That left only his wife, who proved very difficult to pin down. We knew that she was born in England around 1872 but were unable to find a marriage record in New York, so did not know her maiden name. To make things worse, she used the names Emma and Edith interchangeably. Ships manifests revealed that she traveled from England to New York with Harvey in 1902, 1904, and 1906, but they too did not provide her maiden name or any new clues.

The names Harvey and Edith/Emma Watkins are fairly unusual, so it was worth plugging their names into American vital records databases and newspaper search engines in hope of coming up with a hit. Unfortunately, these efforts never yielded a promising lead. Since the couple disappeared only a few years after the death of Harvey's mother, I began to suspect that they had returned to Edith's native England.

In desperation, in 2006 I finally wrote a profile of Harvey Watkins for the SABR BioProject, an initiative that has put close to 2,000 biographical sketches of ballplayers up on the Internet. In the back of my mind, I hoped that someone might read it and solve the longstanding mystery.

Realistically, this was the longest of long shots. Harvey Watkins had no immediate family and his wife was still an enigma. It had been more than seventy years since they vanished and in all likelihood there was no person alive who held the solution to the mystery. And, even if such a person existed, how likely was it that they would stumble upon my biography of Harvey Watkins?

Against all odds, within two months of this biography being posted on the SABR website, I received an email from a woman in Wales named Heather Smith who had also been researching the couple. Like me, she suspected that Watkins and his wife had moved to England. Unlike me, she knew all of the ins and outs of doing genealogical research in the United Kingdom and almost immediately turned up hard proof. Over the next few weeks, she sent me a series of emails containing evidence that the Watkinses were living in London in the 1930s and then moved on to Harrow. The remarkable messages culminated with one that included an obituary and a picture of the couple's gravestone. Harvey and Emma Edith Watkins died together at their home in Harrow on April 29, 1949, when their furnace malfunctioned.

So why was Heather Smith interested in the Watkinses in the first place? She explained that she was helping a friend research the life of his great-uncle, an Englishman who had relocated to Los Angeles in 1890 and become part of the scene that was to become the motion picture industry. The man had died in 1897 and his wife had returned to England and died a few years later, yet they left behind all sorts of tantalizing clues about their interactions with many key figures from the early years of Hollywood.

Heather had been busily following down all leads, one of which was a book passed down in the family that had this intriguing inscription: "With best wishes for Christmas 1915, from Mrs. Watkins, New York." Several additional clues had pointed to this being the wife of Harvey Watkins and she had been searching the web to try to confirm her hunch when she stumbled upon my biography. So the only thing she was hoping for in exchange for all of the material she had provided to me was proof of her theory that his wife's birth name was Emma Edith Butters.

Alas, definitive information about Harvey Watkins's wife had been one of the things I'd been unable to find. Fortunately, this didn't deter Heather Smith in the least. She went on collecting evidence and soon found convincing support for her theory in a passage written by Harvey Watkins for one of the circus route books. Eventually I was able to track down the elusive marriage record: Harvey Watkins had married Emma Edith Butters on October 20, 1894, in East Radford, Virginia. This was nowhere near any place he had ever lived, so no doubt the surprising location was the consequence of the nomadic circus life.

Chapter 13

"I've Been Right Here
This Whole Time"

A GOOD CHANGE OF PACE IS an invaluable tool for a pitcher and the same holds true for writers. So after twelve chapters about the search and pursuit of missing ballplayers, it's time for a bit of a change-up.

When I tell people about my passion for tracking down missing ballplayers, the most frequent response is a look of blank bewilderment. Sometimes that is followed by this question: "Do you have a lot of trouble with imposters such as the elderly man in W.P. Kinsella's *Shoeless Joe* who claimed that he had once played in the major leagues?"

The answer is yes and no. Over the years there have been numerous men who falsely claimed to have been major league ballplayers. Yet major league playing records are compiled with great care, which means that false claims are usually easy to disprove. On a few rare occasions, however, an imposter has actually gone so far as to claim to have been a very specific major leaguer and that has created problems.

For example, in 1959 *The Sporting News* published an obituary for "Gloomy Gus" Williams, who had played for the Browns. It stated that he had died recently in California, noted that his brother Harry had played in the major leagues, and even claimed that he was buried with a ball signed by his Browns teammates.[1] There would have been little reason to question its accuracy except that five years later *The Sporting News* carried another obituary of Gloomy Gus, this one claiming that he had recently died in Sterling, Illinois.[2]

Painstaking research determined that the ballplayer had settled in Sterling and several other pieces of evidence confirmed that the man who died there was indeed the major leaguer. As for the Californian, what can one say? It appears that his name actually was Gus Williams or something similar. Presumably he was a frustrated ballplayer who was unwilling to admit that he was not good enough to reach the major leagues, so claimed to have been the Browns player. In any event, this man — signed ball or not — was an imposter.

It was odd enough that someone would choose to masquerade as Gloomy Gus Williams. Yet that was nothing compared to Fred Strothkamp, who went to his grave maintaining to have been Charles Reipschlager, an obscure catcher who played parts of five major league seasons beginning in 1883. When Strothkamp died in 1960, *The Sporting News* published an obituary stating that the dead man had told friends "when I signed with the old New York Metropolitans I took the name of Ripschlager. My nickname as a youngster in New York was Rip. I am of German extraction and knew the German word for hitter was Schlager. So I told them my name was Ripschlager. Later, someone put an extra 'e' in the name and made it Reipschlager."[3]

It was a rather odd story, but "baseball names" were not uncommon in the nineteenth century so it was certainly conceivable. What was much more problematic was that, based on contemporaneous coverage the ballplayer would have been over 100 years old in 1960, while the dead man was a full decade younger than that. To make things worse, an 1882 drawing of the ballplayer in a national publication depicted a man with a full mustache and a bit of a receding hairline, hardly things one would expect from the then 17-year-old Strothkamp.[4]

So more research was conducted and it was determined that Reipschlager had been playing for men's teams as early as 1878, when the imposter was barely yet a teenager. The rest of Strothkamp's story collapsed like a house of cards and the search began for the real Charles Reispchlager. Eventually Richard Malatzky determined that the actual ballplayer had died in Atlantic City in 1910.

Gus Williams and Strothkamp/Reipschlager were the notable examples that I'm aware of, but this issue may continue to resurface. The post-baseball whereabouts of major leaguers are tracked more carefully these days, but at the same time there is also more temptation for would-be imposters. Major league ballplayers are now among the wealthiest members of society and, with their playing records and vital information public knowledge, they are obvious targets for identity theft. Former pitcher Dennis Bennett, for example, reported that an identity thief had damaged his credit so badly that "for about five years, I couldn't even buy a pack of gum on credit. That's how bad that guy ruined it."[5]

Impersonating a major leaguer for the ego boost also remains a temptation. In 2007, the AP wire service reported the death of Bill Henry, who pitched for six teams between 1952 and 1969. David Lambert, an active member of the Biographical Research Committee, read the obituary and was puzzled. The age listed for Bill Henry was wrong and he was living in Florida, rather than Texas. Even his middle initial was wrong. So he tracked down a phone number for Bill Henry and dialed it.

He found himself speaking to the real Bill Henry, who confirmed that the reports of his demise had been greatly exaggerated. "I've been right here this whole time," Henry subsequently told a reporter. "It was kind of a shock to hear people say they thought I was dead." The Florida man turned out to be a retired salesman with the same first and last name as the ballplayer but a different middle initial. The Florida salesman had idly boasted to his friends about his baseball career and when he died, they passed the information on to the press.

Bill Henry wasn't the first such imposter and it's unlikely that he will be the last. It's just another one of the potential impediments that members of the Biographical Research Committee have to bear in mind.

Chapter 14

The Shafer Brothers

TWO DECADES OF LOOKING FOR missing players has made me very conscious of several recurring patterns. Since any player still unaccounted for after all these years has frustrated generations of researchers, I now work on the assumption that some unhappy event disrupted the life of any missing player. Nineteenth-century professional ballplayers led a nomadic lifestyle that lacked the prestige enjoyed by today's very well-paid major leaguers. Many of them settled down to normal lives after their baseball careers ended, but this was rarely the case with missing players, who were far more likely to go to jail, or be charged with a crime and flee, or desert their wife and children, or struggle with a drinking problem, or go insane, etc., etc.

But there are exceptions to every rule and we also continue to track down missing players whose post-baseball lives were humdrum. Sometimes they were difficult to find because of a very common name or the use of a "baseball name" or just a lack of information about the player. In many cases, however, the biggest problem is where the player chose to live. Some states bend over backward to help genealogical researchers by making vital records available on the Internet. Others provide no help whatsoever, and in some cases even put obstacles in the path of researchers. Similarly, the sportswriters of some cities kept tabs on ballplayers after their careers were over, while others showed little interest. Hence there are areas where missing ballplayers are very rare and places where they are all too common — places such as Philadelphia.

Philadelphia was one of the major baseball hotbeds during the 1860s and 1870s, yet in the decades that followed the city's newspapers rarely published pieces about the stars of that era. Even legendary stars such as Dick McBride and Levi Meyerle faded into obscurity, while lesser players became impossible to track. Making things far worse were the state's extraordinarily restrictive vital record policies. In Pennsylvania, birth and death certificates were long classified as "closed records," which meant that they could only be issued to those able to prove that they were members of the immediate family.

Privacy concerns certainly dictate that access to vital records be restricted. Nobody would argue that filling in a line in the baseball encyclopedias is important enough to expose anyone to even the slightest threat of stalking or identity theft. Yet Pennsylvania kept the same restrictions on the state's vital records no matter how long ago they occurred, as though the privacy of someone who died in 1916 was being violated by allowing a researcher a glimpse at their death certificate.

In December of 2011, the Pennsylvania legislature at long last addressed this issue. In a compromise, Bill SB-361 decreed that death certificates would remain "closed records" for 50 years and birth records for 105 years, but then they would be made accessible to researchers. As of this writing, it is not yet known when the access will include putting those records in an on-line searchable database with an index, as is the case in many states. In any event, research in Pennsylvania will be much easier in the future.

Before the passage of Bill SB-361, members of the Biographical Research Committee were forced to go to great lengths in pursuit of Philadelphia's many missing players. In many cases these were players who would have been very easy to identify and find had they come from any place other than Philadelphia. A perfect example is the case of brothers George and Taylor Shafer.

In stark contrast to the anonymous ballplayers whom we often pursue, the Shafer brothers were colorful characters who were remembered long after their playing days ended. The older brother George became better known as "Orator" Shafer because of a tongue that never stopped. A century before Mark Fidrych, he often seemed to be engrossed in conversation even when he was standing alone in right field.

George Shafer "needs no introduction," a sportswriter explained in 1882. "He has always had a faculty of making himself known wherever he goes." The writer explained that Shafer "possesses the gift of gab to an unusual degree, an accomplishment that needs a tight rein sometimes to curb and keep within proper bounds." But he was quick to add that Shafer was more than just an overly chatty eccentric: "Without exception he is the best right-fielder in the country today, a position in which he has always played, and which he has down to a very fine point. His record of assist on put-outs at first base beats anything that has ever been heard of."[1]

The description of Shafer as the game's best right fielder might be debated, but the claim that his assist totals were extraordinary was no exaggeration. In 1879, Shafer accumulated 50 outfield assists, a total that remains the major league record despite the fact that teams today play more than twice as many games as his team played that season. He is also the only player in major league history to have two seasons of 40 or more outfield assists and the only outfielder with three different seasons of 35 or more assists. His 290 career outfield assists rank tenth all-time.

George Shafer was also adept with the bat, though far from consistent. In 1878, he compiled a .338 batting average with 25 extra-base hits; the sophisticated metrics now popular with statistically inclined analysts rank him as the best hitter in the National League that year. Six seasons later, he finished second in the Union Association with a .360 batting average and lashed out a league-leading forty doubles. In other years, however, Shafer suffered through season-long slumps that left his batting average scarcely above the dreaded Mendoza line. Nevertheless, in thirteen major league seasons between 1874 and 1890, George Shafer was a well-above average player both at the plate and when showing off his terrific arm from right field.

His younger brother Taylor was a much less accomplished ballplayer who batted below .200 in short stints with four major league clubs. Yet his services remained in demand, a tribute to his versatility and defensive skill. Second base was his primary position, but he earned a reputation for being able to fill in capably at pretty much any spot on the diamond.

The Shafer brothers were Philadelphia natives and both ended their major league careers in 1890 on the hometown Athletics. In the early 1890s, George W. Shafer, occupation ball player, and Taylor Shafer, also listed as a ball player, were at the same address in the Philadelphia city directories. So at first it seemed that they would be easy to trace. These census listings pointed the way:

1860 census, Philadelphia Ward 21
John Shaffer, 35 born Pa, drover
Elizabeth, 28 Pa
George, 9 Pa
Susan, 6 Pa
Anne, 3 Pa
Christian, 1 Pa

1870 census, Philadelphia
John Schaeffer, 44 Pa, butcher
Elizabeth, 36 Pa
George, 18 Pa, butcher
Susan, 15 Pa
Annie, 14 Pa
Christian, 11 Pa
Taylor, 5 Pa

1880 census, 1849 North 22nd, Philadelphia
Elizabeth Shaffer, 43 Pa
George, 27 Pa, occupation "no business"
Sussie, 24 Pa
Annie, 21 Pa
Christian, 19 Pa, Dry Goods
Taylor, 16 Pa, Dry Goods

1900 census, Coatesville, Pennsylvania
Elizabeth Gravell, born October 1837 Pa, 5 children, all living, widow,
    Hotel owner, living in the hotel
Christian Shafer, b. March 1866 Pa, Hotel Manager
Annie Ridgway, b. April 1864 Pa, married, 1 child
Taylor Shafer, b. Sept 1870 Pa, single, retired

There were variations in the spelling of the surname and the ages jumped around even more than usual, but the family itself was easy to identify. Also helping out in the search for the Shafer brothers was an abundance of notes about their doings. A particularly detailed profile of George Shafer in 1886 reported that he had played for amateur clubs in Philadelphia for six seasons before beginning his professional career in 1875.[2] There were also plenty of stray notes, such as a mention in 1885 that he had been called home to Philadelphia to attend the funeral of his grandmother.[3]

The notes included a couple of hints about health problems. In 1882, rumors had Shafer planning to retire from baseball as a result of heart disease.[4] Three years later, a prolonged batting slump led to whispers that his eyesight was failing.[5] But Shafer shrugged off all such reports and went on with his career.

The most promising clues were a series of notes that painted a portrait of the brothers as men about to settle into lives of domestic tranquility. In March of 1879, the *New York Clipper* reported that George Shafer had recently become the father of a son.[6] In subsequent years, there were references to a special trip that he made to Philadelphia to visit his wife and to his "wife and daughter" living with him while he played for a minor league team in Nebraska.[7] In 1888, he was included in a list of well-to-do ballplayers and was said to own a house and lot in Philadelphia.[8] George's brother Taylor remained single for most of his playing career, but at the close of his final big league season there were reports that he too was about to tie the knot.[9]

Yet there were also indicators that pointed in a different direction. Less than a year after George reportedly became a father, he was listed as living with his mother and siblings on the 1880 census. The listing stated that he was married, but neither his wife nor any children were living with him and his occupation was also curious: "no business."

The signs of some unwillingness to accept domestic responsibilities continued after his career finally ended. Various notes stated that George was working as a bookie at racetracks in Washington (D.C.), Cincinnati, Guttenberg, Clifton, and Gloucester (the last three all located in New Jersey).[10] Taylor was reported to be one of his associates in one of those articles.[11] Other notes indicated that Taylor was working as a hotel clerk in Coatesville.[12] The latter claim is partially confirmed by the 1900 census, which shows him living at the hotel run by his mother and brother, but the description of his occupation as "retired" makes one wonder how much working he was doing. He was also listed as being single, so obviously the 1890 report of an impending marriage had proven to be just a rumor.

And what of George's family? The 1900 census offered this portrait:

2043 Master, Philadelphia
Ada Shafer, born Oct. 1858 Pa, married 23 years, 1 child, living
George W., born Oct. 1851 Pa, butcher
daughter Regina L., born Jan. 1879 Pa, dressmaker

This had to be the ballplayer, since the 1902 city directory listed both George and Taylor at the same address, which made one thing very clear: the "son" whose birth had been announced in the *New York Clipper* in 1879 was in fact a daughter. Other things were less clear, such as whether George Shafer had in fact returned to his long-ago profession as a butcher. There was one city directory listing of him as a butcher, but most years he was listed without a profession, suggesting that he may still have been spending most of his time at the racetrack.

Then things got very strange. George's wife Ada was listed by herself in the 1906 and 1907 city directories and then as George's widow in the 1908 edition. So had the noted ballplayer in fact died? Not according to a 1911 note stating that he had inherited money after the death of his sister and a 1912 listing of him as the administrator of the estate of "Elizabeth Gravell, deceased."[13] The 1910 census shows George living by himself at 2302 Oxford with his occupation mysteriously listed as "income," while his wife, daughter, and son-in-law are down the road at 1701 Oxford. The son-in-law, interestingly, was Ambrose Farmer, the brother of another major league player, William C. Farmer. The unavoidable conclusion was that George Shafer's marriage was on the rocks.

His brother Taylor was experiencing similar woes. The 1910 census reported that Taylor had been married for seven years, but instead of living with his wife he was at his mother's address. City directories had listed him as working in the real estate business, but on the census he was tersely described as being "retired." A couple of 1907 newspaper notes confirmed that his wife had sued him for non-support.[14]

By 1912, George's wife Ada was again being listed as a widow in the city directory. Taylor joined her at the 1701 Oxford address in 1913 and 1914 and then disappeared. Yet once again George was not dead, as he reappeared in the 1919 and 1921 directories at 1701 Oxford. Then the 1924 directory listed Ada, widow George W. Schafer, at 1427 Widener Place.

So in summary, Ada Shafer was first listed as a widow in 1908, but an abundance of evidence proved that George was still alive. She was again listed as a widow in 1912, but once more he turned up alive and well. A third such listing appeared in 1924 and then the trail grew cold. Had they separated for many years and then reunited in George's last years? Or had the wayward ex-ballplayer once again flitted off to parts unknown? In most places, it would have been an easy mystery to solve, but not in Pennsylvania. The search for George Shafer had reached a dead end.

In the meantime, Taylor Shafer had left Philadelphia in 1914, but he had left a few clues behind. Several city directories had given his middle initial as "Z" and during his 1907 court proceedings he had been referred to as "Zachary Taylor Shafer."[15] So it looked as though he had been named in honor of a U.S. president (as perhaps was also the case with his brother George W. Shafer).

A search of the 1920 census produced a likely candidate in Atlantic City. Taylor Z. Shafer, a 54-year-old native of Pennsylvania, was listed along with his 43-year-old wife Martha, a New Jersey native, and their three-year-old daughter Elizabeth, also born in New Jersey. The 1918 city directory for Atlantic City showed a Zachariah T. Shafer and wife Martha. We couldn't be certain that this was our man, but it was a very good fit.

Unfortunately, the Shafers soon left Atlantic City and proved difficult to trace. At last we found the whole family living on the opposite coast in Los Angeles on the 1930 census. This was an unexpected development but also a welcome one, since California is a much friendlier place for genealogical researchers than Pennsylvania. A search of an online death index turned up a Zachary Taylor Shafer (born on July 13, 1866, in Pennsylvania; died on October 27, 1945, in Los Angeles County), and a Martha Madden Shafer, maiden name Tice (born in New Jersey on December 29, 1876; died in Los Angeles County on January 30, 1942). This was certainly the couple we had been tracing, but was it the ballplayer? There was nothing to do but send for a death certificate and hope to be able to make the connection.

When the anxiously awaited document arrived, it was everything I had hoped for and more. Zachary Taylor Shafer, it stated, was born on July 13, 1866, in Philadelphia, the son of John Shafer and the former Elizabeth Crock. He had lived in California for 18 years and his usual address was 1614 North Fuller, Hollywood, but his place of death was the Ramona Sanitarium in Glendale. His occupation was "retired athlete" and the "kind of industry" was listed as "baseball."

More digging tied up a few loose ends. A search of Philadelphia death certificates turned up the 1904 death of a prematurely born four-day-old infant named Clement Shafer, the son of Taylor and Martha Shafer. Evidently, Taylor and Martha had a son soon after their marriage, then separated for many years after his death, only to reunite and become the parents of a daughter twelve years later.

And what became of the daughter? She died in Elizabethtown, New Jersey, and an obituary provided this summary of her life: "ELIZABETH SHAFER EMERY, 83, FORMER ACTRESS. Elizabeth M. Shafer Emery, 83, of Masonic Homes, Elizabethtown, died there Saturday after a long illness. A resident of Elizabethtown since May, she was formerly of the Philadelphia area. She was a former actress. Born in Atlantic City, N.J., she was the daughter of the late Zachary Taylor and Martha Tice Shafer. She was the last of her immediate family."[16]

The search for Taylor Shafer had reached a successful conclusion, though there were a few nagging questions that still lingered. What, for example, had led him to transplant his family to Hollywood and what did he do during the last two decades of his life? The fact that his daughter became an actress suggests that he may have made the move with that intent, but the details remain unknown. Alert readers may also have noticed that the 1870 and 1880 census listings suggest that Taylor was a bit older than the July 13, 1866, birth date that appears on his death certificate. I'm strongly inclined to believe that he was born in 1864 or 1865, especially since the 1866 date makes him only 17 when he made his major league debut. Unfortunately, such discrepancies are common and actual birth records from that long ago are rarely available, so there is no way to be certain.

The Shafer brothers had always been closely linked, so the discovery that Taylor had died in California made us suspect that George might have ended up there. No good candidate, however, could be found there and a painstaking search of the 1930 census failed to identify a viable candidate. So the search remained moribund and the last known sighting of George Shafer was still his listing in the 1921 Philadelphia city directory. Had he moved off to parts unknown and died there or had he passed away in Philadelphia and his death somehow gone unnoticed in the city where he had once been so well known?

Richard Malatzky at last cracked the case by checking estate records. He located a George W. Shafer who died in Philadelphia on January 21, 1922, and a check of the will revealed that Regina Loretta Farmer, the ballplayer's daughter, was named executrix.[17] Both of the elusive Shafer brothers had at last been located!

I was still curious about whether his passing was mentioned in the local press. The *Inquirer* and the *Public Ledger* are the only Philadelphia newspapers from those years that are readily accessible on the Internet; both of them published brief death notices but neither made any mention of Shafer's contributions to the national pastime. Indeed my full-text searches of the *Inquirer* and *Public Ledger* did not retrieve any mentions of the man once familiarly known as Orator after 1911. Philadelphia is a very difficult place to do research!

Chapter 15

Peter Morris

WHILE I KEEP AN EYE OPEN FOR sightings of all missing players, there are always some who hold a particular interest. As a child, when I received my first copy of the Macmillan *Baseball Encyclopedia*, I checked to see if anyone with my name had ever played major league baseball. I was puzzled by what I found — a ballplayer listed only as "P. Morris." Little did I know that that entry would be my gateway into an enthralling mystery.

The player in question was a shortstop who appeared in one game for Washington of the Union Association on May 14, 1884. When I first started to do biographical research, I asked Richard Topp about him and his response was discouraging. Morris's one game was played in Chicago and he appeared to have been picked up there for the game, as he never appeared on the team's roster. Topp advised me to focus on higher-profile missing players.

Once I had become a seasoned baseball researcher, my curiosity about him returned and I did a bit of digging of my own. While the encyclopedias listed the player as P. Morris with a birthplace of Rockford, Illinois, the evidence suggested that even that limited information was little more than a guess. The few reporters who covered the game identified him as either Morris or Morrison, with one stating that he was from Rockford and another describing him as a Chicago amateur. As for the elusive initial "P," the sporting presses published several notes in February and March about a shortstop named P. Morris who had signed to play a team known as the "Milwaukee reserves." Someone — probably the notoriously sloppy encyclopedia compilers Turkin and Thompson — seemed to have assumed that this man was the missing major leaguer, but extensive research uncovered no basis for that identification.

I had only a vague idea of what the reserve teams were, so I did some research on that topic and my findings were also discouraging. In 1884, the

Union Association challenged the established National League and American Association and refused to honor the reserve clause. The result was an all-out war for players and one of the strategies used by the two established leagues was to sign players for so-called reserve teams, which played among themselves and provided a supply of back-ups for the established clubs. The main purpose of these clubs, however, was to keep promising players out of the grasp of the new circuit and they all disbanded within a month or so of the start of the season.

That being the case, it seemed out of the ordinary for a player to go directly from a reserve team to one in the Union Association. Of course when the reserve clubs disbanded, some of the players did end up in the Union Association, but that didn't appear to have happened with Morris. In the same issue of *Sporting Life* that reported on the one major league game for the mysterious Morris, there was also a mention that the Milwaukee reserves had disbanded and that several players, including Morris, had signed with Stillwater of the Northwestern League.[1]

A couple of newspaper accounts told similar stories. "The Milwaukee reserves have disbanded and three of the men, Schomberg, Morris, and Dealey [sic], have signed with the Stillwater club," reported the *Stillwater Gazette*. "Morris has played shortstop creditably."[2] A newspaper in Fort Wayne added, "The managers for the Milwaukee Base Ball Association have decided to disband the reserve club, as they have found it did not prove profitable. Falch, Roberts and Clayton will join the regular team. Morris, Schomberg, Dealey [sic] will go to the Stillwater club, who have engaged them."[3]

Neither of these articles gave any indication that Morris had played a game in the Union Association in the interim and with that league still at war with the rest of baseball, one had to wonder if a player would have thus jeopardized his career. Worst of all, there was nothing that placed our man in Chicago on the right date. Washington's Union Association franchise spent much of the season picking up new players, many of whom remain unidentified. So I concluded that the listing of the one-game major leaguer as "P. Morris" was likely another one of the guesses that had originated with Turkin and Thompson. With the few things about the player that had appeared to be known now in serious doubt, the search returned to the back burner.

My interest was piqued again a few years later when I found an article in the *St. Louis Post-Dispatch* that gave the mysterious Milwaukee reserve shortstop's name as Pete Morris.[4] More digging turned up a similar reference in the *New York Clipper* and I decided to search for my namesake in the Milwaukee city directories and the 1880 census. But there was no obvious candidate and my interest once again subsided.

Not long afterward, I began writing my first book, *Baseball Fever: Early Baseball in Michigan.* During my research, I discovered that a player named Pete Morris had been a regular for the Aetna Club of Detroit for several seasons. The Aetna Club was founded in 1871, but it was not until 1873 that Morris made his first appearance.[5] He was a regular in 1873 and 1874, starting as a catcher but then playing a variety of positions. By 1875, the Aetnas were making the transition to professionalism and Morris lost playing time to the likes of Charley Bennett and Ed Williamson, both destined to become National League stars.

Intrigued at finding another namesake, I did some more digging but had no success at identifying the ballplayer. The Aetnas had originated at a prestigious Detroit private school run by a man named Patterson and the roster included Frederick Kimball Stearns, the wealthy businessman who later owned Detroit's National League franchise. Yet Morris could not be connected to the school and the 1870 and 1880 censuses yielded no suitable candidates. Only two men by that name appeared in the Detroit city directory, neither of whom could be traced. So I made a mental note that this might be the missing major leaguer, but once again was forced to acknowledge that I had reached a dead end.

Everything changed when a couple of Milwaukee newspapers became available on-line and I decided to take another look for my namesake. Soon I had discovered a wealth of new information. In 1883, a top Milwaukee club called the Maple Leafs had a regular shortstop named Morris. Both the *Daily Journal* and the *Sentinel* included regular references to the club and the ballplayer, with the latter paper referring to him as "P. Morris" and "Peter Morris."[6]

The war against the Union Association began that winter and the first mention of our man occurred on January 31, 1884, when the *Journal* ran a list of Milwaukee signees that included Pete Morris, who was said to hail from Milwaukee.[7] In a follow-up article, Morris was reported to be a member of the reserve team and was described as follows: "Peter Morris, who plays short stop, is bright and active, and though small, understands how to cover a space between second and third."[8]

Both newspapers continued to provide good coverage of the reserve squad during its brief existence and their accounts make clear that Morris was the team's everyday shortstop. On May 13, one day before the missing player's one major league game, the *Sentinel* reported that the reserves were in Chicago to begin a three-game series against that city's reserve nine. A list of the lineup for that day's game accompanied the article and it listed Morris as the team's shortstop. At long last, there was finally proof that the Peter Morris from Milwaukee was in Chicago on the all-important date![9]

The following day's paper noted that the Milwaukee reserves had beaten their Chicago counterparts, but provided no details.[10] One day later, however, both papers published good game accounts of the game on the 14th. Seven of the Milwaukee starters were mentioned by name but Morris's was conspicuously absent. Instead, a substitute named Tom McDermott, normally a catcher, "covered short."[11] No explanation of the change was given but there was an obvious inference: that Pete Morris had chosen instead to play for the Washington Unions.

The reserves had been scheduled to continue on to Akron, Pittsburgh, and Cincinnati after the series in Chicago.[12] Instead, the team returned to Milwaukee and hosted an amateur Chicago team called the Chicago Blues on Sunday, May 18. Morris resumed his normal spot at shortstop and earned praise for his contributions to the team's victory. Alas, it was the last such triumph as the club disbanded after the game.[13]

There had been rumors for several weeks that the demise of the reserves was imminent and most of the players had been casting around for new destinations. As previously noted, Morris and two of his teammates joined Stillwater of the Northwestern League. Intriguingly, one of the other reserves, Pat Dealy, was reported to be joining the Washington Unions.[14] Dealy never actually appeared in a regular season game for Washington but it was an encouraging sign that suggested that a connection had been made between the Washington Unions and the Milwaukee reserves while both teams were in Chicago.

We still had no "smoking gun" to prove that the Milwaukee reserve player was the one-game major leaguer but there was now a very strong circumstantial case. Indeed, the more I examined it, the stronger the case looked. Pete Morris and the Milwaukee reserves were in Chicago for a series, yet Morris was replaced at shortstop on the same day that a shortstop named Morris made his lone appearance in a Washington uniform. Was it conceivable that the Milwaukee Morris needed a day off on the same date that the Washington Unions decided to use a different man named Morris at shortstop? Of course it was — anything's possible — but it would have been an extraordinary coincidence. Shortstop, in particular, was a vital defensive position and it seems unlikely that even a ragamuffin team like Washington would experiment in a regular season game with a player who didn't have credentials as a shortstop. Nor would Milwaukee have given its shortstop a day off without a very good reason.

I was still a bit concerned about the idea of a player going from an American Association reserve team to one in the rival Union Association, so I consulted with David Ball, an expert on the business practices of nineteenth-century clubs. Ball pointed out that the Milwaukee team was contractually obligated to pay a twenty-day severance pay to any released player who wasn't picked up by another team, so it would make sense for them to encourage the players to look around for new clubs. At the same time, the fact that this arrangement might be frowned upon by the parent team would help to explain why game accounts did not specifically identify Morris.

After looking it over from every angle, I was convinced that Peter Morris from Milwaukee was our missing major leaguer and, when I presented all the evidence to Bill Carle, he agreed. There will always be a small flicker of lingering doubt but I'm very comfortable with the listing.

Having finally identified Peter Morris, the next task was to find him. That proved surprisingly easy. Morris's stint with Stillwater did not last long and by August he was back in Milwaukee, playing for a revived version of the Maple Leafs.[15] His name appeared in several box scores that fall, the last of which was played in mid–October.

Less than two months later, this sad item appeared in the *Milwaukee Sentinel*: "Peter Morris, a well-known local ballplayer, was killed by the cars on Tuesday morning, at Columbus, Wis. Morris was a member of the Milwaukee reserves, and later in the season played with the Maple Leafs. He was coupling cars, and his foot caught in the guard rail when the accident occurred."[16] Slightly different version of the article appeared in the *Milwaukee Journal* and the *Oshkosh Northwestern*.

Identifying the ballplayer also proved easy. A few days after Morris's death, the Watertown section of the *Sentinel* included this note: "Peter Morris, the freight conductor killed at Columbus Wednesday morning, while coupling cars, was a resident of Ixonia and well known in this city."[17] Ixonia is a small farming community in southeastern Wisconsin and the 1860, 1870, and 1880 censuses revealed a perfect candidate: Peter R. Morris, who was born in Wales around 1854, and was the eldest of at least eight children of Richard and Sarah Morris. A check of cemeteries in the area proved that this was the right man, as his tombstone gave a birth date of January 1, 1854, and date of death of December 9, 1884.

Naturally, I was anxious to learn more about my namesake and a portrait gradually emerged. Fortunately, my sister Corinne is a Welshophile who earned her doctorate at the University of Aberystwyth and also happens to be an expert genealogist. She advised me that there were two babies named Peter Morris born during the first three months of 1854 and, as a result of several clues, told me that the more likely candidate was one who was born in the St. Asaph district of Denbighshire.

So I sent away to Wales for that man's birth certificate (resisting the urge to claim that it was my own birth certificate). Soon the document arrived and it showed that Peter Morris was indeed the son of Richard Morris and the former Sarah Roberts and had been born on January 1, 1854. His exact place of birth was Hylas Lane in the small town of Rhuddlan.

Why had a young family from northern Wales transplanted itself to Wisconsin? It turned out that there was a Welsh enclave in that part of Wisconsin. In 1840 a Welshman named John Hughes had arrived in Waukesha and found his new surroundings so appealing that "he wrote back to his relative, Thomas Jones in Wales, setting forth its many attractions. Jones had the letter printed in a Welsh magazine and this letter was the means of bringing many settlers to Waukesha county. The Welsh who settled in Waukesha county came mostly from Cardiganshire and Angleseyshire on the west coast of Wales."[18]

According to one of those early settlers, "times were hard and wages low" in that part of Wales, leading more than a hundred Welsh families to join Hughes in Waukesha County during the 1840s. The language barrier created a significant amount of isolation and the new settlers became known as the "Welsh colony." Since most of them were farmers, they soon overflowed into neighboring counties and began to draw new immigrants from all over Wales. Those included young Peter Morris, who was only eight months old on September 30, 1854, when he and his parents arrived in the United States aboard a ship called the *Universe*.[19]

The Morrises had been farmers in Wales and, like so many of the new arrivals, they continued to do so in Ixonia. In 1897, writer and women's rights activist Theodora Winton Youmans explained that members of the "Welsh colony" were "likely to stay upon the farm. Of course some of the growing boys drift off into other pursuits, but there are other boys to take the place of their fathers and the farm is not sold, as in so many cases, for lack of some one to manage it. A very well-informed Welshman told me lately that he thought two-thirds of the boys remained upon the farm, a remarkable showing in this age and country."

Yet while Youmans reported that the Welsh colony was still intact, she had to admit that by then its survival was in jeopardy. "How long it will remain so is an interesting question," she mused. "The language is dying out and in a generation longer its use locally will have entirely disappeared. The children of to-day are thoroughly Americanized and many of them are educated away from home. Will the aptitude for farm life and the bond of a common descent and a common religion suffice to bind together the great great grandchildren of the Angleyshire farmers, so as to in any way differentiate them from their neighbors? Probably not."[20]

My research had established that Peter Morris was one of those Welsh-Americans who chose to assimilate into mainstream American life; sadly, his new career as a railroad conductor cost him his life. Both of Peter's parents had also died by 1886 and all of his known surviving siblings chose to leave the "Welsh colony." His brother William settled in nearby Watertown and became a railroad baggageman, while his sister Agnes married and moved to Chicago. I was especially intrigued to learn that his youngest brother, Edward, moved to Lansing, Michigan, where he became a cook at a hotel.

That discovery in turn got me wondering whether I could make a connection to the Peter Morris who played for the Aetna Club of Detroit. Some more digging turned up proof positive. During the first week of September of 1876, the Aetnas traveled to Milwaukee for a series against the West End Club. When the series ended, the *Milwaukee Sentinel's* correspondent from

Oconomowoc, a town near Ixonia, had this news to report: "'Pete' Morris, of the Detroit Aetnas, was in town Monday making a short visit to his parents and many friends."[21]

By the following year, Morris had returned to Wisconsin. In May of 1877, "Morris (formerly of the Aetnas of Detroit)" played third base for a Milwaukee picked nine.[22] Three months later, he agreed to play for the Brown Stockings of Oconomowoc for the remainder of the season.[23] His whereabouts over the next few years are difficult to trace, so he was probably concentrating on work. Nonetheless, he must have continued to find time for baseball at least occasionally, as in 1879 he played at least one game for the Brown Stockings.[24] Another gap follows before he resurfaces with the Maple Leafs of Milwaukee in 1883. All in all, Morris had been active in baseball for over a decade before making his one major league appearance.

I was still curious to learn how Pete Morris had acquired his passion for baseball. Although Morris had grown up in the United States, he had done so in Wisconsin's "Welsh colony," where the culture of the motherland was lovingly preserved. It seemed highly unlikely that there was much baseball being played there, so my hunch was that his baseball career must have been launched in Detroit.

Returning to the Detroit city directories, I found that there were two men by that name living in Detroit during the mid–1870s: a Peter T. Morris and a Peter Morris with no listed middle initial. Since the ballplayer's middle initial was R, I focused on the latter man, a plasterer who lived at 50 Columbia. More research established that address to be the home of the family of a Welsh-born plasterer named Joseph Roberts. Since the ballplayer's mother's maiden name was Roberts, the explanation now seemed obvious. Peter Morris had been sent to Detroit to learn the plastering trade from a relative, probably an uncle, and it was there that he developed his interest in baseball.

I had taken extensive notes on Detroit's amateur clubs during the research for my book, so I now returned to them to look for a connection. They showed me that a player named Roberts was the regular left fielder for the Alert Club of Detroit in the late 1860s. This reminded me of a reminiscent article about the Alert Club that had appeared in the *Detroit Free Press* in 1889. When I tracked it down I was amazed to read that "Joe Roberts played left field and was an excellent fielder.... He was a son of Roberts, the plasterer."

The 1889 article was the result of an interview with W.S. Rathbone, who was described as "the prime mover in the formation of that famous little club." Rathbone in turn reported that the Alert Club "was organized in 1867 and for a single purpose. It was to take part in the grand tournament gotten up by the Detroit Club, but in which the latter took no part. The Alerts were all young boys going to school, who by hard and constant practice learned to play like clock-work. Their fielding was especially brilliant, and Detroiters became very much excited by the achievements of the club, so much so that any member of the team had only to mention a desire for anything except the terrestrial globe and the admirers of the club fought for the privilege of gratifying the wish."

The Alert Club "dissolved with the close of the season of 1868, most of the members going into business or moving away."[25] But Joe Roberts remained in Detroit and it seems safe to assume that when his cousin Pete Morris arrived in town in the early 1870s he passed along his enthusiasm for baseball. Thus Pete Morris's one major league game was the indirect result of a major tournament staged in Detroit in the summer of 1867.

That tournament, billed as a "world's championship," had the subject of an entire chapter of my book about the origins of baseball in Michigan. In many respects the tournament fell short of its goals, failing to attract any of the great east coast clubs and being marred by hard feelings between the organizers and the eventual champions. Yet it had done much to create baseball enthusiasm throughout Michigan and so it was gratifying to learn that, in a roundabout fashion, my namesake had been one of the converts.

It was a very long and improbable trip from Hylas Lane in Rhuddlan, Wales, to the big leagues, where Peter Morris became the first of only three Welsh-born players in major league history. Reaching the major leaguers after growing up in Wisconsin's "Welsh Colony" was just as impressive of an accomplishment. I was very pleased to have gained an understanding of my namesake's long journey. Biographical Committee chairman Bill Carle reported the find in the committee newsletter under the headline, "Peter Morris Finds Himself."

Chapter 16

George Bristow

SOME MISSING PLAYERS ARE EASY to identify but then remain tantalizingly out of reach, vanishing whenever their trail seems to grow warm. Others are mere ciphers, who elude our efforts to pin them down. One such player was George Bristow, who played in three games for the same woeful 1899 Cleveland Spiders team that gave us the mystery of cigar boy Eddie Kolb.

What made this case particularly maddening was that there seemed to be an abundance of clues. George Bristow had a long enough career for numerous profiles of him to appear in the sporting presses, which made it possible to put together this summary of his career:

1889 Whitings (Chicago City League)
1890 Aurora, Illinois (Illinois-Iowa League)
1891 Rockport, Illinois (unaffiliated team)
1892–93 Fort Scott, Kansas (unaffiliated team)
1894 Des Moines and St. Joseph (Western Association)
1895 Galveston (Texas-Southern League)
1896 Paterson and Newark (Atlantic); Fall River (New England League)
1897 Denison-Sherman and Waco (Texas League)
1898 Hot Springs (Southwestern League)
1899 Cleveland (National League); Kansas City (Western League)
1900 St. Joseph (Western League).[1]

There were several things about this listing that gave pause. To begin with, the record from 1889 through 1897 was for a man who was primarily a pitcher, but the 1899 player was an outfielder and the 1900 player a second baseman. It was an unusual sequence, to say the least, but a careful check of coverage in the sporting press confirmed that a position change had indeed taken place. Another problem was that several notes suggested that the years from 1889 through 1891 might in fact belong to a different player named

Thomas Bristow. After a painstaking review of all the contemporaneous notes that I could find, I concluded that that part of the record was questionable but that the remainder of it definitely did belong to George Bristow.

This coverage also provided many potentially useful clues about the ballplayer's identity. According to several notes, he had been born in Paw Paw, Illinois, in 1870. An 1894 advertisement in *Sporting News* reported that Bristow was a resident of Fort Scott, Kansas, while another ad the following year had him living in Hebron, Nebraska.[2] A note in a Galveston paper on April 11, 1895, stated that he had just received a telegram informing him of the death of a younger sister.[3] Most promising of all was an article a few months later reporting that Bristow had secretly married Emma Gates, the sister of Galveston teammate George Gates, on June 20, 1895.[4] Seven months later, word came that Bristow was planning to travel to Chicago with his new wife so that she could meet his parents.[5]

With so many clues, it seemed as though it would be very easy to identify George Bristow. Not so. Our man was in St. Joseph, Missouri, on the 1900 census, listed as a ballplayer who had been born in Illinois in May of 1870 and whose parents were both natives of New York. Where was his wife? She was back in Galveston, living with her widowed mother and four siblings. A search of Galveston city directories showed that she had gone back to her maiden name in 1899. She was listed as Mrs. George Bristow in a few subsequent years, but her husband was never with her. It looked as though the marriage had been short-lived, which would mean that our best clue was going to be a dead end.

Another promising clue was the April 11, 1895, note stating that Bristow had just been informed by telegram of the death of his sister. Unfortunately, there was no mention of where she had died or even her name, so it hard to do much with this clue. Searches in the obvious places yielded nothing, so we had to file this information away and hope that it would come in handy at a later time.

Worse, no matter how hard we looked, nobody could find him on any census other than 1900 and none of the stray clues panned out. Paw Paw, Illinois, was a small town, and at no point was a Bristow family living there. We tried the surrounding area without success and also made fruitless searches for him in Fort Scott, Kansas, and Hebron, Nebraska. A few notes, possibly about a different Bristow, seemed to connect him to Detroit, so we looked there too but found nothing encouraging. There's a Paw Paw in Michigan, so I investigated the possibility that Bristow hailed from there, but that too went nowhere. A note from 1896 suggested that his father was ailing so we looked for an appropriate death, but once again came up empty. How was it possible that so many notes seemed to identify the ballplayer, yet none of them led us to him?

Richard Malatzky became convinced that George Bristow had to be a "baseball name" and began looking for someone who matched. He searched the town of Paw Paw and found only one infant who had been born in May to parents born in New York (as reported on the 1900 census listing). Unfortunately, that child was named Charles Stevens and he was unable to find any connection to the ballplayer. The town of Paw Paw is at the center of a farming community, so he next tried to find an infant named George in the surrounding region who was a possible match. The only possibility was a baby named George Belden, but his family moved to Kansas and no connection could be made to the ballplayer. There were three other babies born in May — George Wormley, George Avery, and George Reams — but research on these also proved fruitless.

My theory was that some of the information we were relying upon was incorrect, so I set out to find a candidate who matched most but not all of it. I was excited when I discovered that a man named Thomas George Bristow had been born in Illinois on May 31, 1873, and died in San Francisco on May 11, 1956. This man spent most of his life in the military, but his whereabouts prior to 1901 were not easy to trace. Since that was when the ballplayer disappeared, it seemed promising. Unfortunately, his obituary made no mention of baseball and a lot of digging failed to uncover anything encouraging. I continued to consider him a candidate but wasn't sure if I'd ever be able to determine whether that actually was the case.

Another possibility was a George Bristow who was born on January 26, 1864, and died in Kansas City on October 14, 1928. But his age was a major problem and the more I researched him, the less likely it looked that he could be the ballplayer.

Recollecting "Orator" Shafer's on-and-off marriage, I decided to see what I could find about the ballplayer's estranged wife Emma in hopes that they might have reunited. But the name Bristow did not appear in the

Galveston city directory after 1904 and when the former Emma Gates died in a Houston sanitarium in 1919 she was using the name Emma Bianchi. Research on her turned up a confusing picture, but there was no evidence to believe that George Bristow had ever returned to her life.

At this point we had pretty much exhausted all of our leads and the search for George Bristow ground to a halt. It stayed there for years, though every so often we'd find a new clue or a new candidate and follow up on it. Richard Malatzky and I would compare notes from time to time but little changed — he continued to believe that Bristow was most likely a "baseball name" while I still clung to the possibility that Thomas George Bristow was our man.

The stagnant search at last broke wide open when Malatzky found a profile of Bristow that appeared in the *Cleveland Plain Dealer* prior to the start of the fateful 1899 season. Quite a bit of the information was familiar but some of it was new, including an exact birth date: May 13, 1870, in Paw Paw. The profile also reported that Bristow had pitched for the Aurora club in 1890 and that he had worked in a bank for several years after that. Several more clubs were mentioned and then came the intriguing information that Cleveland had tried to sign him in 1898 but that Bristow had instead chosen to enlist in the First Arkansas Volunteers.[6]

There were several potentially helpful clues here, but the suggestion that the ballplayer had served in the Spanish-American War was the one that stood out. This renewed my hope that Bristow might prove to be Thomas George Bristow, who had a lengthy military career that apparently began around 1901. I immediately began trying to find a Spanish-American War service record, but at first it was slow going. It turned out that the 1st Arkansas Infantry never left the United States and were mustered out soon after the end of the brief conflict.

At last, however, I found a record for a George G. Howlett who enlisted in the 1st Arkansas on May 4, 1898, and was discharged on May 20, 1898. Underneath Howlett's names appeared the magic words: "Bristow, George G. (alias)." The record indicated that Howlett/Bristow had filed for a disability pension in 1926 but there was no indication of when or where he died. So it looked as though Richard's theory about a baseball name had been correct all along.

More digging provided confirmation. Living on a farm in the township that surrounded Paw Paw, I found a family consisting of: James Howlett (age 32, born NY), wife Sarah (24, born NY), daughter Mary (2, born Illinois), son Grant (born May 1870 in Illinois), and James's father Horatio. Grant Howlett seemed like a strong candidate and a check of the 1880 censuses showed him listed as George G. Howlett. It now looked as though the ballplayer had at last been identified. Amazingly, Richard Malatzky had already spent a great deal of time looking for just such a candidate, but had passed over Grant Howlett because he lived outside of Paw Paw and his first name was not George.

I continued to trace this family and on the 1900 census found most of them together, but no sign of George. This was another encouraging sign since we already knew that the ballplayer had been enumerated in St. Joseph. The 1910 census brought more welcome news. James Howlett had died in 1904 and Sarah was now listed along with her divorced daughter Marie, her son George, George's wife Nellie, and their seven-month-old daughter Dorothy. The listing added that Nellie was 33 and a native of Ohio and that their infant daughter had been born in the state of Washington. Obviously George Howlett was quite the traveler, just like the ballplayer.

The only problem with this listing was that George was reported as being on his first marriage. On the other hand, Sarah Howlett was listed on both the 1900 and 1910 censuses as the mother of five children, four of them living. By process of elimination, that meant that a daughter named Mandy had died between 1880 and 1900, which fit with the note about the ballplayer losing a sister in 1895. All things considered, it looked like the mystery was at last unraveling.

George soon returned to the state of Washington and proved easy to trace, though his marital situation was a bit perplexing. It turned out that he and his wife, the former Nellie Boninger, had also become parents of a daughter in 1905, though that child must have died in infancy. As of 1920, George was working as a surveyor in Seattle, along with Nellie and Dorothy. By 1930, however, his wife was listed as Elizabeth and when he died in Bellingham on October 17, 1939, the death record gave his wife's name as Ada. So it appeared as though he might have had as many as four different wives, but it was also possible that there was an error in one or more of the listings.

I now had a strong circumstantial case that George Howlett was the missing major leaguer, but I still wanted to find a "smoking gun." Soon I did. It turned out that Horatio G. Howlett, George's grandfather, had been one of the first settlers of that part of the state, arriving in Lee County in 1839 when his son James was an infant. As a result, a 1904 *History of Lee County* included many references to both Horatio and James Howlett. The latter turned out to have been a Civil War veteran whose clothes were struck with bullets on several occasions during the war but escaped without injury each time. After the war he returned to the Paw Paw area and on April 4, 1867, he married Sarah Jane Fowler, also a New York native. As of 1904, he was described as being the father of five children, four of whom were living, including "George G., a professional base-ball player."

That left no doubt in my mind, but I kept digging and found more. Another helpful discovery was a family member compiled by a family member and posted on the Internet. According to it, our man's full name was George Gates Howlett, he had been born on May 13, 1870, in Allen's Grove, Lee County, Illinois, and he had died on October 17, 1939, in Bellingham, Washington. This was once again a perfect match, but what really caught my eye was his middle name — was it really possible that the ballplayer's given names were George Gates and that his first wife had been the sister of a teammate named George Gates?

When I looked over the family tree in greater detail, another piece of the puzzle fell into place. George's sister Amanda Belle Howlett was listed as having been born on April 22, 1873, in Allen's Grove, Lee County, and as having died in Paw Paw on March 28, 1895. So that explained the telegram that George had received in Galveston informing him of his sister's death.

I was intrigued that the 1904 book had used the present tense in describing George as a professional base-ball player. So I checked baseball-reference.com, a website that uses minor league records compiled by members of SABR's Minor League Committee. There I found a player named George Howlett who was listed as having been born on May 13, 1870, and as having played for the following clubs: 1902 Le Mars (Iowa-South Dakota League); 1903 Helena and Portland/Salt Lake City (Pacific National League); 1904 Seattle (Pacific Coast League) and Spokane (Pacific National League); 1905 Victoria/Spokane and Bellingham (both of the Northwestern League); and 1906 Spokane (Northwestern League). Obviously, George Bristow's already lengthy playing career had extended for far longer than I had ever suspected, but for some reason he had begun using his real name after the start of the new century.

I plugged the ballplayer's real name into several searchable newspaper databases and received quite a few hits. By 1905, for instance, the now grizzled veteran was serving as a player-manager according to a note that read: "George Howlett, who did such splendid work for Spokane last year, has charge of the Victoria team."[7] Even after Howlett finally retired, he remained a part of the Seattle baseball scene by taking part in old-timers' games in 1926 and 1932 with the likes of Fielder Jones and Amos Rusie (the legendary pitcher who figured so prominently in Harvey Watkins's managerial tenure).[8]

There were still a few unresolved issues, including the ballplayer's middle name. He had been listed as Grant on the 1870 census, so I theorized that his given names might actually be Grant George or George Grant. But when I wrote to the woman who had assembled the helpful family tree, she informed me that Gates was a family name that had also been his grandfather's middle name. While it was a bizarre coincidence that his given names matched the first and last names of his teammate and brother-in-law, that was indeed the case.

I rechecked the 1870 census and confirmed that the name on it was Grant, so either the listing was in error or a change was made at some point. Perhaps the youngster was initially named in honor of Ulysses S. Grant as a result of his father's war service, but it was later changed. While that sounds far-fetched, such changes to names were not all that uncommon in the nineteenth century, with even U.S. Grant having been born with a different set of given names. It's yet another factor that makes biographical research in turns exhilarating and maddening.

The descendant of the ballplayer did not know a whole lot about him, but she did inform me that many family papers were donated to the Paw Paw Public Library, including some photos of a man in a baseball uniform. At some point I hope to examine these and see if they add to my understanding of George Bristow. In particular, I'd love to find out why he chose to use a "baseball name" for much of his career, only to revert to his real name in 1902. But there are always a few nagging questions and at least the main mysteries surrounding George Bristow have been resolved.

Chapter 17

Early Bloodhound Techniques

B Y NOW, IT SHOULD BE VERY CLEAR how much the Internet has revolutionized the search for missing ballplayers. Today, I can sit in my living
room and, with a few clicks of the mouse, access city directories from Brooklyn, newspapers from San Francisco, census records from Iowa, and put
them all together to solve a mystery that has baffled generations of baseball
sleuths. But since I started doing research in the early 1990s, before the
Internet was a part of the daily lives of Americans, I remain acutely aware
that it was not always this easy.

During several of these chapters, I've expressed my disdain for early
encyclopedia compilers Hy Turkin and S.C. Thompson. Faced with an inor-
dinate number of unidentified players, they repeatedly chose guesswork over
research. To this day, the Biographical Committee continues to try to undo
the damage that was done.

The sloppy work done by Turkin and Thompson is all the more regret-
table because of the assistance they received from a legendary biographical
researcher named Tom Shea. After graduating from Boston College in 1926,
Shea became a traveling textbook salesman. The job meant endlessly criss-
crossing the cities and towns of the east coast and he soon began to use his
spare time to accumulate information on old-time ballplayers.[1]

Soon Shea began to look at every new stop on his route as an opportunity. During the day, he'd find time to visit the local library and peruse
the newspaper collection for clues about old ballplayers. When the day's
work was done, he'd stop by a local watering hole and see if he could find
some old-timers who could fill him in one the local baseball scene. After
all, this was a time when many "missing players" were still alive — while I
feel lucky today to find a knowledgeable descendant of an unidentified
player, Shea could realistically hope to meet many of the men he was seeking.

His mission gradually expanded and he created a list of every major leaguer, then began collecting notes on each of them and filing them in what became known as his shoeboxes. The notes were painstakingly compiled and cross-referenced, allowing them to grow into an invaluable resource. Perhaps best of all, Shea was an astute researcher who recognized fallibility of the sources he was relying upon. His original list of players was based upon one assembled by his friend Ernest Lanigan, a sportswriter and historian, but Shea knew better than to take its entries as gospel. When he found new evidence that showed information to be incorrect, he revised the listing. When the evidence proved contradictory, he didn't rush to a conclusion but just went on doggedly looking for definitive evidence.

By the end of the 1930s, Tom Shea had put together an incomparable resource and he began to look for a way to publish it. But nothing came of several efforts and then wartime austerity made such a project inconceivable. When the war ended, Shea learned that a musician named S.C. "Tommy" Thompson and a sportswriter named "Hy" Turkin had received a contract from publisher A.S. Barnes for a reference work that was going to receive an endorsement from baseball commissioner Happy Chandler and be billed as *The Official Encyclopedia of Baseball*. Shea agreed to share his research with them, apparently under the mistaken belief that he would be credited as a co-author.

Turkin and Thompson published their book in 1951 and Shea was dismayed to find that the only acknowledgment of his contributions was a mention of his name along with other people who had offered help. Thompson unwittingly added insult to injury when he wrote to Shea to boast about the book's sales and to complain about "snipers" who insisted on pointing out its mistakes. "[Turkin] has gotten a fellow writing to him now," grumbled Thompson, "and this jerk is a specialist in finding out that a certain player died on August 5th instead of August 4th as we have him etc. etc. etc. ad nauseum. Nothing new or startling. Just petty junk like that until it got into my hair and I just had to tell Hy off. There is never any full data on some guy who is blank. Just a rehash of stuff we have gone over thoroughly. So I finally wrote this jerk and told him off. I hope he shuts his mouth. Ernie [Lanigan] is the other sniper. He has a funny system. He never writes to me but sends Marcellus notes that he 'don't think' so-and-so is right. We only have these two snipers so I guess we are lucky. I told Hy if we changed the data in the book to conform we would lose all prestige and respect of the sports writers as well as that of the publishers. It is my idea that once you go into print, you simply can't bring out a new edition with a million petty changes like one or two days difference in a player's birth or death without damaging your prestige beyond repair."[2]

The letter is an unwitting indictment of Thompson's lack of interest in the accuracy of what purported to be a reference book. Shortly after receiving this letter, Tom Shea gave up baseball research in disgust.

Hy Turkin died four years later, shortly after his fortieth birthday. S.C. Thompson lived until 1967 and oversaw the publication of several more editions of the encyclopedia. Not surprisingly, however, the later editions saw Thompson follow his avowed philosophy by making little effort to correct the book's many inaccuracies.

As a result, when a spate of new researchers began digging into baseball history after the end of World War II, many of them put too much faith in Turkin and Thompson's listings. Founding SABR member Bob McConnell, for instance, became a diligent minor league researcher and began regularly writing to old-time ballplayers to try to fill in the holes in the fields for batting and throwing hand. When he wrote to octogenarian George Winkelman, who had pitched one game for Washington in 1886, Winkelman wrote back and reported that he pitched with his left hand. The elderly former ballplayer also informed McConnell that Turkin and Thompson's encyclopedia was incorrect in listing him as having played for Louisville. But with S.C. Thompson unwilling to correct his mistakes, it took another five decades before Richard Malatzky determined that the 1883 Louisville player was a different man with a nearly identical name and got the record corrected. The 1950s were thus largely a lost decade for biographical research.

The pendulum began to swing back as a result of the efforts of Cincinnatian Lee Allen. The son of a U.S. congressman, Allen was a journalist by profession and his love of baseball led him to write a series of books about the game's history. In the process, he developed a fascination with arcane details such as ballplayers' middle names.

"I also have a hobby of collecting the complete names of players," Allen explained in 1944, "including middle names. I have dug up many unusual middle names that I know are authentic, and will also be glad to exchange those with you if they interest you."[3] It doesn't sound like a very challenging "hobby" but in fact it was, in large part because Chicago sportswriters such as Charles Dryden loved to add color to their accounts by pinning fake middle names on ballplayers. "Those Chicago writers created more fictitious middle names than you can count," Allen once grumbled.[4] Another obstacle was the ballplayer who felt that his middle name was nobody's business. After tracking down a one-game 1922 player named Louis Lutz, it took all of Allen's considerable skills of persuasion to convince the reluctant player to "give up" his middle name of William.[5]

Lee Allen's interest in collecting minutiae about ballplayers soon expanded and he began compiling data on such topics as schools attended, occupations held, ethnicity, and family members. Upon being introduced to the venerable Arlie Latham, a player whose big league career had begun in 1880, Allen asked him whether he was related to George Latham, another major leaguer of that era. "How the hell old are you anyway?" shot back Latham.[6]

When Allen was appointed historian of the Baseball Hall of Fame in 1959, he made biographical research one of his top priorities. Though the task was a difficult one, Allen made successful use of the Hall of Fame's clout and a regular column in *Sporting News* to solve many longstanding mysteries.

One of the most important things that Allen did in his new position was to write to Tom Shea and encourage him to resume his efforts. "I have often wondered why I never heard from you again," Allen inquired, "and wondered if I could have possibly offended you. I hope not."[7] Shea had lost all interest in his former passion after the 1951 publication of the Turkin and Thompson encyclopedia, but Allen's prodding was enough to revive his enthusiasm. It was a perfect partnership, with Shea's painstaking notes complementing Allen's enthusiasm and connections to make the 1960s a golden era for biographical research.

For Shea, those years must have felt like redemption. For Allen, they provided regular reminders of just how meticulous Shea had been in his research. "I was thinking of you last Saturday morning," Allen wrote in one of many letters to Shea, "for I was sitting in the living room of Edith Hanke, who is the youngest daughter of James H. (Orator Jim) O'Rourke. I had searched for her for many years and finally learned she was living at Madeira

Beach, near Clearwater.... I told Edith about you and what you had written me about O'Rourke's fatherless childhood and the strong Christian character of his mother, all of which she verified."[8]

The Internet and its extraordinary tools were still decades in the future, so Allen built a network of his own. "What we really need is a man in each major city in the U.S.," Allen once told Shea and his letters testify to the wide range of contacts he was able to make.[9] When a mystery arose in Washington, Allen declared, "I am going to write to Ira Smith, who once offered to help me get data in Washington."[10] On another occasion, he boasted of having "a very good man in Cleveland now"— none other than Joe Simenic, the expert sleuth who had helped to initiate me into the world of biographical research.[11] Allen was also able to call upon the services of "a man in Trenton," "a friend in Paterson," "a helpful editor in Marlboro, Mass," "a fellow in Iowa, Jack Smalling," and "a girl named Phyllis Kihn with the Connecticut Historical Society [who] has been very helpful with Hartford players," among others.[12]

When a missing player fell outside of Allen's vast reach, he would stop at nothing to find him. "There is a very cooperative country editor" in Herrick, Illinois, he reported at the end of one successful search.[13] Another search involved a player from South Fork, Pennsylvania, which turned out to be "a place so small that I addressed a letter to Editor, Weekly Newspaper, South Fork, Pa."[14] He offered this summary of how he resolved the mystery of a player named Wyatt Lee: "Traced him to Gilliam, Mo., inserted a notice in weekly paper there, and have just heard from his daughter."[15]

In many cases, Allen wasn't willing to wait in Cooperstown while someone else unraveled the mystery. "The last time I was in Albany," he boasted to Shea during one search, "I phoned every Adams in the phone book to try to determine if William Adams of the Athletics was the same man [as a player named James Irvin Adams]."[16] During another search, he "spent an entire day at Ranger, Texas looking for a trace" of a pitcher with the picturesque name of Sleepy Bill Burns.[17] And when a former major leaguer named Moritz Flohr did not return a questionnaire promptly enough, Allen "drove to [Flohr's home in] Canisteo and confronted [him]."[18]

A fascinating 1964 article revealed the extent of Allen's passion:

> Many baseball players who have known the glamour of the big leagues have disappeared quietly from the limelight, leaving no clues to their where-

abouts or fate. The book is not closed on the stories of these men, however, because of the determined efforts of the National Baseball Hall of Fame in Cooperstown.

The institution's historian, Lee Allen, is attempting to compile data on the approximately 1,000 known living major leaguers and 1,500 deceased ones whose post-baseball careers remain mysteries. Allen's ambition is to make the Hall of Fame a "clearing house for all information" on baseball and the more than 10,000 men who have participated in the history of the big leagues. Officials of the institution want records on every man who played major league ball, whether for a single game or a decade.

Naturally, Allen says, the farther back a player is in the past, the more difficult it usually is to discover what happened to him.

In August 1959, the Hall of Fame began building up its records on the whereabouts of living major leaguers, and dates and places of death of the deceased ones.

Allen, who says he doesn't expect to approach completion of the task in his lifetime, has been assisted recently by a five minute broadcast every weekend on the National Broadcasting System's program, Monitor. Sports announcers Mel Allen and Joe Garagiola read descriptions of ball players who seemingly vanished after their baseball careers ended.

The fates of seven ball players have been uncovered so far as a result of audience response to the broadcasts, which were conceived by Lee Allen and Roy Silver of the NBC Sports Department. The first case solved was that of Princeton Charlie Reilly, a third basemen for the Philadelphia Phillies from 1892–95. The Hall of Fame only knew that Reilly had worked on a cattle ranch in western Colorado 60 years ago.

One of the Monitor listeners was a grandnephew of Reilly's and notified that program that the ball player had died in Los Angeles in 1937.

Another player, Phil Geier, who patrolled the outfield for the Phillies, Reds, Philadelphia Athletics and Boston Nationals between 1896 and 1904 was found in good health at the age of 88 in Spokane, Wash. A friend of his heard the broadcast and tipped off the Hall of Fame to the whereabouts of Geier, who still avidly follows the baseball world in the newspaper. In the meantime Lee Allen conducts his separate investigations and continues to follow up hundreds of leads.

He recalls discovering Jack Warhop, the first pitcher to yield a home run to Babe Ruth, in Islip, L.I., where the ex-hurler was a caretaker on a millionaire's estate.

Another time, Allen was in New York City and on a whim, came across the name of J. Howard Carter in the phone book.

Allen was seeking data on a Cincinnati Reds second baseman with such a name who only got into five major league games. The historian gambled and dialed the number. Carter not only turned out to be the short-lived infielder but also the chief counsel for the *New York Daily News*.

The most famous ballplayer to baffle Allen and other baseball sleuths is George Stacey Davis, a 20-year veteran and star National League shortstop at the turn of the century, who twice served as manager of the New York Giants.

Davis, a native of Cohoes, N. Y., is believed to have settled in East Orange, N. J., in 1910 after retiring from the diamond. He later was baseball coach for Amherst College in Massachusetts, but where and when he died remains unknown.[19]

The article bore the apt title of "Bloodhound Techniques Find Old Ballplayers."

As word got out that the Hall of Fame was seeking missing ballplayers, solutions to some longstanding mysteries landed in Lee Allen's lap. One such example was an 1871 and 1872 player known as Sam Jackson whom Turkin and Thompson had somehow identified as having a real name of Elone J. Jackson. As a result, research on the player went nowhere until, in Allen's words, "a very sweet, old lady walked into my office with her husband. They were up in the 80s and as nice as they could be. Her name is Laura J. Mackey and she lives at 1425 E. Lake Road, Middlesex, N.Y. She told me that she is the daughter of Jackson, but that his name was not Elone, but Samuel (NMI) [no middle initial] Jackson.... [Laura Mackey] was so old and so frail that I worried about her. She and her husband drove here in an old, beaten up car and asked where they could obtain reasonable accommodations for the night. My heart really went out to them."[20]

Several years later, a man from Pittsburgh named Ginsburg walked into Allen's office with his 12-year-old son. To Allen's amazement, the youngster asked to see a list of the heights and weights of the players who debuted in 1871. A few weeks later, Allen received a letter from young Dan Ginsburg, who reported that he had found a missing 1882 one-game player named James Renwick Wylie by calling every Wylie in the Pittsburgh phone book until he located the ballplayer's son![21]

Talking to the son of a missing ballplayer was exciting enough, but in a few instances Allen had the thrill of discovering that an elusive ballplayer was still alive. "I have learned that William A. (Chick) Autry, concerning whom I have sought data for 20 years, is still alive in Santa Rosa, Calif.," he crowed in one of his regular letters to Tom Shea.[22]

Another notable success story involved George Davis, the turn-of-the-century star mentioned in the 1964 article quoted earlier. Allen continued to run down every potential lead and in 1967 reported, "I have a letter from an Amherst alumnus telling me that George Stacey Davis and his wife made a living playing bridge in the 1920s in New York City and that Mrs. Davis wore diamonds as big as eggs. But Greasy Neale, who married a wealthy woman and lives on Park Ave., tells me that he doesn't recall ever hearing of Davis and Neale was high up in NYC bridge circles during the 1920s. I think that Davis died in Orange, N.J. But I can't prove it. I think that because I cannot locate a NY death certificate and he had a niece in one of the Oranges and may have ended up there with her. I went to Cohoes about this case and got nowhere. Some old fool told me that George 'Kiddo' Davis was the son of Geo S., but that is the bunk."[23]

The following year, however, Allen's efforts finally paid off. He duly wrote to Shea to inform him that George Davis had died in Philadelphia in 1940. As he explained, the search had been handicapped by the fact that "the widow refused to tell any of the Davis side of the family even that he had died and they didn't find out until several years later."[24] Davis was elected to the Hall of Fame in 1998 — who can say whether he would have earned that honor if his date and place of death had remained missing?

As the Shea-Allen partnership flourished, Allen became increasingly aware of just how flawed the Turkin and Thompson encyclopedia was. As early as 1950, Allen had expressed dismay over Thompson's unwillingness to correct obvious errors. "I am absolutely at a loss to understand Thompson's attitude," he wrote to Shea. "Last winter, for instance, I received a letter saying that Charles Wesley Jones died in 1910 when struck by lightning. I reported the matter to Turkin and we listed Jones as having died then. When I thought about the incident and decided to check on it, I went to considerable expense and made a trip to Princeton, Indiana, and consumed three days before proving the death notice erroneous. When I asked Hy [Turkin] to erase the Jones death in his records, Thompson considered the whole thing very amusing and proof that I was irresponsible. You figure it out, I can't. Lord knows there are few of us interested in this sort of thing, and I don't see why we can't stick together. Thompson has done a lot of good work, and we all owe him a great deal, but he seems to feel that the research he did years ago is final. I am always open to correction, knowing how tough it is to get accurate data on obscure players from the long ago, and he should feel likewise."[25]

During the 1960s, the Turkin and Thompson's errors became a recurring theme in his letters to Shea. As these chronologically arranged excerpts show, Allen grew increasingly frustrated by the errors and his healthy skepticism over questionable entries eventually turned into an unwillingness to trust any listing in their encyclopedia:

"The T & T book has these death dates switched" [December 16, 1961].

"T & T lists George Ware as manager of the 1878 Grays ... but my guess is..." [January 13, 1962].

"I don't know where T & T got..." [January 15, 1962].

"Lane of the 1901 Boston Nationals, and Baldwin of the 1907 club are definitely 'phantoms.' ... They have been crossed out of my copy of the Encyclopedia" [September 8, 1962].

"I share your skepticism..." [October 24, 1962].

"The Encyclopedia lists ... I was suspicious" [January 7, 1963].

"I had already crossed out the date of death that T & T gives..." [January 21, 1963].

"Another erroneous date of death in T & T is..." (January 21, 1963)

"T & T shows a 1b in one game for Columbus in 1890 named 'Schauer.' There is no such individual" [July 10, 1963].

"Was Lehane with the UA Washington club in '84, or was it LEAHAN[?] I am checking that one out, and I suspect that it was a different man" [July 10, 1963].

"The 1917 death date for Wm. A. Brady in T & T is erroneous. The player who died in 1917 was a minor league player of the 1890s" [May 19, 1966].

"T & T says this was Oliver S. Brown, player with Atlantics in 72. Very doubtful" [August 15, 1966].

"Would this be the man T & T show as Michael Hayes?" [November 8, 1966].

"The death date on Rooney Sweeney in T & T is also erroneous. Rooney was alive and kicking in 1887, frequently mentioned in the press" [January 28, 1967].

"You also once told me that the T & T sketch of Henry William Morgan was the combined record of at least three players" [January 28, 1967].

"I consider Michael Hayes, born Cleveland, to be one of Hy Turkin's flights of fancy" [March 24, 1967].

"T & T leaped to the wrong conclusion" [April 9, 1967].

Of course it's very difficult to prove a negative and Lee Allen, not always being able to consult the primary sources that are now available, often couldn't find definitive proof that a Turkin and Thompson listing was wrong. But time has shown that in each of these cases his suspicions about their "flights of fancy" were well founded.

While many of these were honest mistakes that could be chalked up to the limited resources then available, there were far too many instances in which there was no escaping the conclusion that Turkin and Thompson had filled in missing information with data that couldn't possibly be correct. One of the most egregious examples was James Leon Wood, a legend of the 1860s and '70s whose playing days ended in 1874 when he had a leg amputated, but who nonetheless remained involved in baseball for many decades in a variety of ways. Wood was a minor league manager as late as 1888, and later his son-in-law was one of the owners of the Pittsburgh Pirates. Wood's granddaughter also married a major leaguer and notes about his activities continued to appear in the sporting presses as late as the 1920s, including a remarkable series of reminiscent articles about early baseball that was published in 1916.[26]

Notwithstanding overwhelming evidence to the contrary, the Turkin and Thompson encyclopedia listed Wood as having died in 1886. "Turkin slipped a lot of those deaths from the *Clipper Almanac* into T&T and didn't seem to care to check them out in his anxiety to get data," Allen explained in 1963. "Another wrong death date in T&T is that of Jimmie Woods, or Wood. T&T says he died 11-3-86. The *Clipper* almanac shows plainly that the man who died on that date was Burr Wood, a pitcher from Canastota, N.Y. So Turkin lists the player as James Burr Wood and kills him in 1886."[27]

Yet Allen's pleas were not enough to get the ludicrous listing removed and Turkin and Thompson even credited Wood as playing for Baltimore in 1874. "This is also nonsense because Jimmy Wood by that time had his leg amputated," Allen wrote in exasperation in 1966. "T & T is wrong in almost every respect about Jimmy. He did not die in 1886 and his middle name was not 'Burr' but 'Leon.'"[28] By that time, Allen was in contact with Wood's granddaughter, who remembered her grandfather well and told Allen that he had died in the late 1920s.

Allen's dissatisfaction with their encyclopedia initially led him to "prowl through T & T on an alphabetical basis" in hopes of rooting out the errors.[29]

Before long, however, he came to realize that that approach was not enough and began making plans to incorporate all of his research into a new encyclopedia, to be published by Macmillan. Always conscious of the shortcomings of Turkin and Thompson's efforts, Allen asked Shea if he'd be willing to review the proofs "to make certain we have right club connections for Morgans, Taylors et al?"[30]

Work on the Macmillan *Baseball Encyclopedia* was completed in March 1969 and two months later Lee Allen was dead of a massive heart attack. He was only fifty-four years old.

Allen's death was a tremendous loss to baseball research in general and to biographical research in particular. The priorities of the Baseball Hall of Fame soon changed and Allen's aim of making it a central repository for player information was gradually deemphasized. The Macmillan *Baseball Encyclopedia* went through numerous editions, but it changed editors frequently and was not always able to keep up the high standards that Allen had established.

Biographical research would never again be as centralized as it had been in Cooperstown during the 1960s. Instead, tracking down missing players became the bailiwick of the members of the Society for American Baseball Research (SABR), which was founded by L. Robert Davids in Cooperstown on August 10, 1971. Fifteen other founding members joined Davids on that day, including such major figures in biographical research as Tom Shea, Joe Simenic, Bob McConnell, Bill Haber, Cliff Kachline, Bill Gustafson, Tom Hufford, Ray Nemec, and Dan Ginsburg—yes, the same Dan Ginsburg who, three years earlier as a precocious 12-year-old had amazed Lee Allen by tracking down a missing player.

In the years since, SABR's Biographical Committee has benefited from the talents and dedication of Bob Richardson, Dick Thompson, Pete Palmer, Jack Smalling (Lee Allen's man in Iowa), Rich Topp, Reed Howard, Jay Sanford, Bob Bailey, Peter Mancuso, Bob Tholkes, Bruce Allardice, and far too many others to name all of them. Bill Carle joined the committee in the late 1970s and has served as its head since the late 1980s, doing an outstanding job and keeping the standards at a level that would have made Lee Allen proud.

Richard Malatzky of New York City in particular has brought extraordinary doggedness and ingenuity to the pursuit of missing ballplayers. A protégé of Bill Haber, Malatzky started doing baseball research in the late 1970s but was no longer involved when I got hooked in the early 1990s. Yet by then his discoveries were being regularly cited by other researchers so I was delighted when he returned to baseball research in the late 1990s. Since then he has been of invaluable assistance to me in pretty much every one of my searches and has also tracked down many missing players on his own.

The search for missing ballplayers is thus very much a team effort. Multiple members of the Biographical Committee contribute to most searches and all of us continue to build on the work done by Tom Shea, Lee Allen, and many diligent researchers of the past. A perfect example was James Leon Wood, whom Turkin and Thompson had listed as dying in 1886 despite a mountain of evidence showing that he was alive decades later. Wood's granddaughter told Lee Allen that she believed him to have died around 1926 or 1927 in New York City, but Allen had tried in vain to find a matching death certificate and had died without being able to solve the case.

But Allen had at least established that the 1886 death was bogus, so the search went on and members of the Biographical Committee continued to amass clues. Once death certificates became more readily accessible, I was able to determine that Wood died in 1928 — in San Francisco, of all places. He had no known ties to California but had traveled there from his home in New Orleans for a cataract operation, only to fall ill and die. While I was excited about having solved a mystery that had stumped the likes of Lee Allen, the search was also a good reminder of how fortunate I am to have such an abundance of resources. It was not that way when Lee Allen and Tom Shea were exchanging letters and their diligence never ceases to amaze and inspire me.

Chapter 18

Ed Clark

A SEARCH FOR A BALLPLAYER CAN take researchers all over North America and sometimes well beyond. That unpredictability can be very frustrating, but there's also something fascinating about never knowing whether a missing ballplayer's trail is going to end up in an exotic locale or right under one's nose. A pitcher from Cincinnati named Ed Clark was an extreme example of that, as his path proved so circuitous that one sportswriter described him as a "world tourist, erstwhile prisoner of war in South Africa, and other things 'too numerous to mention.'"[1]

Clark's brief line in the encyclopedias credited him with having pitched in two major league games — one on July 4, 1886, for Philadelphia of the American Association and the second one on August 8, 1891, for Columbus of the same league. It was the kind of curious line that often resulted from Turkin and Thompson's penchant for guesswork and I was immediately suspicious. In this case, my doubts proved to be only partly true, as the 1886 game was well documented as belonging to Ed Clark but the 1891 game turned out to belong to a different pitcher named "Dad" Clarke.

The first task was to get a handle on Ed Clark's career. After apprenticing with the Shamrock and Muldoon Center clubs of Cincinnati, Clark signed his first professional contract with Grand Rapids of the Northwestern League in 1883.[2] He spent time with three Ohio State League teams the following year, but soon received his release from each of them. This was to become a recurring pattern.

Clark and a Cincinnati catcher named Joe Strauss signed in 1885 to play for Columbus (Georgia) of the newly formed Southern League. Clark got off to a very strong start and by August he had already surpassed the 20-victory plateau. The league, however, was on shaky financial grounds and clubs were looking to save money in any way they could. Clark learned this the hard way after a rough outing when he was fined a whole month's salary for what was described as "his suspiciously poor work against Nashville."[3] Soon afterward the league disbanded, leaving its players in the lurch. It was the kind of experience that would make anyone wonder about the wisdom of pursuing baseball as a career.

The 1886 season proved just as discouraging. Clark had stints with three Southern Association clubs and one team from the International League, but didn't stick with any of them for long. By Independence Day, he was back in Cincinnati and he got his shot at the major leagues under very unusual circumstances. The 4th fell on a Sunday, and although Cincinnati was scheduled to host Philadelphia, the visitors expected the game to be canceled due to police enforcement of the Sabbath. When that didn't happen, Philadelphia was caught without a rested pitcher and Clark had to be pressed into duty.

As a local reporter put it, "Ed Clark, a native of this city, who has played for a season with the Southern and Northwestern leagues, was instructed to go in and stem the Cincinnati's tide of victory. He didn't stem much...." Clark surrendered eight runs in his emergency start, but he did pitch a complete game, showing that he wasn't completely out of place on a major league baseball diamond. As a result, it was reported that he would "receive a fair trial from the Athletics and if he comes through the ordeal can affix his name to a contract with them."[4] He didn't appear in another game, however, and was soon back home in Cincinnati.

By the spring of 1887, it looked as though he was ready to give up baseball and move on with his life. "Ed Clark says it is doubtful whether he plays ball next season," reported a *Sporting Life* correspondent in February. "He has a lucrative position at the Stock Yards, and writes a better hand than half the teachers of penmanship. Jim Hart wants him for his new Milwaukee team. Clark's old catcher, Joe Strauss, has signed to play there, you know."[5] Another reason for him to be reluctant to continue his baseball career became evident a few weeks later when this item appeared in a local paper: "Ed. Clark, the well-known pitcher, who played in the Southern League several seasons, was married to Miss Maggie Goodall of Everett Street, last Thursday evening."[6]

Yet in the end Clark decided to give baseball another year and signed with New Orleans. He soon became ill, however, and received his walking papers from both New Orleans and an Ohio State League team. In August, it was reported that Clark was "now better and playing for the Baumgartner Shamrocks [of Cincinnati]. He can be reached at 176 Vine Street, Cincinnati."[7] That led to a chance to pitch for an independent club in Crawfordsville, Indiana, but this too was short-lived.[8]

By 1888, Ed Clark seemed to be done with baseball for good and he spent the year working in Cincinnati for the county auditor. Once again, however, the lures of the diamond proved impossible to resist. His pitching for the local Muldoon Club in the spring of 1889 suggested a return to "his '84 form" and professional teams again began to show interest.[9] After a dalliance with a club in Ironton, the Western Association team in Milwaukee gave Clark a trial in an exhibition game against Cleveland's National League team and his performance was so impressive that he was immediately signed to a contract.[10]

It looked like a rebirth, but that was not to be. Clark was hammered when the Western Association's regular season began and was given his walking papers, only to accept a position as one of the circuit's umpires. By August he had been fired from that post as well and was back in Cincinnati looking for another pitching gig.[11]

Cincinnati columnist Ren Mulford, Jr., had this to say about Clark's return: "If there were a civil service side to base ball, Ed Clark would shine near the top, for when it comes to penmanship there are few people in this town who write a nicer fist than he. Clark is back from the wild west where he landed as one of the Milwaukee pitchers and ended as the umpire who was deposed to make room for ... Herman Doescher. Ed celebrated his return home by umpiring the Muldoon-Hornet game at the Avenue Grounds. He will probably retire from the diamond and resume his old desk in the county auditor's office at work on the tax duplicate."[12]

Mulford may not have intended his comments as a eulogy on Ed Clark's career, but that was effectively the case. Clark would make noises about a comeback from time to time in the years to come, but to all intents and purposes his days as a professional pitcher were at an end.

In 1891, word came that "Ed Clark is now superintendent of the new stock yards in Cincinnati. He has given up all idea of ever again playing professional ball."[13] Three more years passed without any word of him, but just when he seemed to be done with baseball forever, a man named Ed Clark was hired as a Virginia League umpire in 1894 and even made a few pitching appearances. Then a man by the same name spent the next four campaigns as a minor league umpire, the first one in the Southern League and the next three in the Texas League.

Though it looked likely that the umpire was the missing pitcher, there was no positive proof. The fact that he had done some pitching in 1894 was a good sign, but hardly definitive. It was still possible that they were different people or even that there two umpires shared the same common name — the 1894 pitcher-umpire could be our missing ballplayer, but the man who umpired in the Southern and Texas leagues could be a different person. So we proceeded with caution.

The 1898 season was a difficult one for baseball, with the Spanish-American War monopolizing public interest and combining with other factors to keep fans away from the ballpark. Minor leagues all over the country struggled to survive and in early May the Texas League disbanded. Ed Clark had earned enough of a reputation to gain an umpiring berth in the Southern League, but within days of his arrival, it too disbanded. At that point the umpire disappeared as well.

The notes already mentioned provided plenty of clues for our search, including Clark's 1887 marriage to Margaret Goodall, an address of 176 Vine Street in Cincinnati, his possession of expert penmanship at a time when that was an essential clerical skill, and the fact that he had worked for a time at the Cincinnati stockyards. Using this information, it was easy to tie him to a series of city directory listings that culminated in 1892–93 with one for Edward C. Clark, occupation "yardman stockyards" living at 587½ Browne. Over the next four years, Mrs. Maggie Clark was listed in the directories along with her widowed mother, Mrs. Margaret Goodall, but there was no sign of Ed. Of course we suspected that he was umpiring in the South during these years, but in 1898 — when our man was suddenly thrust out of work — the directory listed "Maggie Clark, widow Edward" for the first time. Had Ed Clark died in 1898 and his passing somehow escaped notice?

The censuses also pointed to that conclusion. In 1900, Maggie Clark was listed as a widow with three children: daughter Edna 12, and sons Chester 11 and Alfred 7. Maggie was still living with her mother and three children when the 1910 census was taken, and by 1920 the household consisted of only Maggie and her mother, both listed as widows. In another reminder of the inherent unreliability of census listing, Margaret Goodall was reported to be 75 when the 1910 census was taken, but had shed five years and was only listed as 70 a decade later.

Ed Clark was nowhere to be found on these censuses and we had nothing placing him in Cincinnati after 1893. The next step was to try to pinpoint him in earlier censuses and determine his family, in hopes that they would lead us back to him. This was not easy since Ed Clark is a common name and "Ed" can stand for Edward, Edwin, Edgar, and Edmund, among other possibilities. Eventually, however, we were able to locate a strong candidate and trace him as follows:

> 1860 census, Millcreek, Hamilton Co, Ohio
> John Clark, 33, born Scotland
> Anna, 23, b. Ireland
> Joseph, 2, b. Ohio
> John, 8 months, b. Ohio

> 1870 census, Cincinnati
> Anna Clark, 33, b. Ireland
> Joseph N., 12, b. Ohio
> John B., 10, b. Ohio
> Eddie C., 7, b. Ohio
> Thomas F., 2, b. Ohio

> 1880 census, Marshall Ave., Cincinnati
> Bridget Clark, 43, b. Ireland
> John, 21, b. Ohio, parents born Scotland and Ireland, bookkeeper
> Edward, 17, b. Ohio, parents born Scotland and Ireland, stock clerk
> Thomas, 13 b. Ohio, parents born Scotland and Ireland

The Cincinnati city directories show Ann, Anna or Annie listed as a widow beginning in 1869. Edward Clark was listed along with her for the first time in 1880 as a solicitor. He subsequently was listed as Edmund C. Clark at a variety of addresses between 1881 and 1891, usually as a bookkeeper but sometimes as a clerk or a buyer.

So it now appeared that Clark's true first name was Edmund and that he had been born around 1863. Yet his whereabouts after 1898 remained unknown and none of the new information was of use in that regard. Efforts to find a suitable candidate on the censuses failed and the Cincinnati city directories also yielded no candidate. I tried to trace his two brothers, but that didn't provide a solution either. What could have happened to Ed Clark?

By this time, bogus widow listings for the wives of Seymour Studley, George Shafer, and others made me very reluctant to accept such a city directory entry at face value. Nonetheless, a lot of digging had failed to find any trace of Ed Clark after 1898, which happened to be the first year in which Maggie was reported to be a widow. Had Ed abandoned his wife and three children or had he in fact died in 1898? Or could it be that the umpire wasn't the ballplayer at all and some other fate had befallen him?

The solution to that particular mystery was discovered in a remarkable fashion. In November of 1898, *Sporting News* published a lengthy letter from Clark himself, who offered this explanation of why he had not been heard from in some time:

> Some kind friend was thoughtful enough to send me a copy of *The Sporting News* at this station, and to say that it was eagerly devoured by the base ball cranks of the Eighteenth Regulars would be putting it mildly. Its coming reminded me that I owed it a letter to explain to my friends of the base ball business — and I think I have a few — my disappearance after the Texas and Southern leagues broke up. After the Lone Star organization went up I headed for New Orleans and got a job on the Southern staff, but it lasted only one day, for that league, too, went the way of all things mundane.
>
> Encamped in the Crescent City was the Eighteenth United States Infantry, my old friends from San Antonio, and as they were about to go on to Manila I decided that I would not let them leave me behind, so I enlisted. I was accepted on the spot and assigned to M, one of the "skeleton" companies being organized. We had a delightful trip overland to California. At San Antonio the entire city turned out to give its old favorites a farewell sendoff and there was nothing too good for us. Coming up through Southern California our coaches nearly broke down with the loads of oranges and flowers.
>
> We landed in Camp Merritt at San Francisco and there we stayed for two months and a half. In that time we lost a number of men by sickness, among them Corporal Joe Flynn, a clever little soul known to every ball player who ever worked within the confines of the big Lone Star State. We finally got under way for Manila in August, and after getting out to sea 1,800 miles our transport, the "Arizona," broke her engines, and for six hours we drifted around. While that was going on all of us stripped off and plunged overboard to take a mid-sea dip in the great Pacific ocean, something which few soldiers have ever done.
>
> When we got to Honolulu some of the companies of the Eighteenth were sidetracked, among them ours. We have had a pleasant enough time of it

here, but it is awful monotonous, and we will feel happy when we get on the transport tomorrow. We have football or base ball nearly every day.

Yesterday I pitched for our team against the First New Yorks and beat them 4 to 3. This afternoon the Tenth Pennsylvania team, assisted by four regulars, played the All-Honolulu at foot ball and beat the natives 6 to 0.

All the old-time base ball cranks from Fort Sam Houston, whom the Cincinnatis, Chicagos and other players know so well, are with us out here. Noisy Joe Bennett, whose stentorian lungs often did so much to rattle visiting teams, is now a sergeant in my company, and his old "side-kicker" Pop Jones, is also a corporal in the same outfit. Ex–Provost Sergeant Evans, the most inveterate rooter of them all, is first sergeant of Company D [?], and is disconsolate over the way his favorites, the reds, fell down in the pennant race. "Red" Ewald, Sergeant Cary, Sam Price and a number of well-known old-timers are still with us. "Skinny" Allen, the big first sergeant of "G," is with his company in Manilla [sic], where we soon expect to join them. The transport "Arizona" sails tomorrow and we will go off on her.

I am tied up in this league for three years, and I can not be drafted or released, either. Uncle Sam wouldn't hear of it. If we got into a row with the insurgents I will bench a few of them, for fines do not go in this league. If a bullet or disease does not lay me low I'll be back in God's country in three years' time.[14]

Several other periodicals excerpted this letter or carried similar notes and at least one of them described Clark as a "Cincinnati boy."[15] So it was now clear why the umpire had vanished in the spring of 1898 and, as an added bonus, there was also now little doubt that this man was our missing ballplayer. Nevertheless, it was a bit of a mixed blessing, since the new lead placed him en route to the Philippines at the start of a long conflict.

Over the next few years, the newspapers and sporting presses published numerous updates on Ed Clark's doings and whereabouts. Despite his three-year enlistment, he was discharged in August of 1899 and returned home from Manila aboard the *Tartar*. The press was soon publishing allegations that discharged U.S. soldiers had received inadequate medical treatment aboard the *Tartar*, resulting in the unnecessary deaths of several soldiers. Ed Clark had his own horror story to tell, maintaining that one of the ship's surgeons refused to get out of bed to treat a dying soldier. According to Clark, "There were 407 of us discharged soldiers and we can all tell hair-raising stories."[16]

Clark also had a wealth of stories to share about his time in the Philippines. His regiment was first sent to San Francisco, where Clark and his fellow soldiers "drilled all day, and at nights dreamed of the forward march, right face, left oblique, carry arms, present and attention, and, finally, the bugle call for meals." At last it was time to ship out and "he went with the Second battalion and at length reached the troublous islands. One battalion of his regiment, with a command of volunteers, had entered Manila. The transport which bore him to the new land was ordered to Iloilo. There the *Petrel* and *Boston* bombarded the shore and the troops landed. They brushed with the Spanish and carried the day, and after that the command saw nothing but a dreary year for them. They waited for orders, but the command was left undisturbed."[17]

Then, in Clark's words,

politics began stirring the folks at home and that gave us a chance to fight. The Filipinos were all right, but when we got the order to Jaro, which was in the hands of the natives, who had captured the place from the Spanish and were collecting revenues and doing the right thing, I knew the game of politics was on for sure. I felt that the next move would be to brush the Filipinos, and, sure enough, one regiment took a crack at them in another part of the island, through General Otis' order, and then we were ordered to take Jaro. We did what we were told — that was politics — and we beat the Filipinos; but, sure enough, it wasn't right. So that is the way things went, and they are going that way now. All I had to do was fight, and when the bosses said we should scrap I was there with my Krag-Jorgensen doing my little share in the mix-up.

Now let me tell you about the whole job. They made me the point in the advance guard, and if luck was not running just my way old Clark would have been dropped many times. But I went through without a scratch. That job on the firing line is not so good, after all. When I heard the first clack in a brush, I felt as if a mob was after me for umpiring a bad game. It had me so wild I could have been clubbed to death by the enemy before getting my senses together. Of the two things, I thought then that I would rather be home, having the newspapers roasting my decisions on balls and strikes and a howling mob of rooters rapping me with sticks and umbrellas than be there dodging bunches of bullets. But I got over that and was studying the dope about heroes. I wanted to be one of those heroes, and if it had not been that I was shy a few inches I would have been. They had me in the custom-house. My company was out in the field, and I never knew that the command was going to fight. I was in command of the custom-house, with the privilege to sleep and eat. The boys got into a brush, and in the skirmish they used up all of the ammunition. That was a desperate situation. A runner, a native, came there saying the general wanted more ammunition. Who would take it? That was the question I asked myself. Surely not the runner. He could be a traitor. That would never do; so I made a Fourth of July speech to myself, saying I was the one man who could save the day. I said that the world was looking at me with 20-cent field glasses; the president was in a cold sweat waiting upon my action; it meant the turning point of civilization. What did I do? What would any hero do? I got the ammunition and a team and started out to the regiment, holding the lines in one hand and a six-shooter in the other. I drove over the rough roads with all possible speed, nearly killing the mules. When I approached the troops I heard the boys yell. My head bobbed from one side to the other, and I thought they were yelling because Papa Clark had saved the day. But it wasn't that — they were giving me the laugh. You see, the enemy had taken a sneak and left the boys in possession. That was my nearest strike to being a hero.

Let me tell you, Aguinaldo is a good fellow. He is as sharp as a steel trap, and the people are with him. They will do anything he asks, and that is all rot about the troops taking him. He is pretty slick and does not let himself get tripped up so easily. If it had been left to Generals Lawton and MacArthur, Aguinaldo would have been caught long ago. They had him hemmed in, and MacArthur wanted to push forward and crush the greatest strength of the Filipinos and take Aguinaldo. But Otis, with his political head, said there was no sense in doing that, and forced the generals to execute another movement, which let Aguinaldo and his army slip out. MacArthur can end the war any time, if the president and the politicians let him alone; but it is all a political trick, and the situation down there depends upon how the flea is going to jump here.[18]

Another account reported that Clark "spent nearly a year hiking through the Isle of Panay, getting mixed up in a score of skirmishes with the 'Goo-gooes,' and incidentally having his epidermis punctured by a few Filipino bullets. The wounds were all slight, however, and he finally transferred to Manila, where he was made chief clerk in the quartermaster's department."[19] While stationed in Manila, Clark also "organized clubs in the army and navy and was to the Philippines what Col. Nick Young is to America as a baseball authority."[20]

Ed Clark never explained why he returned to the United States after little more than a year in the Philippines, but it wasn't because his services went unappreciated. Several years later, he had a chance encounter with his commanding officer, First Lieutenant Alfred Aloe, who told reporters that Clark "displayed great gallantry" during the capture of Iloilo and added that the former ballplayer's record was so impressive "that he was offered a non-commissioned office if he would re-enlist, in fact he was offered the first sergeantcy of company M, but this offer he declined."[21]

Upon his return to the United States, Clark talked about organizing teams in Galveston and Houston that would "give the Texas coasters a run for their money this summer."[22] But the lure of adventure was still in his blood and in June he headed off to South Africa, then in the throes of the Boer War. He denied any intention of taking up arms, however, declaring that his plan was to "look around the country, then come back and follow baseball again. ... it will be steerage all the way. Going as a muleteer. That'll do about war. I have [had] enough for a long time, and when I go to South Africa, neither the English nor the Boers will get me to handle a gun. It is sight-seeing that I am after, and when I get enough I am coming back to settle down."[23]

The claim that he would be sightseeing was a laughably implausible one and Clark dropped the pretense upon his return to the United States in January. "Well, I'm back in God's country once more, and tickled to death at that," he exclaimed. "I left New Orleans last July as foreman of a British mule transport for South Africa and when I got down there organized a party to get through the British lines and join the Boers. Some one of the party got 'cold feet' at the last minute and informed the authorities, who clapped us into a military prison. After six weeks' confinement I escaped and made my way to East London, where I shipped on the steamer Fernfield for the United States. Our destination was Brooklyn, but when we put into Cape Vincent for coal, our orders were changed to Baltimore, which suited me to a dot, as I had relatives there. I spent a few days with them there and came on to Washington, where I was lucky to secure a position in the government printing office, under the brother of Gus Land, the old St. Louis player. My address is No. 1116 E street N.W., Washington, D.C. I've had enough of soldiering and knocking around the world for the past 30 months. I am open for an engagement next year and would like to get on the Southern League staff of umpires."[24]

Clark later gave a more detailed description of how he escaped from prison:

[I]f it had not been for a Salvation army captain, I would be a prisoner of the British on the island of St. Helena at the present time instead of being out in wide, free Texas. I started out with seventeen other men to join the Boer army last fall but after we had got some distance up the railway which leads north from Capetown in South Africa, one of our detachment changed his mind and gave us away to the British. We were sent to East London. While there, I induced this captain of the Salvation army to listen to me. I found that he was not in sympathy with the unchristian methods of warfare which the British are pursuing in Africa and finally induced him to let me get on board a ship that was departing for the United States.

You see, you can't go anywhere in South Africa now without a permit, but of course the British never thought of suspecting that a Salvation army captain and an Englishman at that would lend a hand in setting free a prisoner. I'll never forget that Salvation army man and ever since then, any time I have had the chance to do the Salvation army a good turn, I have not failed to do it.[25]

As planned, Ed Clark umpired in the Virginia–North Carolina and Southern leagues in 1901.[26] But once the season ended, Clark made three more trips to South Africa, serving as foreman of the hostlers aboard the steamer *Mount Temple* as it brought horses to the troops.

Not surprisingly, Clark was well informed about the conflict and more than willing to share his views. When a reporter asked about stories that Americans were being taken prisoner by the British and forced to work, he replied:

There is considerable amount of truth in these stories and yet looked at from the British standpoint Americans should be slow in passing adverse criticism. South Africa is under martial law at present; the military rules everything. When an American or a native of any other land debarks from a ship he is asked to join the army. England needs soldiers badly. The man doesn't have to join at that time but if he permits his ship to get away from him he is impressed, or at least if he still refuses to join the army he is put to work on the breakwater at Durban or on other governmental work at some other point. In the first place a person debarking from his ship knows what he is doing. He is warned that martial law prevails and if he then permits his ship to sail without him, he has none to blame but himself. I dare say any other nation would do the same as England is doing. I believe England, under international law, has the right to take this course.

I wish you could see the big signs the British have posted up at all their coast towns in South Africa appealing to the patriotism of the British to join the army and help end the war. They are offering all sorts of inducements. They not only call upon Englishmen but they appeal to men from the colonies. A man joining Brabant's Horse or Kitchener's Horse gets five shillings a day and he gets a land grant of 160 acres and 25 head of cattle from the government — the latter to be delivered when the war is at an end. Speculators are getting rich buying up these coupons. They pay two pounds for a coupon which calls for 160 acres and 25 head of cattle when the war is at an end. You have no idea the number of acres of land and number of cattle England will owe when peace is declared.

England at present has about 250,000 men in the South Africa, either in the field or guarding the railroads and block houses. Block houses have been established all over South Africa, but they do not seem to bother the Boers. In my opinion the Boers at present are getting five recruits where the British are getting one. Men from all over continental Europe are joining Delarey and DeWet.

Speaking of these latter two, you have no idea the awe with which some of the British around Durban speak of these men. They regard them as devils incarnate, and the entire military service wakes up every morning expecting to hear of some intrepid deed by one or the other of these men. You see in the United States, or even in England, the public hears of but few of the achievements of these great fighters. I dare say news of not more than one in fifteen of their victories reaches the general public.

In spite of the thousands upon thousands of horses and mules that have been sent to South Africa, the British service is constantly crippled by lack of animals. Here's an instance of the way the Boers do away with horses shipped to South Africa by the British. On my last trip with the Mount Temple we were going from Capetown to Durban, where we were to land our load of 1100 horses. A coast signal service is maintained by the British, and we were signaled from shore our first morning out of Cape-town to make all speed for Durban. We made the run of 870 miles in something less than three days. Upon arriving at Durban we found that three nights before the Boers had raided to within thirty miles of that city and had captured 8,000 horses, which practically took all the reserve animals the British had in that section of Africa. The Boers do not give the British a chance to recapture horses. They pick out all the good ones and cut the throats of all which they have no use for. Nine or ten ships would be required to transport 8,000 horses from the United States to Africa, so you see what a loss it was to the British. Yet news of this raid never reached this side of the water — or at least none of my friends had heard of it when I returned.

When asked how longer he believed the Boers could hold out, Clark declared, "The Boers can keep up the war just as long as they please. If they had the privileges accorded the British of transporting supplies and men through Portuguese East Africa or of getting supplied in the United States, or even if the British were prevented from getting supplied in the United States, I believe the Boers would eventually whip the British."[27]

Clark was back in Texas by the spring of 1902 and resumed his umpiring career. The Boer War ended that year so he remained in San Antonio that winter. According to a reporter, "Clark is a character in his way — a good umpire, but if he wanted to engage in clerical work he need never hunt a job, because he is a fine bookkeeper and expert accountant."[28] Yet he seemed to prefer umpiring and continued to weather the abuse of fans and players for several more years.

Then around 1905 he gave up umpiring for good and his name disappear from the San Antonio city directory. All efforts to pick up his trail were unsuccessful. Had Ed Clark really died this time? Had he gone off on another overseas jaunt and never returned? Or had another fate overtaken him?

Military records seemed the obvious place to check and Richard Malatzky was able to find two separate enlistments. The first one took place, as expected, in New Orleans on May 23, 1898. Edmund C. Clark was reported to be one month shy of his thirtieth birthday, an umpire by profession, and a native of Cincinnati. After serving in the Eighteenth Infantry in Iloilo, he was discharged as a private on August 23, 1899, and a notation described his service as "good." Although he had fudged on his age by some five years, there was no doubt that this was our man.

His second enlistment took place on June 15, 1907, while at sea en route to Manila. This time Clark enlisted in the 26th Infantry and his card mentioned his prior service in the 18th. He was described as a bookkeeper and his age was given as 38 years, 2 months, meaning that he had managed to shed another year. He completed his three-year tour of duty on June 14, 1910, and was discharged at Fort Wayne, Michigan; though still a private, his service was reported to have been "very good."

So where had he gone next? The new clues made it possible to locate him in Detroit on the 1910 census, where he was reported to be 41 years old and a private in the U.S. Army. But he didn't remain in Detroit after being discharged and once again his trail went cold.

The only possible candidate on the censuses was an Edward C. Clark who showed up in Florida in 1914 and lived there until his death on September 19, 1949. Much of his information matched the ballplayer's, but there were also some significant discrepancies and the more we investigated him, the less it looked as though this was the right man.

So I kept searching and finally found a pension card for Edmund C. Clark that listed both of the missing player's enlistments. The card in turn led me to record showing that he entered a home for disabled veterans in 1914 and lived in various such institutions until his death at the National Home in Hampton, Virginia, on November 7, 1927. Although I had found no indication that he ever returned to Cincinnati after leaving his wife and family in the early 1890s, his next of kin was listed as one of his brothers back in his native city. Clark was buried at Arlington National Cemetery, Section 17, Grave #21085.

Chapter 19

Joe Gannon

I DON'T REALLY HAVE A favorite among the many missing players I have found, though if forced to pick one I'd probably choose Walter Walker. But any short list of my favorites would have to include Joe Gannon, because he is one of the best embodiments of what I hope to get out of every search. Joe Gannon started off as an anonymous cipher but in the process of looking for him I gained an understanding of the person who compiled that short line in the baseball record books. As such, it is fitting for his saga to be the final chapter in this book.

On August 28, 1898, the St. Louis Browns plucked a pitcher named Joe Gannon from a local amateur club called the Empires and gave him the chance to start against the Baltimore Orioles. Back in Chapter 5, I discussed the descent into chaos of the Browns and owner Chris Von der Ahe during the 1895 season. Von der Ahe's downward cycle continued in the years that followed and his travails included another divorce, being kidnapped and brought across state lines because of unpaid debts, and a fire that consumed part of his ballpark in April of 1898. The situation on the field was no better, as the Browns claimed only 29 victories against 102 defeats in 1897 and followed up with a 39–111 record in 1898.

In contrast, the Orioles remained a powerhouse. After three straight National League pennants, Baltimore had finally been nosed out by Boston in the final week of the 1897 season, but they still featured an extraordinary lineup. The batters Joe Gannon would face on that day included five future Hall of Famers — John McGraw, Wee Willie Keeler, Hughie Jennings, Joe Kelley and Wilbert Robinson. So over half of the batters Gannon faced in his major league debut were Hall of Famers.

It was a classic David versus Goliath match-up and, not surprisingly, David got pinned with the loss. Gannon's new teammates made five errors behind him and he was hit hard in a 13–2 loss. Still, it could have been a lot worse, as Gannon pitched a complete game and held the hard-hitting Orioles to a respectable total of thirteen hits.

The St. Louis papers had long since ceased to show much interest in Von der Ahe's charges, but one local sportswriter offered the assessment that Gannon "is a promising youngster, and a few seasons in the minor league will do him great service. He was nervous at the start, and a couple of bases on balls by him proved costly. Toward the close he settled down and, while being hit freely, did not receive the best support in the world. But five of the Birdies' runs were earned, a fact which speaks well for young Gannon."[1]

Instead, Joe Gannon never played another major or minor league game. Prior to the 1899 season, Von der Ahe's time as an owner had come to a merciful end and St. Louis was only too happy to forget the final years of his tenure. Joe Gannon vanished into complete obscurity, leaving behind not even a record of the hand with which he pitched. Turkin and Thompson couldn't figure out who he was, so they made another one of their blind guesses and credited the game to an outfielder named William Gannon.

Eventually another researcher rectified that mistake, but the obstacles to finding Joe Gannon remained daunting. There was nothing to go on except his name and hometown, so the only thing to do was to pick the best candidate from the censuses and city directories, try to trace him, and then hope at some point to be able to prove him to be the ballplayer.

Fortunately, there was only one Joseph Gannon of appropriate age in the St. Louis city directory. Here is his listing on the 1900 census:

> 2322 Rutger, St. Louis, Missouri
> Catherine Gannon, born August 1854 Ireland, widow, 3 children all
>   living
> son Joseph S., born February 1876 Missouri
> nephew Patrick E., born August 1869 Ireland, immigrated 1882
> nephew Eugene, born August 1870 Ireland, immigrated 1900
> daughter Kate M., born April 1881 Missouri
> daughter Mary L., born August 1886 Missouri

Also living with them were her married son Frank A. Gannon (born March 1873 Missouri), his wife Minnie A. (born March 1879 Missouri) and their newborn daughter Hortense (born March 1900).

There was an obvious contradiction between the statement that Catherine Gannon had given birth to only three children and the fact that four members of her household were described as being her children. Richard Malatzky went to work reconstructing her family and determined that Catherine was actually the mother of five children.

The St. Louis Public Library has an excellent on-line index of the *St. Louis Post-Dispatch*, a newspaper that is available in microfilm at the MSU Library, and these two resources enabled us to make a lot of additional progress. The index led to an 1894 obituary for Catherine Gannon's husband, Michael, a police sergeant in the Fifth District. In it, Michael Gannon was described as the brother of Mr. Patrick Gannon, his address was given as 328 South Garrison Avenue, and he was buried in Calvary Cemetery.[2] The same method led us to this obituary for their youngest son: "James Edward Gannon, 17 years, 2 months, 328 S. Garrison, youngest son of Catherine Gannon (nee Dwyer) and the late Sergeant Michael Gannon, and brother of Frank and Joe Gannon."[3]

More digging established that Catherine Gannon died on March 9, 1913, but at that point the family unit effectively broke up and the surviving members became hard to trace. Joseph Gannon vanished from the St. Louis city directory that year and there was no listing that looked promising until 1929 when Joseph Gannon, employee Barrett Co, was listed at 3325 9th Street along with Joseph M. Gannon, clerk. This entry and a follow-up one in 1931 led researcher Jay Sanford to a Joseph Gannon who died on March 19, 1931. Sanford sent away for the death certificate, which stated that the deceased had been born on February 22, 1877, was single, and was the son of Michael Gannon and Catherine (nee Dwyer).

So we'd found the man we'd been tracing and since he seemed to be the only Joseph Gannon in St. Louis of appropriate age, it was likely that he was the major leaguer. Yet we had no proof of that and it was not going to be easy to obtain such evidence about a man who appeared in only one professional game and who did so during the dismal final season of Von der Ahe's tenure.

The best hope was to find a detailed obituary, but none of the available St. Louis newspapers published one. The next best option was to find this Joseph Gannon listed with the occupation of baseball player in either the city directory or census. This was a long shot considering the brief duration of his career, but Richard Malatzky tried anyway and the results were perplexing.

Michael Gannon had been a policeman for some time, which made the family fairly easy to trace. But on the 1880 census, Michael and Catherine Gannon's three children were listed as Thomas T. (7, b. Missouri), Michael J. (4, b. Missouri), and James E. (1, b. Missouri). Obviously Michael J. Gannon had to be the man later known as Joseph S. Gannon, so perhaps Joseph was actually his middle name. But if so, where did the middle initial "S" come from? Even more confusing was the oldest son's name, who had been Frank A. Gannon by the time of the 1900 census, yet here his name was given as Thomas T. Gannon. There seemed to be no logical explanation and the St. Louis directories didn't really clear things up: Joe was consistently listed as Joseph S. Gannon, but his older brother was listed as Frank A. Gannon, Frank T. Gannon, and Thomas T. Gannon. More discouragingly, Joseph Gannon was never listed with a baseball-related profession.

The only thing left to do was to try to find an article connecting our prime candidate to baseball. The good news for me was that the MSU Library has an excellent microfilm collection of the *St. Louis Post-Dispatch* and that newspaper had very good coverage of amateur baseball during the 1880s and 1890s. The bad news was that the *Post-Dispatch* was not part of any of the text-searchable Internet collections. That meant that looking for mentions of Joe Gannon was painstaking work indeed, but after a lot of time spent hunched over a microfilm reader this is the picture that emerged.

The earliest mention I could find that looked like it might be Joe Gannon occurred in the spring of 1884, when he would have been only seven or eight. A club for boys of ten-and-under called the Ewings included J. Gannon as pitcher, M. Gannon at third base, and a third Gannon whose initial was difficult to read but might be a B. The contact person for this club was James Gannon of 825 Ewing, an address that was already familiar to me as the home of Joseph's uncle Patrick. So it looked as though young Joseph was playing on a team captained by his cousin James.[4]

This established a likely connection between our prime candidate and baseball, but St. Louis was a baseball-mad town at the time and it would have been odd for any youngster not to be on a team. What I really wanted to find was a connection between this Joe Gannon and the Empire Club (the club from which the major leaguer had graduated), so I kept searching. A day-by-day search of fourteen years of a newspaper is an extremely time-consuming endeavor, so I focused my efforts on the early months of each season when the lineups of that year's clubs were usually published in the *Post-Dispatch*. Here is what I found.

In 1888, a player named Gannon played right field for a 14-and-under club called the Randolph Stars. No initial was given but the team's captain lived at 2724 Bernard, right across the Gannon home at 2727 Bernard. Since Joe Gannon was the only one of the Gannon boys whose age was appropriate for a 14-and-under club, this was another good sign.[5]

Two years later, "J. Gannon" was listed as the pitcher of "The Bulks," a 15-and-under club. This team's captain and secretary was W. Crane of 532 Argyle Avenue, while the Gannon family was now living at 328 Argyle. Since this was when Joe would have been 13 or 14, this pretty much had to be him and the fact that he was now a pitcher was extremely encouraging. It was also noteworthy that the team's right fielder was named "D. Dwyer," likely a relative on Joe's mother's side.[6]

The next glimpse came in 1892 with the formation of the Willows, a 16-and-under club that had a pitcher and shortstop named J. Gannon.[7] When the Willows reorganized for the 1893 season, their contact person was none other than the same W.F. Crane who had acted in the same capacity for the Bulks.[8] The Willows remained active for at least two more seasons and in 1895 it was reported in *Sporting News* that Joe Gannon was the team's pitcher.[9]

It all added up to a very strong circumstantial case that our prime candidate was the missing ballplayer, but I still hoped to make it stronger. Unfortunately, during Von der Ahe's final years as owner of the Browns local interest in baseball fell off dramatically and newspaper coverage followed suit. Though I went through the *Post-Dispatch* for most of the summer, I found only a few mentions of Joe Gannon and the Empire Club and these articles told me nothing new.[10]

I now felt confident about the identification of the ballplayer but I still wanted to find indisputable evidence. So I began searching for a descendant and eventually discovered that Joe's younger sister Catherine had married a man named Grover Bell. The union produced three sons, one of whom became a Catholic priest. Some more digging determined that Father Ira Bell was retired but still in the St. Louis area. So I wrote to him in search of more information and soon received a wonderful letter in reply.

Father Bell reported that he had only met his uncle once but that his mother frequently talked of Joe as "a person who had talent, gifted at mathematics and no matter how good a job he had, when the Spring came he quit it so that he could go and play baseball." While Father Bell didn't know much more about his uncle's baseball career, he was able to confirm all the details we had reconstructed about the family.

The mystery of Joe Gannon was now solved but that wasn't the end of the story. My interest inspired Father Ira Bell to contact another relative and work with her to put together a lot of information about the family's history. I did my best to help them out and she was kind enough to send me a picture of Joe Gannon that I hung in my living room. A year or two later, the other relative let me know that Father Bell had passed away, and told me that she was grateful that they had been able to gather threads of the family history that might otherwise have been lost. I was touched.

Afterword

THE PRECEDING CHAPTERS HAVE told the stories of only a few of the missing players I've pursued during the last two decades but I hope they've given a sense of why this hobby has had an enduring fascination for me. Each new search begins with a simple line in the encyclopedias, but there is never any way to predict where they will go and where they will end. My first search began with a trip to Ionia, but since then they have taken me in every conceivable direction.

There had been Ed Clark, who was on hand for both the Boer War and the conflict in the Philippines. There was Harvey Watkins, who traveled far and wide with Barnum & Bailey and who ended up in England. I had even found a ballplayer with my own name and learned that his journey had also been a remarkable one.

Others have ended up surprisingly close to home. Walter Walker spent time in Lansing, as did Pete Morris's brother, and both men's careers were influenced by the events I chronicled in my first book. Bert Miller lived in the area for much of his life and at one point even resided on the same street that I was living on while searching for him.

There were a host of other obstacles to overcome. Players such as Art Sunday, Al Nichols, and George Bristow all turned out to have used different surnames during playing careers. Confusion about the correct first names of Ebenezer Johnson, Wallace Goldsmith, Patrick Murphy, Edmund Clark, and Joseph Gannon hindered those searches. And, as explained in the chapter on the Shafer brothers, just being from Philadelphia was a daunting impediment.

And after all of this work, the best that could happen was to add a line to the record of an obscure major leaguer. So why bother? It's a question I've tried to answer at various times in this book and I hope I've been able to convey the thrill of the chase. But along the way I've discovered one other reason and I'll close with that.

Today, extraordinary talent is a prerequisite for playing major league baseball. Each big league team has an extensive staff of scouts who are paid to scour the fifty states, Latin America, Canada, and — increasingly — the entire globe for the very best baseball talent. Determination and dedication are still enormous plusses and there are players such as Jamie Moyer and David Eckstein who succeed in the major leagues despite having less-than-dazzling raw tools. Yet even examples such as these are blessed with far more innate ability than the vast majority of us.

It wasn't that way in the nineteenth century. Possessing great talent was the easiest route to the major leagues, but plenty of men with very limited ability got there for at least a few days because they were in the right place at the right time. Eddie Kolb, the hotel cigar boy who talked his way into a major league game, was an extreme example but there were plenty of others who owed their big league cup-of-coffee to happenstance. Today's structured farm systems didn't exist until many decades later, so when an injury occurred, managers were often looking for any warm body to fill the void. Joe Gannon, Ed Clark, Walter Walker, and Pete Morris all had big-league trials that lasted exactly one game, while several of the other players featured in this book spent only slightly longer in a big league uniform.

But what these men lacked in talent they made up for in determination. Their devotion to baseball came at quite a price in many instances — Joe Gannon sacrificed numerous career opportunities to pursue baseball, Walter Walker's former partner used his love of baseball against him in an election campaign, and Ed Clark was one of many ballplayers whose marriages appear to have suffered because they made baseball their priority. Were these wise decisions? Probably not, especially in hindsight, but the intense desire to reach the major leagues is one that millions of Americans can understand.

So I'm pleased that I've been able to give these and other "missing" major leaguers their due by sorting out their life stories and getting their vital information correct. Along the way, I've been privileged to work with many amazing researchers and to meet or correspond with some wonderful descendants of these ballplayers who have generously shared their recollections with a stranger. Perhaps the most gratifying part has been the many ways in which unearthing the stories of these ballplayers' journeys has enriched my understanding of the national pastime.

Chapter Notes

Chapter 1

1. *New York Clipper*, June 3, 1893.
2. *Ionia Sentinel*, August 25, 1876.
3. *Ionia Standard*, February 9, 1883, and November 23, 1883.
4. *Detroit Free Press*, April 9, 1884.
5. *Isabella County Enterprise*, March 22, 1889.
6. *New York Clipper*, June 3, 1893.
7. Pontiac Valley Asylum records, case no. 3509, State Archives of Michigan.
8. *Detroit Free Press*, July 8, 1905.

Chapter 2

1. The Bureau of Investigation (BOI) was established in 1908 and became known as the Federal Bureau of Investigation (FBI) in 1935.
2. The 1860 census gives this picture of the family: Rochester, NY, Luther Studley 52 land agent; wife Lucy Ann 44; son Samuel [sic] 19; son Henry 15; daughter Frances 4.
3. *New York Clipper*, August 23, 1878.
4. *Rochester Democrat and Chronicle*, July 13, 1901, 14. The Studleys were living at 42 West Alexander in the 1861 city directory.
5. *Washington Critic*, May 6, 1873.

Chapter 3

1. Hy Turkin and S.C. Thompson, *The Official Encyclopedia of Baseball* (New York: A.S. Barnes, 1951).
2. Lee Allen to Tom Shea, April 8, 1963, Lee Allen Collection, A. Bartlett Giamatti Research Center, National Baseball Hall of Fame.
3. *Atlanta Constitution*, December 30, 1907.
4. *Cleveland Plain Dealer*, August 13, 1879.

5. *Chicago Tribune*, March 7, 1880.
6. The American Association that was founded in 1882 was a major league that it not related to the twentieth-century minor league by the same name.
7. David Nemec, *The Beer and Whisky League* (Guilford, CT: Lyons Press, 2004), 35.
8. *Sporting Life*, February 3, 1886.
9. *New York Clipper*, November 8, 1879, 261.
10. *New York Clipper*, May 10, 1879.
11. *San Francisco Call*, December 8, 1893.
12. *Montgomery Advertiser*, April 3, 1907.
13. *Grand Forks Herald*, August 28, 1906.
14. "Famous Player in Bread Line," *San Francisco Call*, May 24, 1906, 6.

Chapter 4

1. According to the 1900 census, Minnie Kolb was the mother of six children, five of them living.
2. *Cincinnati Enquirer*, April 14, 1899. According to the article, the Norwoods previously had been known as the Ivanhoes.
3. *Cleveland Plain Dealer*, October 16, 1899, 16.
4. Ibid.
5. *Cleveland Plain Dealer*, October 16, 1899, 16; J. Thomas Hetrick, *Misfits!* (Jefferson, NC: McFarland, 1991), 171, 181.
6. *Sporting Life*, March 10, 1900, 9; *Portsmouth Daily Times*, August 14, 1901, 4.
7. *Sporting Life*, January 25, 1902, 9.
8. *Champaign Democrat*, February 19, 1903, 2.
9. *Sporting Life*, January 9, 1904, 6.
10. *Sporting Life*, March 11, 1905.
11. *Cleveland Plain Dealer*, March 30, 1905, 12.

12. *Cleveland Plain Dealer*, September 10, 1905, 25.

13. *Sporting Life*, April 20, 1907, 3.

14. *Sporting Life*, May 11, 1907, 22.

15. *Cleveland Plain Dealer*, November 6, 1907, 6. The league was alluded to the previous winter in *Sporting Life*, February 9, 1907, 3, with Miller Huggins's brother Clarence helping Kolb with the scheme.

16. *Sporting Life*, November 7, 1908, 6.

17. *Sporting Life*, November 14, 1908, 5.

18. *Cleveland Plain Dealer*, March 30, 1905, 12.

19. *Cincinnati Enquirer*, reprinted in the *Anaconda Standard*, September 28, 1908, 8.

20. *Sporting News,* November 12, 1908; *Sporting Life*, November 7, 1908, 2 and 6; *Cincinnati Enquirer*, reprinted in the *Anaconda Standard*, September 28, 1908, 8.

21. *Sporting Life*, October 10, 1908, 5.

22. Hetrick, *Misfits!*, 181.

23. *Calgary Herald*, October 2, 1949.

24. *Cincinnati Enquirer*, quoted in *Columbus Ledger-Enquirer*, October 10, 1911; *Calgary Daily Herald*, September 14, 1911, 8.

25. "Who Is the Big Scout in Calgary?" *Calgary Daily Herald*, September 14, 1911, 8.

26. *Sporting Life*, November 21, 1914, 15.

27. "E.W. Kolb to Open Another Restaurant," *Calgary Daily Herald*, March 30, 1914, 1.

28. *Calgary Daily Herald*, February 12, 1916, 11 and 14.

29. *Calgary Daily Herald*, February 15, 1916, 6.

30. *Calgary Daily Herald*, May 7, 1919, 11.

31. "Pro. Ball League for Next Season Being Discussed," *Calgary Daily Herald*, July 17, 1919, 20.

32. "Professional Baseball League to Include the Calgary Team in 1920," *Calgary Daily Herald*, September 13, 1919, 28.

33. "New Café to Be Opened Thursday," *Calgary Daily Herald*, November 28, 1928, 14; advertising copy in the following page of the same issue.

34. *Calgary Daily Herald*, June 14, 1945, 15.

35. "Buck Ewing Best Baseball Catcher; This Is Opinion Expressed by Connie Mack in Letter to Ed. Kolb," *Calgary Daily Herald*, April 12, 1930, 7.

36. "Solution Found for Calgary Problem in Community Kitchen," *Calgary Daily Herald*, March 11, 1933, 21.

37. "Kolb Dismissed from Relief Post," *Calgary Daily Herald*, March 2, 1936, 9.

38. "Dismissal of Kolb Ungrateful Reward, Says Col. Sanders," *Calgary Daily Herald*, March 7, 1936, 12.

39. "Activities at Oil Wells Near Calgary," *Calgary Daily Herald*, August 22, 1914, 1.

40. *Calgary Daily Herald*, April 7, 1923, 14.

41. "Absorption Plant at Illinois Well to Start at Once," *Calgary Daily Herald*, April 23, 1923, 9.

42. *Lethbridge Herald*, June 23, 1942, October 28 and December 14, 1946.

43. *Calgary Daily Herald*, August 17, 1944, 7.

44. "Former Major League Baseball Star Lives in this City," *Calgary Daily Herald*, January 29, 1938, 7.

45. "Old Ball Jerseys Finally Hit Ashcan," *Calgary Daily Herald*, January 8, 1941, 6.

46. An article published three years later gave this similar version: "A broken leg [in 1905] brought to a sudden end a brilliant baseball career that had extended from 1900 — three years with Cleveland Indians and three with Cincinnati" ("Old Ball Jerseys Finally Hit Ashcan," *Calgary Daily Herald*, January 8, 1941, 6).

47. "Former Major League Baseball Star Lives in this City," *Calgary Daily Herald*, January 29, 1938, 7.

48. Bob Mamini, "Sports Booster Passes," *Calgary Daily Herald*, October 4, 1949, 19.

Chapter 5

1. The Brown Stockings were often known as the "Browns," which confuses some into assuming that they were the predecessors of the American League St. Louis Browns. Von der Ahe in fact founded the franchise now known as the St. Louis Cardinals. The change of nickname was probably designed to distance the team from the dreadful clubs that Von der Ahe fielded in the 1890s, but when St. Louis received an American League franchise, the name Browns was adopted as a way

to link the new team to the glory years of the 1880s. Similar transformations occurred in Boston and Chicago, where the American League Red Sox and White Sox took on nicknames abandoned by their cross-town rivals.

2. *Sporting News*, May 16, 1896. It was common for articles in *Sporting News* and most nineteenth-century periodicals to be unsigned, so the attribution of a specific article involves speculation. But Spink seems to have written most of the unattributed material in *Sporting News* during these years, and his attacks on Von der Ahe were so regular during these years that it is a fairly safe assumption.

3. *St. Louis Post-Dispatch*, August 11, 1895.

4. Ibid.

5. *Philadelphia Record*, quoted in *Sporting News*, August 24, 1895.

6. *Sporting News*, August 17, 1895, 4.

7. An inquiry to Notre Dame's archives by researcher Cappy Gagnon produced records for a Frank Phelan seven years older than our man.

8. *St. Louis Post-Dispatch*, August 11, 1895.

9. *Chicago Tribune*, July 17, 1897.

10. *Cleveland Plain Dealer*, December 15, 1894, 5; quoting another judge who had cited Taft's ruling in sentencing Debs.

11. *Cleveland Plain Dealer*, July 14, 1894, 8.

12. *Washington Post*, October 14, 1908.

13. J. Thomas Hetrick, *Chris Von der Ahe and the St. Louis Browns* (Lanham, MD: Scarecrow, 1999), 176.

14. *Sporting Life*, October 12, 1895, 5.

15. *Sporting Life*, November 2, 1895, 7.

16. *Washington Post*, February 12, 1896, 8.

17. *Sporting News*, December 21, 1895.

18. *Chicago Tribune*, July 17, 1897.

Chapter 6

1. Johnson also played a few games for Terre Haute/Toledo of the Western League in 1895.

2. "Anson Gets Revenge," *Chicago Record*, June 30, 1897, 3.

3. *Sporting Life*, July 24, 1897, 8.

4. Dennis DeValeria and Jeanne Burke DeValeria, *Honus Wagner: A Biography* (New York: Henry Holt, 1995), 30.

5. *Sporting Life*, September 18, 1897, 11, reported both transactions as part of National League secretary Nick Young's September 10 bulletin. (The listing has "L. Johnson" going from Louisville but that is clearly a mistake as there was no Louisville player by that name.)

6. *Utica Daily Press*, undated article on Old Fulton NY Post Card website, apparently from March 10, 1904.

7. Another Wagner biography records the trade as Wagner for Johnson, Hach and $2100 (William Hageman, *Honus: The Life and Times of a Baseball Hero* [Champaign, IL: Sagamore, 1996], 16), though Dennis DeValeria and Jeanne Burke DeValeria's *Honus Wagner: A Biography* does not list any other players being involved in the final deal.

8. *Utica Daily Press*, letter from Johnson in an undated article on Old Fulton NY Post Card website, apparently from March 10, 1904.

9. *Sporting Life*, May 21, 1904, 15.

10. *Sporting Life*, June 18 and July 2, 1904.

11. *Sporting Life*, June 3, 1905, 15.

12. *Sporting Life*, March 30, 1907, 13; "Fifty Years Ago," *London Free Press*, March 21, 1957.

13. *Sporting Life*, May 13 and August 26, 1911.

14. *Sporting Life*, March 23, 1912, 13.

15. Albert Johnson, Jr., letter to National League secretary Harvey Traband, apparently dated March 18, 1935, Abbie Johnson Hall of Fame File, Cooperstown, New York.

16. "Fifty Years Ago," *London Free Press*, July 2, 1955.

17. *Sporting Life*, April 28, 1894, 9.

18. "Fifty Years Ago," *London Free Press*, March 21, 1957.

19. Albert Johnson, Jr., letter to National League secretary Harvey Traband, apparently dated March 18, 1935, Abbie Johnson Hall of Fame File, Cooperstown, New York.

Chapter 7

1. *Kalamazoo Telegraph*, coverage of 1897 season, especially April 23, July 2 and 15.

2. *Louisville Courier-Journal*, June 28, 1897, 6.

3. *Sporting News*, July 24, 1897, 5.

4. *Sporting Life*, July 24, 1897, 8.
5. Ibid.
6. *Hastings Banner*, April 29, 1897.
7. *Hastings Banner*, June 25, 1896.
8. *Sporting Life*, August 21, 1897, 21.
9. *Hastings Banner*, June 25, 1896. The *Saginaw Globe* of June 23, 1896, confirmed that this was Bert Miller by describing the new pitcher as the "Hastings wonder."
10. *Fort Wayne News*, February 18, 1899.
11. *Lake Odessa Wave*, September 1, 1893.
12. *Lake Odessa Wave*, February 16, 1900, 1.

Chapter 8

1. *Brooklyn Eagle*, April 20, 1890, 17.
2. *Sporting News*, July 30, 1887.
3. *Sporting News*, November 12, 1887, and January 4, 1890.
4. Bill O'Neal, *The Texas League, 1888–1987: A Century of Baseball* (Austin: Eakin Press, 1987), 6.
5. *Sporting Life*, November 13, 1889, 4.
6. *National Police Gazette*, December 21, 1889.
7. *Sporting News*, October 1, 1892.
8. *Sporting News*, October 7, 1893.
9. Wild-card searches allow a researcher to type in a partial name and get hits, which can be very helpful in light of the many misspellings in census listings.
10. *Carson City Daily Appeal*, October 4, 1926, 1.

Chapter 9

1. Marshall Wright, *The National Association of Base Ball Players, 1857–1870* (Jefferson, NC: McFarland, 2000), 199, 208, 251, 305.
2. William Ridgely Griffith, *The Early History of Amateur Baseball in the State of Maryland, 1858–1871* (Baltimore, 1897), 91.
3. *Sporting News*, December 6, 1890.
4. *Sporting Life,* March 23, 1901.
5. James H. Bready, *Baseball in Baltimore: The First 100 Years* (Baltimore: Johns Hopkins University Press, 1998), 2.
6. *Chicago Inter-Ocean*, October 18, 1896, 11.

Chapter 10

1. Quoted in *Louisville Courier-Journal*, September 12, 1877.
2. For more on the scandal, see Daniel E. Ginsburg, *The Fix Is In: A History of Baseball Gambling and Game Fixing Scandals* (Jefferson, NC: McFarland, 1995); William A. Cook, *The Louisville Grays Scandal of 1877: The Taint of Gambling at the Dawn of the National League* (Jefferson, NC: McFarland, 2005); and J.E. Findling, "The Louisville Grays' Scandal of 1877," *Journal of Sport History* 3:2 (1976), 176–187.
3. *Brooklyn Eagle*, March 19, 1875.
4. *Chicago Tribune*, April 24, 1875, 7, special New York correspondent.
5. *St. Louis Democrat*, May 21, 1875.
6. *New York World*, quoted in *Forest and Stream*, August 12, 1875.
7. *Louisville Courier-Journal*, July 11, 1876.
8. *Louisville Courier-Journal*, July 7 and 12, 1877.
9. *New York Clipper*, September 6, 1884.
10. *Sporting Life*, April 15, 1885, 6; *New York Clipper*, April 18, 1885, 68.
11. *New York Sun*, April 7, 1885, 3.
12. *Sporting Life*, February 24, 1886, 6.
13. *Sporting Life*, February 17 and 24, 1886.
14. *New York Sun*, May 6, 1888, and February 2, 1889; *Philadelphia Press*, February 16, 1890.
15. *New York Herald*, March 15, 1891, 28.
16. *Sporting Life*, September 17, 1892, 2.
17. *New York Sun*, reprinted in *Sporting Life*, July 6, 1901.
18. *Sporting News*, September 10, 1887; *Philadelphia Press*, February 16, 1890; *New York Sun*, reprinted in *Sporting Life*, July 6, 1901.
19. *Sporting Life*, November 23, 1887, 5.
20. *National Police Gazette*, October 1, 1887, 14.
21. *Sporting Life*, February 12, 1890, 3, Chadwick's signed column.
22. Chadwick Scrapbooks, unidentified clipping.
23. Lee Allen to Tom Shea, April 9, 1967, Lee Allen Collection, A. Bartlett Giamatti

Research Center, National Baseball Hall of Fame.

24. *San Diego Union*, December 7, 1913.
25. *Staten Island Advance*, May 16, 1934.
26. Cook, *The Louisville Grays Scandal of 1877*.
27. Annie was listed as Catherine Ann on the *Belle Wood*'s passenger list, but all subsequent records indicate that her name was in fact Martha Ann.
28. A confusing listing on the 1910 census has a 14-year-old son named Walter also living with Al and Mary. But no such son was listed on the 1900 census and Mary is listed as has given birth to three children, one living on both censuses. Since Edna was still alive, it seems most likely that Walter was a relative who was living with them. It is also possible that he was an adopted son, but no other trace of him has been found.
29. *Newtown Register*, October 27, 1892, 5.
30. *Newtown Register*, January 19, 1911, 5.
31. Charles Hughes, "Barn Dances Filled Winter with Fun in Old Glendale," *Brooklyn Eagle*, June 29, 1941, 8A.
32. Charles A. Hughes, "Moving Days in Old Glendale," *Brooklyn Eagle*, October 19, 1941, 5E.
33. *Brooklyn Eagle*, June 29, 1941, 8A.
34. Charles A. Hughes, "Indians Played Good Baseball but Forgot to Touch Home Plate," *Brooklyn Eagle*, March 1, 1942, 4E.
35. Charles A. Hughes, "A Little Boy Remembers His Trips to Rockaway Beach in the '80s," *Brooklyn Eagle*, November 23, 1941, 5E.

Chapter 11

1. *Sporting Life*, July 4, 1891.
2. *Columbus Evening Dispatch*, April 16, 1890; *Sporting News*, May 17, 1890.
3. *Indianapolis Morning Star*, October 10, 1911; *Indianapolis News*, October 10 and 11, 1911.
4. *St. Paul and Minneapolis Pioneer Press*, March 11, 1888.
5. T. P. Sullivan, "Stories of the Diamond," *Sporting News*, March 21, 1912. This article appeared five months after Pat Murphy's death, but that wasn't significant because it was very likely a reprint that had originally appeared before Murphy's death.

6. *Sporting Life*, March 20, 1889.
7. *Indianapolis News*, June 28, 1892.
8. *Sporting Life*, February 27, 1889.
9. *Sporting News*, July 2, 1942.
10. *Sporting News*, September 25, 1913.
11. Mrs. John J. McGraw, edited by Arthur Mann, *The Real McGraw* (New York: David McKay, 1953), 94, 231.
12. Hugh Jennings, *Rounding Third* (unpublished manuscript), Chapter 74.
13. *Sporting News*, September 25, 1913.

Chapter 12

1. *Billboard*, November 29, 1913.
2. *New York Herald*, December 3, 1893.
3. Louis E. Cooke, "Reminiscences of a Showman," a series of articles published in the *Newark Evening Star* in 1915 and 1916, reprinted on the Circus History website (www.circushistory.org).
4. Harvey L. Watkins and Bert Davis, *Barnum & Bailey Official Route Book Season of 1890* (Buffalo: The Courier Co., 1890).
5. *Bandwagon*, Vol. 4, No. 4 (July–August), 1960, pp. 9–11, 14.
6. New York marriage records show that Harvey Watkins married Annie G. Macconer in Manhattan on October 8, 1889. According to the *1893 New York Clipper Annual*, page 5, Watkins's marriage to Rose Meers was annulled in May 1892. The *Clipper* did not elaborate on the reasons, but New York Supreme Court records reveal that Harvey Watkins and Annie G. Watkins were separated but not legally divorced when he eloped with Rose Meers. As a result, the Meers marriage was annulled and then Harvey and Annie Watkins obtained their divorce.
7. *New York Sun*, August 9, 1894.
8. *Chicago Tribune*, August 22, 1895; *New York World*, August 22, 1895; *Sporting Life*, March 9, 1895, 5.
9. *Sporting Life*, September 26, 1896, 16.
10. *New York Herald*, August 22, 1895, 10.
11. *Washington Post*, August 20, 1895; *Sporting News*, August 24, 1895.
12. *Sporting News*, August 24, 1895.
13. *New York Herald*; reprinted in the *Washington Post*, August 21, 1895.

14. *Auburn Weekly Bulletin,* August 12, 1906.
15. *New York Herald,* August 22, 1895, 10.
16. *New York Herald,* August 22, 1895, 10.
17. *Sporting Life,* September 7, 1895, 8.
18. *Sporting Life,* December 7, 1895, 5.
19. *New York Herald,* December 18, 1895, 15.
20. *Chicago Tribune,* December 6, 1895.
21. *Sporting Life,* February 1, 1896, 4.
22. *New York Herald,* February 16, 1896.
23. *New York Herald,* June 22, 1896, 9.
24. *Sporting Life,* September 26, 1896, 16.
25. *Sporting Life,* October 24, 1896, 9.
26. *New York Times,* October 29, 1897.
27. *Boston Globe,* January 13, 1898.
28. *Sporting Life,* March 5, 1898, 7.
29. *Sporting Life,* March 12, 1904.
30. "The Great Triumvirate," *Billboard,* May 19, 1906, 10.
31. *Show World,* October 12, 1907; reprinted on the Circus History website.

Chapter 13

1. *Sporting News,* February 25, 1959.
2. *Sporting News,* May 2, 1964.
3. *Sporting News,* September 28, 1960.
4. *National Police Gazette,* December 23, 1882, 12.
5. Quoted in Mark Armour, "Dennis Bennett," The Baseball Biography Project (*http://bioproj.sabr.org/bioproj.cfm?a=v&v=l&p id=931&bid=1364*).

Chapter 14

1. *Cleveland Leader,* March 23, 1882.
2. *Official Baseball Record,* May 27, 1886.
3. *Sporting Life,* June 10, 1885.
4. *Detroit Free Press,* March 21, 1882.
5. *Sporting Life,* September 2, 1885, 4.
6. *New York Clipper,* March 15, 1879.
7. *St. Louis Post-Dispatch,* May 7, 1884; *Sporting News,* October 1, 1887.
8. *Sporting News,* November 24, 1888.
9. *Sporting News,* November 29 and December 20, 1890.
10. *Sporting Life,* February 7, 1891, and April 1, 1893; *Sporting News,* September 3, 1892, and April 27 and October 19, 1895; *St. Louis Post-Dispatch,* April 17, 1893.

11. *Sporting News,* April 27, 1895.
12. *Sporting Life,* April 1, 1893; *Sporting News,* March 2, 1901.
13. *Philadelphia Inquirer,* November 1, 1912.
14. *Philadelphia Inquirer,* May 11 and August 31, 1907.
15. *Philadelphia Inquirer,* August 31, 1907.
16. *Lancaster New Era,* October 15, 1999.
17. The ballplayer's daughter's name was listed as Regna, rather than Regina, on several occasions. I'm inclined to believe that each such instance was a typo, but it's possible that her name was in fact spelled without an "i."

Chapter 15

1. *Sporting Life,* May 28, 1884.
2. *Stillwater Gazette,* May 21, 1884.
3. *Fort Wayne Daily Journal,* May 24, 1884.
4. *St. Louis Post-Dispatch,* March 29, 1884.
5. *Detroit Free Press,* February 24, 1889.
6. *Milwaukee Sentinel,* May 18 and July 5, 1883.
7. *Milwaukee Daily Journal,* January 31, 1884.
8. "For the Reserve Nine," *Milwaukee Daily Journal,* March 18, 1884.
9. *Milwaukee Sentinel,* May 13, 1884, 2.
10. *Milwaukee Sentinel,* May 14, 1884.
11. *Milwaukee Sentinel,* May 15, 1884.
12. *Milwaukee Sentinel,* May 13, 1884, 2.
13. *Milwaukee Sentinel,* May 19, 1884, 2.
14. *Milwaukee Daily Journal,* May 20, 1884.
15. *Milwaukee Sentinel,* August 10, 1884, 3.
16. *Milwaukee Sentinel,* December 11, 1884, 3.
17. *Milwaukee Sentinel,* December 14, 1884, 10.
18. Theodora W. Youmans, "Early Welsh Settlers; John Hughes Located at Genesee in 1840," *Milwaukee Sentinel,* April 18, 1897, 11.
19. New York Passenger Lists, 1820–1957.
20. Theodora W. Youmans, "Early Welsh Settlers; John Hughes Located at Genesee in 1840," *Milwaukee Sentinel,* April 18, 1897, 11.
21. *Milwaukee Daily Sentinel,* September 6, 1876, 2.
22. *Milwaukee Daily Sentinel,* May 4, 1877, 5.

23. *Milwaukee Daily Sentinel*, August 7, 1877, 2.
24. *Milwaukee Daily Sentinel*, August 11, 1879.
25. "Old Time Base Ball," *Detroit Free Press*, January 6, 1889, 10.

Chapter 16

1. *Galveston Daily News*, April 7, 1895; *Sporting Life*, April 27, 1895.
2. *Sporting News*, January 20, 1894, and March 23, 1895.
3. *Galveston Daily News*, April 11, 1895, 6.
4. *Galveston Daily News*, June 29, 1895, 8.
5. *Galveston Daily News*, January 26, 1896.
6. *Cleveland Plain Dealer*, April 6, 1899.
7. *Sporting Life*, May 27, 1905.
8. *Seattle Daily Times*, September 27, 1926, and July 4 and 7, 1932.

Chapter 17

1. My main source of information on Shea is Dick Thompson, "Tom Shea," *National Pastime* 18 (1998), 94–102. Thompson inherited Shea's correspondence, which served as the basis of this article. In revised form, the article can now be found on the SABR BioProject website.
2. S.C. Thompson to Tom Shea, July 20, 1951, quoted in Dick Thompson, "Tom Shea," *National Pastime* 18 (1998), 94–102.
3. Allen to S.C. Thompson, May 6, 1944, Lee Allen Collection, A. Bartlett Giamatti Research Center, National Baseball Hall of Fame.
4. Allen to Tom Shea, June 30, 1961, Lee Allen Collection, A. Bartlett Giamatti Research Center, National Baseball Hall of Fame.
5. Allen to S.C. Thompson, October 16, 1944, Lee Allen Collection, A. Bartlett Giamatti Research Center, National Baseball Hall of Fame.
6. Allen to Tom Shea, April 9, 1967, Lee Allen Collection, A. Bartlett Giamatti Research Center, National Baseball Hall of Fame.
7. Allen to Tom Shea, March 5, 1960,

Lee Allen Collection, A. Bartlett Giamatti Research Center, National Baseball Hall of Fame.
8. Allen to Tom Shea, January 23, 1968, Lee Allen Collection, A. Bartlett Giamatti Research Center, National Baseball Hall of Fame.
9. Allen to Tom Shea, April 9, 1967, Lee Allen Collection, A. Bartlett Giamatti Research Center, National Baseball Hall of Fame.
10. Allen to Tom Shea, June 30, 1961, Lee Allen Collection, A. Bartlett Giamatti Research Center, National Baseball Hall of Fame.
11. Allen to Tom Shea, September 8, 1962, Lee Allen Collection, A. Bartlett Giamatti Research Center, National Baseball Hall of Fame.
12. Allen to Tom Shea, November 21, 1961, January 19, 1962, January 21, 1963, March 24, 1967, and January 13, 1962, Lee Allen Collection, A. Bartlett Giamatti Research Center, National Baseball Hall of Fame.
13. Allen to Tom Shea, January 7, 1963, Lee Allen Collection, A. Bartlett Giamatti Research Center, National Baseball Hall of Fame.
14. Allen to Tom Shea, April 5, 1961, Lee Allen Collection, A. Bartlett Giamatti Research Center, National Baseball Hall of Fame.
15. Allen to Tom Shea, May 30, 1963, Lee Allen Collection, A. Bartlett Giamatti Research Center, National Baseball Hall of Fame.
16. Allen to Tom Shea, January 13, 1962, Lee Allen Collection, A. Bartlett Giamatti Research Center, National Baseball Hall of Fame.
17. Allen to Tom Shea, April 18, 1963, Lee Allen Collection, A. Bartlett Giamatti Research Center, National Baseball Hall of Fame.
18. Allen to Tom Shea, September 27, 1966, Lee Allen Collection, A. Bartlett Giamatti Research Center, National Baseball Hall of Fame.
19. "Bloodhound Techniques Find Old Ballplayers," *Otsego Farmer*, March 26, 1964.

20. Allen to Shea, August 12, 1961, Lee Allen Collection, A. Bartlett Giamatti Research Center, National Baseball Hall of Fame.

21. Lee Allen, "Cooperstown Corner" column, *Sporting News*, November 9, 1968.

22. Allen to Shea, March 28, 1963, Lee Allen Collection, A. Bartlett Giamatti Research Center, National Baseball Hall of Fame.

23. Allen to Shea, April 9, 1967, Lee Allen Collection, A. Bartlett Giamatti Research Center, National Baseball Hall of Fame.

24. Allen to Shea, August 15, 1968, Lee Allen Collection, A. Bartlett Giamatti Research Center, National Baseball Hall of Fame.

25. Allen to Shea, October 22, 1950, quoted in Dick Thompson, "Tom Shea," *National Pastime* 18 (1998).

26. James Leon Wood (as told to Frank G. Menke), "Baseball in By-Gone Days," syndicated series, *Indiana* (Pennsylvania) *Evening Gazette*, August 14, 1916; *Marion* (Ohio) *Star*, August 15, 1916; *Indiana* (Pennsylvania) *Evening Gazette*, August 17, 1916.

27. Allen to Shea, January 21, 1963, Lee Allen Collection, A. Bartlett Giamatti Research Center, National Baseball Hall of Fame.

28. Allen to Shea, August 15, 1966, Lee Allen Collection, A. Bartlett Giamatti Research Center, National Baseball Hall of Fame.

29. Allen to Shea, October 24, 1962, Lee Allen Collection, A. Bartlett Giamatti Research Center, National Baseball Hall of Fame.

30. Allen to Shea, March 10, 1968, Lee Allen Collection, A. Bartlett Giamatti Research Center, National Baseball Hall of Fame.

Chapter 18

1. "In South Africa; Umpire Ed Clark, Recently Returned, Relates Interesting Experiences," *Fort Worth Morning Register*, April 12, 1902, 4.

2. *Grand Rapids Daily Democrat*, August 8, 1883.

3. *Sporting Life*, September 2, 1885, 4.

4. *Sporting News*, July 12, 1886, 1.

5. *Sporting Life*, February 16, 1887, 4.

6. *Cincinnati Enquirer*, March 20, 1887.

7. *Sporting News*, August 6, 1887.

8. *Sporting Life*, August 31, 1887.

9. *Sporting Life*, May 1, 1889, 6, column by Ren Mulford, Jr.

10. *Cleveland Plain Dealer*, April 25, 1889; *Sporting Life*, March 26 and May 1, 1889.

11. *Sporting News*, August 10, 1889.

12. *Sporting Life*, August 14, 1889, 5, column by Ren Mulford, Jr.

13. *Sporting Life*, November 28, 1891, 2.

14. *Sporting News*, November 19, 1898, 1, letter from Ed Clark in Honolulu dated October 22.

15. *San Antonio Daily Light*, September 8, 1898, 3; *Sporting Life*, November 19, 1898, 4; December 3, 1898, clipping from unidentified source.

16. *Chicago Tribune*, November 25, 1899, 5. Clark was referred to as Ed C. Clark of the 18th Infantry, so there's no question it was the ballplayer-umpire.

17. "Umpire Ed Clark Back from Manila with a Grievance Against Otis and His Political Backers," *New Orleans Times-Picayune*, June 18, 1900, 8.

18. "Umpire Ed Clark Back from Manila with a Grievance Against Otis and His Political Backers," *New Orleans Times-Picayune*, June 18, 1900, 8.

19. *Dallas Morning News*, March 23, 1902. One week earlier, the same newspaper had reported that while in the Philippines Clark "was in more than a score of engagements and was wounded seven times" ("Ball Players Coming," *Dallas Morning News*, March 16, 1902, 6).

20. *Dallas Morning News*, April 7, 1900, 3.

21. "The World is Small; Think the Two Soldiers Who Met after a Separation of Two or More Years," *Fort Worth Morning Register*, June 4, 1902, 2.

22. *Dallas Morning News*, April 7, 1900, 3.

23. "Umpire Ed Clark Back from Manila

with a Grievance Against Otis and His Political Backers," *New Orleans Times-Picayune*, June 18, 1900, 8.

24. *Sporting News*, January 5, 1901, 2.

25. "In South Africa; Umpire Ed Clark, Recently Returned, Relates Interesting Experiences," *Fort Worth Morning Register*, April 12, 1902, 4.

26. *Sporting News*, August 10, 1901.

27. "In South Africa; Umpire Ed Clark, Recently Returned, Relates Interesting Experiences," *Fort Worth Morning Register*, April 12, 1902, 4.

28. "Ball Players Coming," *Dallas Morning News*, March 16, 1902, 6.

Chapter 19

1. *St. Louis Globe-Democrat*, August 29, 1898.

2. *St. Louis Post-Dispatch*, August 3, 1894.

3. *St. Louis Post-Dispatch*, April 27, 1896.

4. *St. Louis Post-Dispatch*, April 29, 1884.

5. *St. Louis Post-Dispatch*, May 5, 1888.

6. *St. Louis Post-Dispatch*, April 27, 1890.

7. *St. Louis Post-Dispatch*, April 4, 1892.

8. *St. Louis Post-Dispatch*, March 23, 1893.

9. *Sporting News*, April 27, 1895; *St. Louis Post-Dispatch*, April 9, 1894.

10. *St. Louis Post-Dispatch*, August 14 and 28, 1898.

Index